D0861957

Words of Praise for *Beneath the Tyrant's Yoke*

"I must compliment you without reservation. The book you have written is according to my judgment the best book that has ever been written concerning the German occupation of Norway and the Norwegian Resistance. You have a total grasp of the situation in this country in the years 1940-1945. Very good indeed!"

—KRISTIAN OTTOSEN, SERVICE IN BRITISH-NORWEGIAN INTELLIGENCE SERVICE 1940-19[42]

"Fuegner's work tells the story of a heroic people's confrontation with the Nazi regime and its collaborators. Along with information on the men and methods of sabotage against the German occupiers, there are valuable insights into the ideological struggle of the Norwegian Church and the establishment of an illegal press."

—JOSE M. SANCHEZ, PROFESSOR OF MODERN EUROPEAN HISTORY, ST LOUIS UNIVERSITY

"I have greatly enjoyed reading this book. A thorough account, well researched, compellingly told, and helpfully illustrated. I will certainly mention it to audiences when I do my presentation of the war."

—KATHLEEN STOKKER, PROFESSOR OF NORWEGIAN, LUTHER COLLEGE

Books by Richard S. Fuegner

Beneath the Tyrant's Yoke

Gaslight Square Illuminated

Dawn of Courage

A Nation Defiant

A
NATION
DEFIANT

A NATION DEFIANT

POLISH RESISTANCE TO THE GERMAN OCCUPATION OF POLAND

RICHARD S. FUEGNER

The front cover shows: The monument commemorates the Polish heroes
of 1939–1945, including participants in the defense of Warsaw in September 1939, the
Warsaw Ghetto Uprising, the Warsaw Uprising, and the victims of Nazi terror in the
the occupied capital. The figure on top of the pedestal is the goddess of victory: Nike,
which is also the symbol of Warsaw.

ISBN 13: 978-1-59298-936-2

Library of Congress Catalog Number: 2014905225

Printed in the United States of America

First Printing: 2014

18 17 16 15 14   5 4 3 2 1

Cover and interior design by James Monroe Design, LLC.

Beaver's Pond Press, Inc.
7108 Ohms Lane
Edina, MN 55439–2129
(952) 829-8818
www.BeaversPondPress.com

To order, visit www.BeaversPondBooks.com
or call (800) 901-3480. Reseller discounts available.

DEDICATION

For God
For Family
And for Country
. . . In that order

CONTENTS

ACKNOWLEDGMENTS

I would like to thank the following persons for their assistance while I was conducting research in the final preparation of the manuscript. All were most helpful. My sincere thanks to Toni Reavis and to Teresa Wetzel both of whom provided me with first hand information and photographs from their mother, Elzbieta (Bisia) Krasicka, who served as a sworn member of the Polish Home Army resistance during the German Occupation.

I am indebted to Ronald J. Rychlak, Professor of Law at the University of Mississippi whose book entitled *Hitler, the War and the Pope*, was most helpful, and who took time to review sections of the manuscript and provide me with helpful suggestions concerning the persecution of the Catholic Church in Poland.

I am particularly grateful to Henry Sokolowski and the Polish Combatants' Association, Toronto, Ontario for providing me with source material dealing with both the ground and air war in the early stages of the German invasion.

I would also like to thank Pat Rohan, the head of the Reference Department and Information Services Manager at the Kirkwood,

Missouri Public Library for her timely efforts in locating and obtaining bibliographical material throughout the course of my research.

I want to express appreciation to Adam Komorowski for the use of photographs taken from *The Secret Army*, a book written by his father, T. Bor Kokorowski.

I am also grateful to Professor William Brennan of St. Louis University for very useful advice and suggestions that facilitated the final preparation of the manuscript.

Thanks also to James Gallen, President of the Military History Club at the Missouri Athletic Club, St. Louis, Missouri who also provided me with helpful data.

And among those to whom I am beholden I would especially like to thank my Editor and Publishing Mentor, Katy Jo Turner, whose genuine interest, enthusiasm and suggestions were a real source of help and encouragement in turning a manuscript into a published book. And I am equally grateful to my designer, Jay Monroe, whose concern and creative imagination resulted in a particlarly attractive and satisfying cover design.

INTRODUCTION

Poland has not yet perished
So long as we still live.
What the foe by force has seized,
Sword in hand we'll gain.

—POLISH NATIONAL ANTHEM

Nowhere in Europe during the Second World War were the emotions, passions, and sensibilities of the ordinary civilian population strained and tested more severely, than in Poland during the German occupation. Having to live daily face-to-face with the foreign occupying forces, alone and without the help of Allied assistance, these beleaguered citizens dealt with conditions and experiences the scale and extent of which far exceeded anything comparable in other countries of occupied Europe.

This book is but one attempt to describe life in Poland during the most savage war in human history, a war in which the genocidal policies of the Nazis resulted in the deaths of millions of innocent people.

The war in occupied Poland involved more than clearly defined battles fought by conventional military forces. There was that, of course. But it is also a story of dedicated men and women—both young and old—ordinary people who never wore uniforms, who harbored a great love of country matched with a resolve to do extraordinary things, oftentimes sacrificing their own safety and self-interest—and in many cases their own lives—in an unequal struggle against the brute force of a far-superior alien power. In their refusal to accept tyranny, they exemplified the finest qualities of the human spirit.

For the people of Poland, the occupation was a *state of mind*, a *spirit of defiance* and a *deep-seated rejection of the German occupying power.*

The distinctive features of the occupation were perhaps most accurately described by one of its more well-known personalities and eye witnesses, Karol Wojtyła, later to become Pope John Paul II, who stated that life in Poland was *"a trial by fire, a period of fear, violence, extreme poverty, death, and tragic experiences of painful separation, endured in the absence of all security and freedom; recurring traumas brought about by the incessant bloodshed."*[1] The German invasion and occupation of Poland was nothing less than a policy of extermination, the purpose of which was to eliminate the country as a viable nation. From the very beginning and within the heartland of Poland itself, the locustlike German invaders unleashed a reign of terror to facilitate a plan for genocide.

The people's response was an organized resistance movement that grew to dimensions unmatched in any other occupied country in Europe and that would test the mettle of the nation for almost six long years. Those involved in the Resistance consisted of men and women possessed of a self-assurance that, whether things went well or amiss on any particular day, drew on a sense that one was doing the right thing. Whether living in large expanses of woodlands that served as bases for partisan units involved in sabotage, raids on German offices and army facilities, and assassinations of traitors and detested German officials, or in concealed attics operating clandestine radios in communication with London, all had a strong sense of human dignity that was something more than a phrase. They saw people literally dehumanized before their very eyes and simply refused to bear it.

The intelligentsia and educated classes suffered brutal mistreatment. All universities and secondary schools were closed, as were as all theaters, museums, cultural activities, radio stations, and newspapers. All of the elements of normal national life prior to the occupation were now underground activities. Courageous citizens established an underground press for publishing books, as well as numerous clandestine newspapers, secret tracts, and pamphlets that were meant to boost morale and spread the news of what was happening on other war fronts.

Those who resisted also included civilians living in their homes, often with children, and old people keeping the activists alive by simply providing other resisters with the means to carry on the fight. Groups of actors, for example, secretly performed ballads, concerts, and plays in private apartments and cellars to counteract depression, anxiety, and other forms of stress brought on by daily life under the occupation.

From 1939 to 1945, approximately six million Polish inhabitants were lost in a total population of thirty-five million; damage to cities such as Warsaw, Wroclaw, and Gdańsk was estimated at 75 to 85 percent; three-quarters of the industry had to be reconstructed and 80 percent of the farmland was laid waste.[2] That work of destruction, which was symbolic of the nation's fate in World War II, was also mute testimony to the audacity of the Polish people.

With no Allied assistance, it was their unshakeable resolve, spirit of defiance, unwavering resilience, and indestructible national consciousness that defied eradication. This remarkable history of the

Polish people not only makes for one of the most memorable pages in the annals of the European Resistance, but also records one of the most unrecognized tragedies of the Second World War.

This book is in no way meant to be a full-scale picture or comprehensive study of the Polish Resistance. All I have been able to do is lift one corner of the veil and afford a glimpse of the throbbing life and suffering of those who took part in the midst of the struggle. It is but an endeavor to describe a time in Polish history that deserves to be long remembered by later generations. I hope that this book will move readers to reflect upon the prowess of a people who, during those bitter years, not only survived severe testing against overwhelming odds, but who also strengthened a national identity unsurpassed in moral grandeur. It is also my hope that those who read this book and who have never lived under tyrannical rule will appreciate all the more the freedoms and individual liberties that they enjoy and so often take for granted.

I, of course, take full responsibility for any of the book's short-comings, omissions, or inaccuracies.

CHAPTER ONE

The Polish Phoenix

Interwar Europe was a pile of kindling waiting for a spark. The economic deprivation of millions, the rise of blood-thirsty ideologies, outbreaks, national and racial hatred— all spoke of a social and spiritual crisis at the very heart of European civilization.

—*LEGENDS OF MODERNITY:*
ESSAYS AND LETTERS FROM OCCUPIED POLAND, 1942–1943
CZESLAW MILOSZ (1911–2004)

The terms of the Versailles Treaty that brought the First World War to a close re-established Poland as an independent nation, a status the country lost in 1795 by the joint intervention of Russia, Prussia, and Austria as they partitioned and annexed Polish lands.[1] This century-long division dissolved in the spring of 1919 when the Allied Powers redrew the borders of Germany and Russia, establishing the independent nation state of Poland. The newly reformed Polish republic was formed out of the Polish-speaking parts of Russia and Germany, which included large areas with minority populations, most notably German. The Poles were granted the largest expanse of land carved out of Germany.

A particular point at issue was the Baltic port city of Danzig, predominantly ethnic German in population, which was declared a demilitarized free city under the protection of the League of Nations. The settlement separated Danzig from Germany and created a Polish land corridor between the German territories of Pomerania and East Prussia, both of which were awarded to the newly independent Poland, which gave Poland access to the sea.[2]

During the early months of their newly found freedom and after having lived under foreign rule for 123 years, many Poles experienced a patriotic zeal and feverish exaltation toward a country that was, to them, like a phoenix rising from the ashes. The unexpected enthusiasm that news of the treaty brought to the Polish people, however, was not enough to help the citizenry deal with two formidable problems facing the country from the first day of its independence. The newly formed nation faced a geopolitical situation, the result of the Versailles Treaty and the Treaty of Riga signed in 1921, which was both difficult and complex. The latter pact was a compromise agreement that ended a six-year Polish war with Russia and that divided disputed Ukrainian and Byelorussian lands between the two contending countries. Only a narrow strip of territory, the "Danzig (Polish) Corridor," connected the center of landlocked Poland with the Baltic Sea.

Surrounded on 60 percent of its frontiers, Poland was bordered by two antagonistic powers opposed to the very existence of the new Polish state: Germany on the west and Soviet Russia on the east. For Germany, Poland—even more than France—was the hated "upstart of Versailles"; for Soviet Russia, it was an obstacle to Communism's westward expansion, the main barrier separating the Red Army from Germany.[3]

The Germans were never willing to regard the Polish acquisitions as permanent. In 1922 Germany entered into a covert working relationship with Soviet Russia involving arms technology by the Rapallo Treaty. The pact was vital to the Germans, who had been required to dismantle their armaments industry by the Versailles Treaty. The agreement enabled Germany to secretly extend arrangements for the joint manufacture of arms in Russia, and even to have German pilots and tank crews trained there.[4] For all practical purposes, the alliance largely targeted Poland.

This hostility from Germany and Soviet Russia produced a serious strain on Poland's resources. The nation could dedicate only about one-third of the its budget to national defense; World War I had left the country in a state of devastation and impoverishment, thereby drastically reducing the remaining portion of the modest national income available for reconstruction purposes. The nation's heaviest financial burden involved the physical rehabilitation of its cities, farms, industries, and communications systems.[5]

During the 1920s and early 1930s Poland's security depended on the alliance with France and Romania, as well as on the weaknesses of Soviet Russia and Germany. Although the Rapallo Treaty allied the two latter countries, their armed forces and economies were initially weakened by the war. In 1921, Poland, under the foreign policy leadership of Józef Piłsudski, "the founder and father of the Polish Army," formed an alliance with France, one that the Poles hoped would strengthen the military ties uniting the two countries. France, however, eliminated the provision requiring both partners to come to one another's aid in case of a German attack. Instead, France wanted the military responsibilities to be based on a vaguely defined responsibility from mutual membership in the League of Nations.[6]

In January 1932, faced with the rise of Stalinist Russia on its eastern border, Piłsudski signed a ten-year nonaggression pact with

Joseph Stalin, assuring the Soviet leader that Poland would never side with Germany against the Soviet Union.[7]

Poland's continued relationship with France throughout the early 1930s and beyond, as we will see, was ambivalent and subject to much vacillation. In March 1933, shortly after Adolf Hitler's rise to power, Piłsudski contacted the French prime minister, Édouard Daladier, and warned him that German rearmament would soon increase at a rapid pace. He recommended launching a joint preventive war by France, Great Britain, and Poland to crush Hitler, thereby preventing German rearmament. In fact, Piłsudski was so certain of a future German invasion of Poland that he offered to create an incident at the Polish military depot at Westerplatte in Danzig as a necessary pretext to destroying Hitler's regime before it became too strong. However, the proposal failed after Daladier consulted with London. A month later Piłsudski made the offer again, only to have the French refuse it once again.[8]

In the spring of 1933, Germany's political and military positions could not have been worse. The Third Reich was diplomatically isolated, and domestic conditions in Germany were precarious, with 40 percent of the workforce unemployed. Some one hundred thousand men, deprived of tanks and military aircraft, comprised the armed forces. Poland had an army of three hundred thousand men. Piłsudski believed that, having won the Polish-Soviet war only twenty years earlier without anything other than a tough and determined infantry, a hardened war-experienced cavalry, and unsophisticated equipment, his country would not require much more than that in the future, so long as Poland had the support of the combined forces of France and Great Britain.[9]

Polish Foreign Minister Józef Beck, in 1936, after Piłsudski's death and shortly after the German occupation of the Rhineland, proposed the idea of a preventative war. But yet again, after consulting with the British, the French refused to act. Thus key European players forever lost the opportunity to overthrow Hitler without causing a general war.[10]

When Hitler came to power, he not only promised the German people that he would eliminate the shame of Versailles, he would also put the 40 percent of the total German workforce who were unemployed back to work. Above all, Hitler, who was an exalted nationalist, was determined to restore a defeated and chaotic Germany to a far greater status than it had ever enjoyed before. His vision included raising the new German state to a heightened grandeur unlike anything the world had ever witnessed, and he would do it with a program based on racial purity.

Hitler fashioned his ideal future German state on an underlying requirement: greater territorial expansion, or *Lebensraum*—living space—for the German people. Hitler said that current Germany territory alone would fail to meet the living standards of the expanding population. Therefore, Germany required more agriculturally productive space, and he had in mind the more sparsely populated regions of the Slavic lands of Eastern Europe, which included the western, Prussian-controlled provinces of Poland. This meant the following:

> *The new Reich must again set itself on the march along the road of the Teutonic Knights of old, to obtain by the German sword soil for the German plow and daily bread for the nation. . . . Today we count eighty million Germans in Europe! This foreign policy will be acknowledged as correct only if, after scarcely a hundred years, there are two hundred and fifty million Germans in Europe!*[11]

But before German forces could obliterate Poland, Hitler saw that it must separate from its alliance with France. After coming to power, Hitler enacted one of his first foreign policy decisions, namely entering into a nonaggression pact with Poland in 1934 to neutralize the possibility of a French-Polish military alliance against Germany, before the latter had a chance to complete its rearmament.[12]

In March 1935, Hitler began rearmament in public defiance of the Versailles Treaty. In March 1936, he issued German troops with formal orders for the reoccupation of the Rhineland, which had earlier been demilitarized by the treaty. The German generals did not want another world war. The experiences of World War I had left deep impressions in the minds of the German people and the generals were far from certain about the country's ability to wage another major war. Nevertheless, in March 1938, Hitler, acting against the advice of his apprehensive generals, decided on a military occupation of Austria, which, without offering up any resistance, was absorbed into a greater Germany.[13]

In September 1938, Germany also acquired the ethnically German Sudetenland region of neighboring Czechoslovakia; this occurred after Hitler successfully intimidated Britain and France at the Munich Conference by threatening armed force against the rest of the Czech state if the two countries refused his terms. The final settlement ceded to Germany eleven thousand square miles of territory in which 2.8 million Sudeten Germans and 800,000 Czechs dwelt.[14]

The ease with which Britain acquiesced at Munich, along with the accompanying French passivity, encouraged Germany. As a result and in violation of Hitler's assurance that he would have no further territorial demands in Europe, German forces entered Prague in March 1939, thereby completing the total annexation of Czechoslovakia.[15]

Hitler, however, was not yet ready to invade Poland. For the time being, he only wanted Danzig returned to Germany, as well as free access to East Prussia via a yet-to-be-established German highway and railroad across the Polish Corridor. The position of both Danzig and the Polish Corridor made for a geographically abnormal division and was a bone of contention from the beginning, but it was something the Poles obstinately refused to relinquish.

On March 29, the possibility of an imminent attack by Germany on Poland, which the Polish government considered in their vital interest to resist, prompted the British to provide a guarantee against any German action threatening Polish independence. For Hitler, that Polish Guarantee was a "manifest provocation" to incite a world war.[16]

On April 3, after receiving news of the guarantee, Hitler issued a top-secret directive code-named Case White—*Fall Weiss*—ordering the *Wehrmacht* to destroy the Polish armed forces. He intended to unleash a punitive measure and a short, localized war, with no interference from Britain or France.

In mid-May the Polish government sent its minister of war, Tadeusz Kasprzycki, to Paris, where he obtained a signed, formal agreement from the French General Staff. This document promised that, on the outbreak of war between Germany and Poland, the French would respond with air action against Germany, followed by a major military offensive of the full French army within fifteen days of mobilization.[17]

At a military conference on August 22, 1939, Hitler told his generals, "I shall give a propagandist reason for starting the war—never mind whether it is plausible or not. The victor will not be asked afterward whether he told the truth or not. In starting and waging a war it is not right that matters, but victory." And in a typical Teutonic torrent of rage, he thundered,

Close your hearts to pity! Act brutally! Eighty million people must obtain what is their right . . . the stronger man is

*right . . . Be harsh and remorseless! Be steeled against all signs
of compassion!*

*Whoever has pondered over this world order knows that
its meaning lies in the success of the best by means of force . . .*[18]

But Hitler was still wary of an all-out major conflict. He realized
that the only way by which he could successfully wage a war against
Poland—his next target of opportunity—was by gaining the support
of Russia, the only power that could otherwise give direct support to
Poland and be a deterrent to Germany.[19]

On August 23, 1939, Hitler entered into a secret nonaggression
pact with Soviet Russia, despite his fear and hatred of Communism.
For the time being, both leaders were willing to put aside their ideological differences and "bury the hatchet" in Poland, despite their mutual
distrust. The agreement provided that both parties would "desist from
any act of violence, any aggressive action, and any attack on each
other." An additional secret protocol to the pact stipulated that both
Germany and Soviet Russia split up Eastern Europe into spheres of
influence, with Russia getting the eastern territories in Poland and the
Baltic countries of Estonia and Latvia. The protocol was amended on
September 28, granting the Soviets Lithuania as well. The Germans
would receive all the Polish territory that lay west of the Vistula and
Bug rivers.[20]

Hitler believed that neither Great Britain nor France would take
action against him. The German leader knew that Poland was a country too far out of reach from Great Britain to constitute a real threat.
And the pact with Russia now enabled Hitler to invade Poland without fear of Soviet intervention. In essence, he had all the assurance he
needed to accelerate his steps toward *Lebensraum* with impunity.

By the late spring of 1939, all diplomatic negotiations between
Poland and Germany had come to an end, and war with Germany

rose as a real probability. Poland then partly mobilized its forces in secret during the summer of 1939, with the intention of declaring full mobilization in late August. However, the French insisted that Poland halt the announcement for fear it might antagonize Hitler. Poland nevertheless declared mobilization on August 30, but France again objected, threatening to withhold assistance and demanding a revocation. Poland complied, but reissued its mobilization the following day. A fully mobilized Polish army would have numbered about 2.5 million, but various preliminary mobilizations had set the number of Polish troops at about 600,000. When full mobilization began, Poland's forces probably consisted of only 150,000 to 200,000 fully equipped men in place to meet the German invasion on September 1.[21]

The Polish Army also faced a serious geographic problem. Polish forces were dispersed along a frontier with Germany that was about 1,250 miles long. The Slovakian border added another 500 miles to defend. The Poles had built practically no fortifications anywhere, except to a limited extent on the Narew River in the northeast part of the country. Permanent fortifications would have simply cost too much money, something they did not have. Besides, no nation could have fortified frontiers of the length of Poland's. Various army field commanders had to assume the responsibility of building field defenses and antitank ditches at critical locations, or not to build them, as they chose. During the summer of 1939, the army commanders were reluctant to dig up the farmland before the farmers had gotten in their crops.[22]

Matters were made worse because the French were unable to begin their full-scale offensive action until September 17—fifteen days after mobilization. This inability to have troops in place earlier arose from the complicated French mobilization system; it was clearly outdated and relied on a conscript army, which could not go effectively into action until the mass of trained reserves were called up from their civilian jobs and the formations were made ready to operate. An additional delaying factor involved the French Command's persistence in outdated tactical ideas, particularly the idea that a massive artillery bombardment, along the lines of what had happened during the First World War, must precede any offensive action. Finally, the French command had to take the greater part of their heavy artillery out of storage; they could not make it available until the last stage of mobilization, on the sixteenth day. These conditions governed preparations to deliver an offensive.[23]

All of this gave rise to genuine concerns, but the Poles refused to be frightened. They believed themselves to be militarily stronger than they actually were. And they believed the Germans to be weaker than they proved to be. They knew that they would incur losses and a good deal of suffering. Nevertheless, the Poles displayed remarkable equanimity in the face of war. They believed that Britain and France would quickly join the conflict and that their own forces, serving with those of the Western Allies, would prevail. From initial defeat would come victory. These were the Polish hopes and expectations before the leaves began to fall in the autumn of 1939.

CHAPTER TWO
The September Campaign

The German invasion was among the most trying and tragic in the millennial history of the Polish nation. Left alone to fight Nazi Germany and abandoned by their allies, throughout the war the Polish people faced a seemingly hopeless situation.

—M.K. DZIEWANOWSKI (1913–2005) POLISH HISTORIAN

As a pretext for starting its invasion, Germany preceded its attack on Poland with a border provocation on the evening of August 31, 1939. A small group of German SS operatives posing as Poles staged a simulated attack on a local German radio broadcasting station near Gleiwitz on the German-Polish border in Upper Silesia. To further imply that the attacking force consisted of Poles against German troops, the local head of the Gestapo, Heinrich Müller, took some twelve or thirteen condemned German concentration camp inmates, dressed them in Polish uniforms, and left them for dead on the ground at the scene of the incident. For this purpose, the Gestapo gave the men fatal lethal injections and shot their bodies so they appeared to have been killed during the attack. The station was "held" long enough for a Polish-speaking German to transmit an anti-German message in Polish, thus reinforcing the appearance that the attack had been the work of Polish saboteurs. Shortly after the assault, foreign journalists arrived on scene and viewed the bodies where the incident occurred.[1]

On the following morning, Friday, September 1, 1939, without any prior warning or declaration of war, motorized armored formations of *Wehrmacht* troops prepared to overrun the borders of Poland on three fronts that extended from the Baltic Sea to what had until recently been Czechoslovakia. The German attack came from East Prussia and Pomerania in the north and from the west, and Slovakia in the south, where German troops broke through all Polish defenses along the frontier. From there, they advanced toward Warsaw, the nation's capital, in a massive encirclement attack west of the Vistula River. The invading force consisted of five armies and reserves. German forces totaled 1.8 million soldiers. There were 2,700 tanks, 10,000 artillery pieces, and more than 2,000 aircraft. All fell under the command of General Walther von Brauchitsch.[2]

The typical Polish infantry division roughly equaled its German counterpart in number, but came up short in terms of antitank guns, artillery support, and transport. Poland had thirty active and seven reserve divisions, as well as twelve cavalry brigades, and one mechanized cavalry brigade. The Border Defense Corps (KOP), an elite force designed to secure the frontiers from infiltration and engage in small-unit actions as well as diversion, sabotage, and intelligence gathering, supplemented these forces. A National Guard, equipped with older-model weapons, also stood ready for local defense. Armored train groups and river flotillas operated under army command. The Poles had 180 tanks and 420 operational aircraft.[3]

German Wehrmacht troops entering the city of Warsaw.

It was all too clear that the Polish army was utterly unprepared for the invasion. Having no offensive capability against the German onslaught, Poland's plan in the event of an attack by Germany, known as Plan Z, was based on a defensive withdrawal to the southeastern part of the country—to friendly Romania—with the aim of holding out for an Anglo-French counterattack in the west. This would reduce German pressure and enable Polish forces to be resupplied by the Allies through Romania.[4] Expressing the state of the nation, the eminent historical analyst Samuel L. Sharp noted, "Her defenses were aptly compared to a thin eggshell containing a soft yolk which presented almost no problem to the German war machine."[5] Despite the scarcity of good roads and the numerous lakes and forests in some areas, the open Polish plain offered flat and fairly uninhibited terrain that was all too well suited for the German offensive.

Germany did not have the resources to fight a prolonged engagement with Poland while simultaneously defending itself against an attack by the Western Allies.[6] Consequently, Germany conducted what came to be known as blitzkrieg—lightning warfare—a tactic developed in Germany based upon speed and surprise. It entailed a lethal combination of light tank units supported by motorized infantry, armored artillery, motorized service forces, and aircraft—all trained to work in close coordination. The instantaneous control of the Polish air space by the *Luftwaffe* made retreat virtually impossible. And there was no way for the Poles to block roads or junctions against the motorized German army, which could simply leave the roads and drive through the fields. The Germans achieved tactical surprise from the very beginning of the assault.

Strategically, the German plan was based on two wide-ranging pincer movements. One German force striking upward from Silesia in the south was to converge on Warsaw, meeting forces coming down from East Prussia and German Pomerania in the north. A second pincer movement was to stem from the same bases but meet much farther to the east—approximately in the region of Brest Litovsk.[7]

Germany made careful preparations for the use of the *Luftwaffe,* the initial mission of which was to defeat the Polish Air Force. However, an early morning mist over many of the airfields frustrated the early morning attacks on the prewar runways. Contrary to a widely held belief, the Polish Air Force was not destroyed on September 1 on its airfields. Most of the Polish aircraft were dispersed to new and secret airfields in eastern Poland on August 31, in anticipation of a German attack. The only airfield destroyed by the *Luftwaffe* on the morning of September 1 was the prewar airfield at Rakowice near Kraków, where twenty-eight unusable aircraft were decimated.[8]

The *Luftwaffe* controlled the sky over Poland only because so few Polish planes counteracted the opposition. As one source records, "The one exception was Warsaw, where the Polish Pursuit Brigade intercepted a number of bomber attacks throughout the day, scoring 16 confirmed kills with a loss of 10 Polish fighters and 24 damaged."[9]

With the out-of-reach planes in eastern Poland and having lost a number of others in the first week of the war, Poland faced a drastically restricted ability to respond. Much of the problem stemmed from the lack of fuel at the new airstrips. Nevertheless, the small Polish Air Force fought well against tremendous odds. Polish aircraft had 121 confirmed kills of German aircraft, but later research into German records indicates that Polish fighters accounted for the loss of at least 160 aircraft. However, the overwhelming numerical strength of the *Luftwaffe* made it virtually impossible for the small Polish squadrons to challenge German air supremacy.[10]

The first assault operation occurred just before dawn at 4:40 a.m., when a massive indiscriminate *Luftwaffe* carpet-bombing raid of Stuka dive-bombers suddenly and brutally attacked the inhabitants of the defenseless city of Wieluń in central Poland. More than 1,200 people died, hundreds more suffered injuries, and 90 percent of the town center was destroyed.[11]

No one can compile the tears, agony, and rage that a people feel when the brute force of an alien power destroys the nation in which they live. Newspaper headlines cannot accurately tell of the unthinkable mass of sorrow. Nor can one ever describe the distraught faces of a Polish civilian population turned up toward the clouds as the dive-bombers—sixty and seventy in a flock—went into earthward dives, their specially built sirens activating blood-curdling shrieks that surely maximized the panic on the ground below, raining death and destruction.

**Polish peasants tremble, cry, and pray as
German troops approach Warsaw.**

Farther north, at 4:45 a.m., on the Baltic Sea coast, the German battleship SMS Schleswig-Holstein, on a so-called goodwill visit, opened fire on the small, isolated Polish naval depot and garrison maintained by a small force of 182 men on the Westerplatte peninsula, in what was then the free city of Danzig. Polish defenders held off the Germans until further attacks followed. At the Polish post office, postal workers and Boy Scouts resisted for most of the day until they were forced to surrender. The Germans then summarily executed the defenders.[12]

At 5:30 a.m. on the German-Silesian border in southwestern Poland, huge numbers of German tanks amassed in preparation for an all-out invasion. Within minutes, armored formations rolled down the main street of the Upper Silesian capital city of Katowice.

The inhabitants, awakened by the sustained clamor of the mobilized panzer armor, opened their windows only to have their worst fears realized. The invading German armies now raced from city to city, largely unopposed. These incidents were just the beginning of what came to be known as the most devastating period in Polish history: the onset of the Second World War.

In advance of the main lines of attack, the *Luftwaffe* successfully disrupted the mobilization of Polish army units by bombing all road and rail junctions and concentrations of Polish troops. Within a few days, the invading forces destroyed so many bridges and railroad tracks that practically all railroad activity halted. German forces deliberately bombed towns and villages, creating a fleeing mass of terror-stricken civilians that blocked the roads and hampered the flow of reinforcements to the front. Flying directly ahead of the panzers, the dive-bombing aircraft, in waves of forty or fifty, laid waste any obstacles in the German path of destruction. Being taken completely by surprise, Poland did not put their antiaircraft guns into action until the second raid. People were stunned to hear of news of the occupation of such large towns as Katowice, Poznań, Kraków, Łódź, and Lublin, one after the other.

German panzer and motorized armored forces, led by tank tactician General Heinz Guderian, made their way into the base of the Polish Corridor just below Danzig and Gdynia. The battle here was especially intense. At about five o'clock in the afternoon of that first day of the invasion, a broad wave of the Polish 18th Lancer Cavalry Brigade and a company of the 81st Armored Troop held the northernmost Polish positions, while the remainder of the brigade withdrew southward. Daylong fighting with the German 20th Motorized Infantry Division resulted in severe losses.

At seven o'clock Polish troops suddenly located a German infantry battalion in a forest clearing. The Polish regimental commander,

Colonel Kazimierz Mastalarz, decided on a mounted saber charge. However, a column of tanks and motorized German troops unnoticed by the cavalrymen appeared from around a bend and opened fire before the mounted troops could turn their horses around. Some twenty Polish troopers, including Mastalarz, were killed before the squadron could withdraw behind a nearby hill.[13]

This particular three-day battle for the Polish Corridor soon became a legend and source of German propaganda, which falsely reported to Italian war correspondents that Polish cavalry, armed with sabers, had attacked German tanks. Some Western military historians still believe this myth even today. In fact, "the occasional encounters between mounted troops and German armored vehicles usually resulted in the Poles trying to escape such a hopeless skirmish in order to deal with them by using anti-tank rifles from dismounted positions."[14] Polish cavalrymen easily realized their inability to attack German armor.

When and where they were in position, Poles sometimes got the better of the fight. At one point in East Prussia, the Polish Podlaska Cavalry Brigade counterattacked, crossed the border, and actually captured a few small German villages.[15] But after three days of hard fighting in the Polish Corridor, the German superiority in infantry and armor was too much for the Poles, who waged a heroic, but ultimately futile, struggle against vastly overwhelming odds.

German success was even more rapid in the south. By September 3, the Poles were unable to contain the German Army Group South. By September 5, each of the three German armies that made up the group made a breakthrough about sixty miles within Polish territory. Despite furious resistance, the German 8th Army made a breakthrough toward Łódź. The 14th Army had captured the entire Silesian industrial basin and was driving toward Kraków, which would surrender the next day, while the tanks and infantry of the 10th Army continued the drive toward Warsaw, only seventy miles away.[16]

It became increasingly evident that, in order to survive, Poland needed the promised French offensive and British bombing attack on Germany. In Warsaw on the day of the German invasion, the Polish foreign minister, Józef Beck, called in both the French and British ambassadors to find out when their countries would enter the war. On September 2, both countries delivered ultimatums to the German government: unless German forces withdrew from Poland, Britain and France would fulfill their obligations to honor the Polish Guarantee. The French were initially reluctant to go along with Britain, but finally conceded. The German refusal to respond to the ultimatum moved both Western Allies to declare war on Germany on September 3.

Meanwhile, for the Poles in the field, one of the worst problems was a breakdown in communications. The telegraph and telephone system that the Polish Army had relied upon broke down in western Poland as the German armored columns, driving across the country, pulled down the wires. As a result, Polish General Headquarters had no clear idea of the location of many of its own divisions or what they were doing. The proximity of the German troops to Warsaw prompted the Polish High Command and its commander, MarshalRydz-Śmigły, to relocate to southeastern Poland. Orders came to form a defensive line behind the Vistula River.[17] Civilian volunteers in Warsaw wasted no time building barricades and antitank trenches in anticipation of the panzer elements that they would soon encounter.

On the evening of September 8, advance armored elements of the German Army Group South arrived at the Warsaw workers' suburb of Praga. On the following morning, they waged an attack on the city itself, only to discover that the defense of the capital was far stronger than they expected. Under a flag of truce, the Germans delivered a demand to the Poles for unconditional surrender. But instead of giving up, the citizens began to fortify the city. To tell the world that the capital was still in Polish hands, the city repeatedly transmitted a Chopin polonaise repeatedly throughout the city. Norman Davies, the distinguished English authority on Poland, provides a vivid description of Warsaw at the time:

> *Men, women, and children worked into the night digging trenches in parks, playgrounds, and vacant lots. Wealthy Warsaw aristocrats were chauffeured to defense sites where they toiled alongside office workers. Trolley cars were thrown across thoroughfares; barricades of cars and furniture were erected in narrow streets.*
>
> *When the German tanks jumped off for the attack . . . they were stopped dead—in many cases by civilians who dashed boldly into the street to toss burning rags under the vehicles, causing them to catch fire and explode. German infantrymen were pinned down by snipers.[18]*

It was clear to the invaders that Polish resistance was stiffening.

On September 8 and 9, the Poznań army, consisting of four infantry divisions and two cavalry brigades, counterattacked from the north against the German forces heading toward the center of Warsaw. By noon on September 10 a Polish offensive that surprised the German Army Group South halted the German advance, forcing it to divert away from the capital. But German superiority in tanks and aircraft and reinforcements allowed them to regroup and stop the Poznań Army's push southward.[19] The counterattack became a battle of encirclement. On September 12 it was clear to the Poles that they could not cut through the entire German Army Group South. Thus they redirected their attack eastward in an attempt to break into Warsaw either to relieve the capital or join its garrison.

On September 13, Army Group South, commanded by General

Gerd von Rundstedt and heavily reinforced, attacked the Poles from the west and the south. Part of Army Group North closed the ring from the north. The center of the Polish force was situated in the small city of Kutno, where the struggle became known as the Battle of the Kutno Pocket. The battle lasted until September 17, when the Polish defenses broke down. The Germans took fifty-two thousand prisoners. Only two Polish divisions escaped to aid in the defense of Warsaw.[20] By the middle of September Polish losses were severe and the German advance had captured half of the country.

It was not long before surviving Polish field forces tried to cut through unruly crowds that were heading east and filling the unpaved roads outside the cities. And in the midst of the chaos, the Polish soldiers ceased to exist as a unit. All semblance of order disappeared. The expressionless refugees trudged along in unending columns, some pushing hand carts with quilts tied over the tops of mounds of furniture, others pushing an occasional baby carriage or bicycle; still others pulled wagons under the weight of suitcases, mattresses, and whatever other necessities they could handle. The *Luftwaffe* seemed to concentrate on the roads near the frontier, where the refugees were all in desperate retreat toward the safety of the Romanian border.

Poland dismissed any hopeful expectation of relief or assistance from Britain and France on September 17, when the French failed on their commitment to launch a full-scale offensive against the German forces in Poland within the promised fifteen days after French mobilization. Britain and France had also promised to conduct bombing attacks in Germany. But now both governments were concerned that bombing raids in Germany would provoke Hitler and lead to prompt retaliatory raids on civilian populations in London and Paris.[21]

**Civilians leaving the battered city of Warsaw
after the invasion.**

If the Polish people had any remaining ray of hope it was extinguished on that same fateful September 17 when Soviet Red Army forces invaded Poland's eastern territories. In typical Soviet-Russian fashion, the invading armies prepared hasty propaganda to justify the intervention. The document stated that the Soviet Union was "obliged" to intervene because the Polish nation was disintegrating and no longer showed any signs of life. It was therefore incumbent on the Red Army to protect the kindred Ukrainian and White Russian people who were "living in a state of national oppression" on Polish territory, but who were blood brothers to major nationalities within the Soviet Union. Moreover, the Soviet government said that it intended to "take all measures to extricate the Polish people from the unfortunate war into which they were dragged by their unwise leaders." When the Polish ambassador at the Soviet ministry received this document, he rejected it forthwith.[22] Poland was now caught between Scylla and Charybdis, with next to no hope that she could survive as a free nation.

Militarily, the Soviet move had little influence on the outcome of the September campaign. The Polish forces could not reform their front line: there was none since the German breakthrough during the first few days of September. Aside from isolated pockets of resistance, the Soviet troops moved into a political and military vacuum.[23] Nearly all the Polish troops had withdrawn from the eastern border to fight the German onslaught.

Only a few units of the Border Defense Corps, aided by local volunteers, resisted. Outnumbered one hundred to one, the Poles refused to surrender. A Soviet rifle division attacked one such force at a Polish line of bunker and trenches near Sarny in Western Ukraine close to the Russian border. For three days the Poles defended the bunkers, but on September 20, facing encirclement, they were forced to withdraw. In some places the Poles resisted until September 25. Lieutenant Jan Bolbot commanded a platoon of fifty men who were holed up in their bunker where they fought to the last man, despite hopeless odds. Unable to defeat the Poles with their own weaponry, the Soviets piled debris around the bunkers and set the piles on fire. Bolbot and his entire force died in the flames.[24] Still, some Poles fought on. An effective Polish resistance mounted in the Pripet Marshes of east central Poland did not surrender until all of its ammunition was gone and its forces were outnumbered by the prisoners it had taken.[25]

Polish defenses in the southeast collapsed as authorities ordered troops to fall back across the Romanian and Hungarian borders. Fighting continued to rage around Warsaw, beleaguered and ruthlessly bombarded day and night both from the ground and the air. Finally, German artillery and bombers destroyed the water supply system and exhausted the city's food supply. Radio Warsaw played Chopin's *Funeral March* on September 28 as the proud, besieged city capitulated. As one survivor remembers it,

> *In the western suburbs of the city we saw abandoned guns and street barricades, sometimes reaching to the second stories of the houses. The city resembled an overturned ant heap. The streets were full of rubble, already with pathways trodden through and over it by people hurrying in all directions.*[26]

Polish forces continued to mount an effective defense on the Hel Peninsula, one of the longest-defended pockets of Polish Army resistance. Against overwhelming odds, some three thousand soldiers of the Coastal Defense Group defended the area until October 2, when Germans finally forced them to capitulate. And then on October 6, 1939, in the Pripet Marshes of east central Poland beyond the Bug River at the Battle of Kock, an independent operational unit, Group Polesie, waged the final battle that ended the Polish conflict.[27]

The legitimate although powerless Polish government was now forced to move from place to place during that first month of the invasion. In their flight, Polish officials left the impression that they had abandoned their people. Nevertheless, the government finally decided it must leave Poland, cross over into Romania, and made its way to France, where the now-exiled government would resume the fight.

General Government

Polish territories incorporated into the Reich

Polish territories occupied by the Soviets in 1939 and incorporated into the Soviet Union; occupied by the Germans after June 22, 1941. Ceded to the Soviet Union at Teheran and Yalta.

Cities visited by the author on his secret trips

Partition of Poland: Russia received the eastern territories of Poland; Germany received all of western Poland west of the Vistula and Bug Rivers.

After thirty-six days of unrelenting conflict, the Germans, with relatively minor assistance from the Soviet army, killed 66,500 Poles and captured about 700,000 more. The German losses amounted to some 14,000 killed and another 30,000 wounded. The German victory facilitated the capture of 200,000 Polish soldiers by the Red Army while sustaining only 700 casualties.[28]

The major Soviet offense included the mass deportation of an estimated two million anti-Soviet and "socially inadaptable elements" from eastern Poland, and some Western Ukrainians and Byelorussians who were transported to Siberia, the Gulag Archipelago, and Kazakhstan in the terrible railroad convoys of 1939 to 1940. At least one-half of those who were transported died within a year of their arrest. Others were recruited into the Red Army or sent to work inside Russia.[29]

Fighting gradually wound down as the German or the Soviet armies eliminated the remaining elements of resistance. But at no time were orders for a total surrender ever given nor did any general surrender ever take place.

Afterthoughts on the September Campaign

With neither an ultimatum nor a declaration of war, Germany invaded Poland on all fronts. The *Luftwaffe* bombed every Polish city. No one could doubt Hitler's objective: the military conquest of the entire country; the status of Danzig was no longer an issue.[1] Polish sovereignty had been violated. Legally, under her guarantee with Poland, Great Britain was bound to declare war on Germany immediately; it had pledged to act at once. But she did not. Foreign Secretary Lord Halifax simply sent a note to Berlin that was "in the nature of a warning and is not to be considered as an ultimatum." Britain did not consider a violation of her Allies' borders a cause for war. France responded similarly to the invasion, expressing a willingness to negotiate, though refusing to send any deadline for a German response. Prime Minister Neville Chamberlain noted that Hitler was a busy man and might not have the time to review the note from Berlin.[2] Even Parliament, which had been waiting for Chamberlain's announcement, was stunned by the prime minister's lack of action.[3]

Despite the British declaration of war fifty-three hours after the invasion started and France's six hours later, neither country provided the promised active assistance at any time. Aside from propaganda leaflets dropped over a few German cities by the RAF, Britain conducted no bombing raids against Germany. And France mounted no massive land assaults against the Germans in Poland. Thus the first country to resist the German onslaught was left to face the enemy alone.

With the exception of a relatively small German force of second- and third-line divisions guarding the Siegfried Line at the border with France, the major part of the German Army massed on the Polish western border and in East Prussia, targeting Poland.

The French Army, from its secure base behind the Maginot Line, was superior in men, tanks, artillery, and aircraft. Yet there was no substantial French assault on the Siegfried Line. On land, 106 French divisions faced only 23 German divisions throughout the Polish campaign, but French General Maurice Gamelin, the Allied commander in chief, said privately that no major offensive could be launched before at least two years.[4] A concerted French push into western Germany would well have resulted in a disaster for Hitler's Third Reich. Even German Field Marshall Wilhelm Keitel, head of the Oberkommando der Wehrmacht (OKW), noted that had France conducted a full-scale invasion of Germany, Germany would have fallen immediately.[5] Had the Allies acted, the bloodiest war in human history might well have been averted. Yet both Allied powers stood aside and did nothing. Instead, the French conducted a pathetically small offensive—nothing more than a preliminary probing attack—on the German western frontier at the Saar River, resulting in a French retreat after advancing only six miles after coming under enemy fire.[6]

With the French and British vacillation, indecision, and ultimate failure to act in time, accompanied later by confused mobilization procedures, the hopelessly outdated Polish Army could have done little—with their misguided reliance on First World War tactics—against the use of blitzkrieg tactical warfare, a far more modernized German Army, and superior air force. Nonetheless, this tough, resilient, and intransigent Slavic nation demonstrated to a basically indifferent world that no price was too high to pay in the defense of one's homeland and its basic freedoms, no matter the outcome in terms of human life.

And now the tenacity of this nation that for almost a century and a half had enjoyed no more than a twenty-year breathing spell of restored self-confidence and national independence would be tested for the next six years to a degree that can only astound civilized world.

CHAPTER THREE
The Occupation under German Rule

The power and the certainty of being able to use force without any resistance are the sweetest and most noxious poison that can be introduced into any government.

—Hans Frank, Governor General of occupied Poland

The German administration of occupied Poland was vastly different from the occupation regimes in Western Europe, and especially in Scandinavia and the Low Countries. Hitler believed the people in Norway and Denmark to be racially pure and of Germanic origin—except for the few who had Jewish blood in their veins—and that in Holland, a common hereditary bond existed, both racially and nationally; non-Jews were treated comparatively well there. In Poland, however, Hitler viewed the subjugated people as *Untermenschen*—"subhuman"—and dealt with them accordingly.

In October 1939, at the conclusion of the military campaign, the German occupation divided Poland into two areas. The western and northern provinces, which included Polish Pomerania, Posnania, and Upper Silesia, and fragments of central Poland including the district of

Łódź, were annexed outright into the Greater German Reich.[1]

Persecution was the most brutal in these annexed western provinces, especially in the area called Warthegau, as Great Poland was named. It was here that the barbarity of Nazi leadership took place rapidly and with little direction or specific orders from above. There were no restrictions on the use of measures deemed necessary to ensure compliance with the objectives that authorities in Berlin had outlined for maximum and swift "Germanization." The Germans waged assaults on every aspect of economic and social life. They banned Poles from professions and from running businesses. They seized farms and commercial properties. They forced Poles to work longer hours for far less than what was paid to Germans. Poles could only shop at certain times. They were discriminated against in public conveyances. Local policemen were told not to show any leniency toward Poles and not to put them on the same level as Germans, who were the "people of culture."[2]

Nor did any laws protect the Poles from the deadly retribution that German authorities could impose arbitrarily and at any moment. The people were absolutely at the mercy of their Nazi masters. Large numbers of Poles were brutally punished for trivial offenses or taken to concentration camps. Public hangings took place almost daily, the bodies left on improvised gallows as a warning to others.[3]

The Nazis expelled thousands en masse from Pomerania, Poznań, and other towns of Great Poland; they systematically cleared all streets of inhabitants. Occupants were forced to leave all their property for use of the Germans who had come from the Reich or the Baltic countries and were placed in Polish homes. Polish leaders were eliminated by execution and many of the inhabitants were driven out from the "annexed" provinces and transferred into forced labor in Germany. This was also the lot of many thousands of youths from Central Poland. The Nazis forced those people who remained to renounce their Polish citizenship and accept German nationality. Those Poles who were economically the weakest and who remained on the spot were more severely oppressed, as was the only refuge left to them, the Catholic Church.[4]

The second area of occupation was called the General Government, which consisted of the more extensive central and southern areas that included the cities of Warsaw and Kraków; it was organized as a separate entity and completely surrounded by closed and well-guarded frontiers. It was a vast area of confinement for about twelve million Poles who had no right to cross the borders unless they had frontier permits; these were only issued in special cases when the journey of a Pole was in the German interest.[5]

The General Government was a police-run state in which a reign of terror replaced the rule of law. It was entirely controlled by the diabolical *Schutzstaffel* (SS) and run by Dr. Hans Frank, Hitler's former legal expert; appointed the governor general, he made it all too clear what the people could expect of life under the New Order. From the beginning of the occupation, the Germans used every means of violence and physical liquidation to transform Poland into a colony for exploitation. From beneath the swastika flag that hung over his residence in the Wawel Castle in Kraków, the capital, Frank issued unequivocally stated instructions to his subordinates:

The General Government will comprise all that is left of historic Poland, and it is essential that Poles residing here understand the nature of their new state. It is not a nation governed by law. It is a nation governed by the demands and desires of the Third Reich. The Poles have no rights whatsoever. His only obligation is to obey what we tell him. He must continually be reminded that his duty is to obey.

A major goal of our plan is to finish off as speedily as possible all troublemaking politicians, priests, and leaders who fall into our hands. I openly admit that some thousands of so-called important Poles will have to pay with their lives, but you must not allow sympathy for individual cases to deter you in your duty, which is to ensure that the goals of National Socialism triumph and that the Polish nation is never again to offer resistance.[6]

When asked what the ultimate plans were for Poland and its people, Frank was no less specific:

Every vestige of Polish culture is to be eliminated. Those Poles who seem to have Nordic appearances will be taken to Germany to work in our factories. Children of Nordic appearance will be taken from their parents and raised as German workers. The rest? They will work. They will eat little. And in the end they will die. There will never again be a Poland.[7]

After the war, at the Nuremberg Tribunal, when asked about the extermination of innocent Poles during the occupation, Frank responded, "If I wished to order that one should hang up posters about every seven Poles shot, there would not be enough forests in Poland with which to make the paper for the posters."[8]

In the early months of the occupation, Germany established control over the population by a strict, rigidly enforced racial apartheid. With methodical precision, *Reichsführer*-SS Heinrich Himmler organized a program to classify and segregate the various sections of the population. Nazi authorities required all Poles to register and allocated them to one of four racial categories: Germans born within the Reich were *Reichsdeutsche*; those who could claim German ancestry within three generations were German Nationals or *Volksdeutsche*; those non-Germans who could prove themselves to be free of all Jewish connections were (non-German) *Nichtdeutsche*; and the non-Aryan "subhumans" were *Juden* (Jews).[9]

These groups were further subdivided according to the people's work abilities and political loyalties, identifiable by their identity passes and ration cards. The *Reichsdeutsche* in Poland received coupons for four thousand calories a day; a Polish worker had to survive off of nine hundred; and a nonproductive Jew very often had nothing. False papers, stolen ration cards, and spurious genealogies began to emerge on all sides and gave rise to confusion, corruption, and brutality. Even the Nazi officials competed among themselves. In Danzig, the German governor registered all Poles as Germans just to spite the SS.[10]

Once classification was complete, segregation could begin. German authorities set up enclosed Jewish ghettos in the towns. In larger cities such as Warsaw, Kraków, and Łódź, local authorities expanded ghettos to accommodate Jews who had been deported from the countryside and from other countries. Polish homes in the more desirable middle-class suburbs were expropriated without any compensation to the owners in order to facilitate the influx of German officials and their families. In all public places, Nazis enforced strict racial apartheid. Streetcars, park benches, and the better shops and hotels were clearly marked *Nur Fur Deutsche*—Germans only. Jews were forbidden to leave the ghetto on pain of death.[11] All non-Germans were confined to their own quarters and forbidden to congregate in groups of more than three persons, except when in church.

Authorities also prohibited non-Germans from possessing radios, although many people concealed them, despite the order. One Warsaw family, for example, hid a radio in their bedroom. Each night as they tuned in, the first four chords of Beethoven's *Fifth Symphony* announced the beginning of the BBC broadcast. One afternoon, on a streetcar filled with Germans, the family's little boy began to sing those very notes. As a result, a Gestapo informer followed the boy home and the German authorities arrested both parents.[12]

Martial law was in force in all of the annexed territories in Poland. Nowhere did the population enjoy the protection of civil law, and the only two forms of stipulated punishment for *any* infraction of obedience were death or sentence to a concentration camp.[13] The military control of conquered Poland lasted until October 25. During that three-week period, German officials ordered 714 mass executions and 6,376 Poles, mainly Catholics, were shot.[14]

The German civilian authorities immediately put a number of decrees into effect. One such decree required Poles of either sex to step into the gutter when they saw a German soldier approach. People were reminded that the streets belong to the victors, not the vanquished. Poles were forbidden to give the German salute of raising the right arm or the "Heil Hitler" salute. Dr. Zygmunt Klukowski, who wrote in his diary of a most ugly incident to which he was a witness, described the extent of permissive German public behavior:

> *Across from the hospital where I work are a few burned-out Jewish homes. An old Jew was standing with a few Jewish women next to one when a group of three German soldiers came by. Suddenly one of the soldiers grabbed the old man and threw him headfirst into a deep cellar. . . . The soldiers then calmly walked away. I was puzzled by this incident, but when he was brought to me for treatment of his head wound I was told that Jews must stand at attention and men have to take their hats off whenever German soldiers pass. The old man was talking with the women and had overlooked the Germans.[15]*

Shop and markets had to serve German forces, members of their families, and German nationals first. Only afterwards could they serve Poles. No Pole was allowed to wear a Polish uniform or other identifiable badges, and that included Polish national emblems by Polish railway and postal employees. Gatherings in the streets and at street corners, particularly of juveniles, were strictly forbidden. Anyone molesting a German woman would receive severe punishment, and Polish women accosting or molesting a German would be sent to a brothel. In addition, the German officials required that all bicycles be fitted with head and rear lights, and until they were so fitted, the owners had to dismount at dusk. Those Poles who did not comply with these decrees would be shot.[16]

Mieczysław Maliński, a boyhood friend of Pope John Paul II, said that it was not a question of knowing whether you would be alive next year. Given the indiscriminate horror dealt out by the Nazis, the question was whether you would be alive the next day. He recalls that when his brothers and sisters left home for work, the family never knew whether they would see them for supper that same evening. And at home, people were not free from fear, either. At any time the police or the Gestapo might show up, break down an apartment door, and drag someone off to prison or to Auschwitz. Police roundups, deportations to camps, and forced labor in Germany or some other unknown place were common occurrences, as were beatings by SS men and death by shooting in the street. People frequently heard shots at night after curfew hours when the police arrested people caught walking the streets without passes; the police fired at anyone who did not stop when challenged. All of these incidents were part of daily life. People lived in a constant state of terror and intimidation.[17]

The Nazis also took prominent citizens as hostages, making them responsible for public order in the city. Stefan Korboński, who was later to become the chief of the civil resistance, described the terror that the Polish people had to live with daily:

> *One morning I was awakened by a violent banging at the door
> and a voice shouting, "Open the door." When I got up and
> opened the door, a Gestapo, accompanied by two gendarmes,
> entered the room and read my name and occupation on a list.
> "You will come with us." My hands were trembling and all sorts
> of thoughts flashed through my mind. The Gestapo man stood
> watching and urging me to hurry. My wife, pale but calm,
> handed me the various things I might need, a towel, a cake
> of soap, some underclothing. At last we left the house. A truck
> was waiting in front of the door and in it I noticed two crouch-
> ing shapes. I thought their faces were familiar. . . . After a few
> minutes drive we were led into the great hall of the university
> in the Kraków Suburb Avenue which was filled with several
> scores of people as frightened as we were ourselves. After about
> half an hour, we were informed that as prominent citizens we
> had been taken as hostages. Should any riots occur we would
> be shot.[18]*

In November 1939, German authorities began a relentless persecution of the Polish intelligentsia and other leading classes. They
arrested deported, and in some cases killed professors from Poznań
University, and closed the university; it reopened in 1941 as a German
university. They closed the Jagiellonian University in Kraków, the
second oldest university in east central Europe, arresting 184 faculty
members and transporting them to the Sachsenhausen concentration camp in Germany, where many of them died.[19] After the faculty
arrests, the Germans looted the university, wrecking libraries and
laboratories. All other universities, indeed all educational institutions,
including secondary schools, were also shut down.[20]

Theatres, cinemas, and radio stations were "Germanized." The occupiers confiscated collections from art galleries and burned large numbers of Polish books taken from libraries, thereby refusing the Poles the right to their own cultural pursuits. They subjected the Catholic Church, regarded as a bulwark of Polish national feeling, to a massive onslaught. German authorities imprisoned most of the clergy or sent them to concentration camps; more than one in ten of them were killed.[21]

Although the number of deaths in the first years of the occupation was far less than in the later period, the Germans instituted two separate, early programs that were harbingers of the Holocaust to come. The first such action was the Euthanasia Campaign of 1939 to 1940, which eliminated all "cripples and imbeciles" from the country's hospitals. The other was the (AB-Aktion) Extraordinary Pacification Campaign of 1939 to 1940 in which some fifteen thousand Polish priests, intellectuals, teachers, and political leaders were transported to Dachau, Buchenwald, and Sachsenhausen or shot in the Palmiry Forest near Warsaw.[22]

Other violence was largely confined to local reprisals and intermittent fighting in the countryside. The war against partisan units in the outlying country was ruthless and bloody. Even German soldiers were appalled by the horror that was the fate of innocent villages and villagers, innocent victims marked for punishment. As Sergeant Hans Becker recalled in his autobiography, "Retribution was usually meted out according to a standard procedure. On the very same evening that the 'crime' had been committed, the village would be surrounded by troops . . . The entire village was set on fire and the entire population systematically slaughtered."[23]

This was the environment in Poland that generated a climate of hatred and vengefulness toward the Nazi enemy, and the atmosphere became more and more intense with the passage of each day. After having absorbed the first shock of the war and the dislocation it created, people now faced issues of survival, ingenuity, and improvisation: in short, they had to muster the will to live through the infernolike catastrophe.

CHAPTER FOUR
Life under Soviet Rule

The efficiency of the NKVD is everywhere inside our lines.
People in the Russian zone have simply stopped talking to their friends.
The fear is on the streets, in the air. Of our top echelon, political and
military, nothing remains; those who are alive are in the Lubyanka,
and out of contact.

—Alan Furst (1941–), American author,
The Polish Officer

After having entered into a nonaggression pact with Germany in August 1939 and within two weeks after the German invasion of Poland, the Soviet Union, in the absence of a war declaration, attacked Poland in the east. The joint German and Soviet occupations of the country enabled the two tyrannical powers to work in close collaboration. The Soviets strengthened that relationship by delivering raw materials to Germany for the latter's war effort. Russia transported oil to Germany through Poland in support of the German invasion of France and the Battle of Britain. In August 1940 the Soviets helped the Germans in one of their most daring naval missions of the war.

Far north of the Soviet Union lay a German ship called the *Komet*, which appeared to be a normal merchant ship but was actually an armed German raider. It was only with the help of Soviet icebreakers that the German vessel was able to pass through the ice fields at the top of the Soviet Union and emerge into the Pacific Ocean, where it attacked and destroyed seven Allied ships.[1] When Stalin's forces attacked Finland, the Baltic States, and Romania, Hitler's troops did not interfere. Nor did Stalin interfere in the German conquest of Denmark, Norway, Holland, Belgium, Luxemburg, and France.

The German "racial enemy" was virtually indistinguishable from the Soviet "class enemy." Both tyrannical nations looked upon the Poles with unmitigated hatred.[2] They orchestrated exchanges in which the Gestapo received German "criminals" and Jewish "agitators" in return for Communists and Ukrainians. Yet because of the more extensive experience dealing with the techniques and logistics of political terror gained from the Stalinist purges and collectivization campaign in the mid-1930s, the work of the Soviet NKVD in eastern Poland proved far more destructive than that of the Gestapo in the west.[3]

Just as the Germans had treated the Poles, the Soviets screened, classified, and segregated the eastern population, physically removing all unfavorable elements as soon as officials identified them. They quickly sovietized the annexed lands, introducing compulsory collectivization. They confiscated and nationalized all private and state-owned Polish property.[4] In the process, the Soviet banned all political parties and public associations and they either imprisoned or executed the local leaders as "enemies of the people." In line with their antireligious policy, the Soviets persecuted members of churches and religious organizations.[5]

According to an NKVD decree issued in February 1940, the Soviets unleashed a campaign of terror against all anti-Soviet elements in occupied Poland. They forcibly deported some two million people. Among the major categories of those subject to deportation included members of prerevolutionary parties; officers of the former Tsarist army; followers of Trotsky, Mensheviks, and anarchists; members of anti-Bolshevik armies; officials of the Lithuanian ministries; refugees and political émigrés; clergymen and members active in religious communities; aristocrats, business proprietors, and landowners.[6]

The sovietization of the eastern territories also involved an intensive war against all religion and every vestige of Polish cultural influence. The Soviets, like the Nazis, made every effort to obliterate Polish society. They sought to remove all trace of Polish history of the area under their control. The name "Poland" was banned from use. Soviets tore down Polish monuments. They closed all Polish universities, putting in place new Russian directors who taught dialectical and historical materialism aimed at strengthening Soviet ideology. Authorities burned books of Polish literature and language studies, replacing them with Russian or Ukrainian texts, even in the primary grades. The new pro-Soviet curriculum included classes in Byelorussian, Ukrainian, and Lithuanian.[7]

In the absence of a war declaration, the Soviet Union never viewed Polish military personnel as prisoners of war, but rather as insurgents against the new Soviet government in Western Ukraine and Western Byelorussia. The reign of terror by the NKVD began in 1939 as an inherent part of the sovietization process. The first victims of the Soviet new order were approximately 250,000 Polish prisoners of war captured by the Soviets during and after the invasion. Since the Soviet Union had not signed any international convention on rules of war, the Soviets denied Polish prisoners legal status. They murdered almost all captured officers, and sent a large number of ordinary soldiers to the Soviet Gulag.[8]

The West has largely ignored the horrors that the Soviets

committed during the twenty-one months when the eastern part of Poland was under Soviet occupation. The truth did not emerge until long after the Second World War, during the Cold War when the Soviets were no longer considered an ally of the Western Powers. The Western public had not yet been conditioned to recognize the Soviet barbarity, even though it was known long before Solzhenitsyn's *Gulag Archipelago* brought it to the attention of Western readers.

At the start of the Soviet invasion, the Soviets encouraged local Ukrainian nationalists to attack Poles, which resulted in sporadic killings that were forerunners of greater atrocities to come. People were deported in large railroad convoys between February 1940 and June 1941, when Germany invaded Soviet Russia.[9] Soviet authorities shipped off more than 1.5 million political offenders to do hard labor in Siberia and other far reaches of the Soviet wilderness; this number included women and children, all whose only "crime" was that they were Poles.

Nevertheless, while the Germans were still preparing the techniques and logistics of terror at Auschwitz, Treblinka, and Majdanek for mass extermination, an estimated two million Poles and West Ukrainians were transported to Arctic Russia, Siberia, and Kazakhstan in the terrible railroad convoys of 1939 and 1940 for slave labor; at least half died within a year of deportation.[10]

In September 1939, fifteen thousand Polish army officers and their families were arrested and transported to western Russia. Most were reservists mobilized after the German offensive. All were well trained and educated professionals: doctors, scientists, civil servants, and teachers. Because these prisoners were key figures in Polish society, they were viewed as potential threats. Because the Soviets did not consider them normal prisoners, they were placed in three special Soviet detention camps. The NKVD, whose members interrogated them, hoped that they might be willing to collaborate with the Soviets. The vast majority proved obstinate, however, and refused to deal with their captors. Then in the spring of 1940, some 15,000 prisoners suddenly disappeared from Soviet captivity. Among those who were never to be seen again were 4,321 Polish army reserve officers.[11]

Later in December 1941, when Poland and Soviet Russia were allies, General Władysław Sikorski, the head of the Polish government-in-exile and its commander in chief, along with a delegation of Poles, met Stalin and asked about the whereabouts of the thousands of missing Polish officers. Stalin said that after the German invasion of Russia, amnesty had all been granted to all Poles (for crimes that had not been committed), and they were free. He claimed that they had escaped to Manchuria. Sikorski knew that the Soviet dictator was lying. He also knew that many of the Polish relatives of the army officer-prisoners who were still in exile in some of the worst possible places in the Arctic had not heard from their prisoner-relatives since the spring of 1940, when they had suddenly vanished. In some cases, letters from the family members were returned to them stamped "Addressee Unknown."[12]

In April 1943 the Germans announced that they had discovered the mass graves of more than four thousand Polish officers in the Katyn Forest near Smolensk in Byelorussia. The site revealed a massacre in which those same Polish officers had been shot in front of open graves, their hands tied behind their backs and a bullet in the base of their skulls. There was no doubt of the identities of the bodies when documents were found in their pockets. Berlin claimed that the victims had been killed by the Soviets in May 1940. The Soviets claimed that the Nazis had killed the victims in the winter of 1941; that explanation proved false when it was discovered that the Poles had been wearing summer uniforms. The Kremlin nevertheless continued to deny the allegation. When the Sikorski government asked the International Red Cross to investigate the matter, Stalin broke off all diplomatic relations with the Polish government-in-exile in London.[13]

The Polish government in London relied on the support of the Allied forces' governments in its controversy with the Kremlin, but both Britain and the United States wanted nothing to do with the Katyn massacre. The British government and the press either would not believe—or pretended not to believe—the Soviet guilt. Newsreels in England made no mention of the disappearance of the Polish officers, but the British press accused the Germans of the crime and said the Polish government "had slandered an ally and had acted with blatant political stupidity." As Tadeusz Pilch, one of the most well-informed members of the Polish legation, maintained, "You are greatly mistaken to think that the British are guided in politics by moral considerations and by the search for objective truth." The British wanted to win the war, and knew that they could not do so without Russia.[14] It was quite clear both in London and Washington that the preservation of Allied unity took precedence over any other considerations.

In point of fact, the Katyn massacre was the only "Nazi war crime" on Soviet territory that the Soviets never mentioned.[15] In the minds of some, the matter remained a mystery, but to most neutral observers Soviet guilt was established beyond a reasonable doubt. Nevertheless, the Soviets continued to maintain their denial until a Russian military investigation uncovered the truth in the 1990s.[16]

In the summer of 1940, while Hitler was preoccupied directing the war in the west, Stalin was reaching down into the Balkans. This was of great concern to Hitler, who realized that, in order to continue the war effort, Germany had to be certain of two things: full control of the economic resources from the Balkans, especially oil from Romania, and continued deliveries of grain from the Soviet Union. By the end of August, he was so concerned of the likelihood of further Russian encroachments that he ordered twelve additional divisions to southern Poland "to guarantee the protection of the Romanian oilfields in the event of a sudden demand for intervention." Hitler believed that "the sooner Russia is crushed the better. . . . If we start in May '41 we will have five months in which to finish the job."[17]

In the late spring of 1941, a massive German buildup of assault forces in eastern Poland, combined with the recent *Wehrmacht* conquests of Yugoslavia and Greece and its occupation of Romania, Bulgaria, and Hungary, was a source of serious concern to the men in the Kremlin. By June Germany could not conceal the movement of hundreds of divisions of German troops by road and by rail toward the Soviet frontier. It was an all too-obvious sign to everyone except Stalin, who remained unconvinced, that the Nazi-Soviet Pact was coming to an end. For almost two years the Soviets had provided the Germans with food, stocks of oil, and other vital raw materials to fuel the Nazi war machine. Nevertheless, on June 22, 1941, Hitler launched Operation Barbarossa, the invasion of the Soviet Union.

For the Poles, the fortunes of war—at least for a brief period—shifted in their favor. By an ironic fate, the German attack on Russia saved the Poles. There can be no doubt that if the Nazi-Soviet pact had not dissolved, the Polish nation would have been obliterated. Isolated from any outside help, Poland would not have survived in any recognizable form the collaborative brutalities of the cobelligerents. And despite the five long years of unimaginable suffering that the Poles endured, the Germans alone were incapable of destroying the nation and its people. The people's response was an organized resistance movement that grew to dimensions unsurpassed by any other occupied country in Europe. It is to that movement that we now turn.

CHAPTER FIVE
The Civilian Resistance

Civilians faced with the sudden eruption of a military conflict succumb to a frenetic, hallucinatory state in which they want to be everywhere and with everyone, to remain involved, to participate in the general drama while realizing that much of what man can undertake matters very little in a world where everything collapses . . . and the cruelty of human beings . . . is identical in its results with the cruelty of nature.

—Leo Tolstoy (1828–1910) Russian author, *War and Peace*

Unlike the mood in the French cafés, where daily existence during the German occupation was one of resignation and where, unless you were a Jew, you were left alone so long as you did not bother the occupying forces, the mood in Poland was one of defiance. For the Poles, the unprecedented savagery and unpredictability of German terror to which the Polish citizenry was subjected from the beginning of the invasion created a state of intolerable oppression that ultimately drove virtually the entire population into action. The people's response was an organized resistance movement that flourished from the beginning of the occupation and grew to dimensions unmatched in any other occupied country in Europe.

Unlike some countries under German rule, there had been no Polish equivalent of a Nazi puppet government such as Norway's Vidkun Quisling, or Holland's Anton Mussert, or France's Pierre Laval, which all believed collaboration to be established policy. Given the barbarity of the German occupation policies throughout the country, which were unequalled anywhere else in Europe, no Pole of any political stature would consider collaboration. Parties of the extreme Right in Poland were unequivocally anti-German. Nor was there any meaningful support for Communism even among the disaffected minorities such as the Byelorussians and Ukrainians. For the Poles the issue never arose seriously.

In relation to the country as a whole, the number of those who did collaborate was not significant. Those who did collaborate were, for the most part, the dispossessed rabble of society, especially criminal types. Most collaboration occurred because of greed. Living conditions were so bad that collaborating with the authorities was a way for some to make money or gain access to scarcely available goods. There were occasions where some collaborated out of fear of being killed or because of threats that family members would be deported. Then there were those captured members of the Resistance who were forced to become double agents through various forms of torture.[1] According to the postwar Israeli War Crime Commission statistics, out of a population of more than twenty million ethnic Poles, only about seven thousand collaborated with the Nazis.[2]

The Poles were given a simple choice: submit completely as slaves or resist. Since they gained nothing by submitting, the vast majority of the citizenry turned to resistance, which before long spread throughout the country. Whole villages in remote areas faced the Hobson's choice of either resisting or being massacred. Rather than being massacred or starving in what was left of their shelters, they went into the forest or the marshes, depending upon what part of the countryside was closest to them, to avoid the German onslaught. The more virulent the terrorism became, the more unified the population became as it reaffirmed its desire to resist.

Any form of systematic, organized resistance required considerable support from ordinary citizens who "only" practiced civil and passive resistance.[3] In the face of increasing misery and the growing difficulties of day-to-day existence for which the occupying power was held responsible, a wave of hatred swept over all of enslaved Europe. This reaction was swifter and far more violent among the traditionally anti-German Poles.[4] At first resistance was small, but numerous isolated incidents that occurred daily testified to the growing Polish hatred of the Germans and elevated Polish morale.

Initial enmity took the form of spontaneous acts of what Resistance historian Henri Michel called "prickly xenophobia, the instinctive aversion to the presence of the foreigner, particularly in a position of authority,"[5] for example, a woman giving wrong directions to a German on the street; a lone vocalist on a streetcar singing Polish or anti-German songs to the delight of the Polish passengers; an old couple on opposite sides of the street warning pedestrians not to walk any further, or to change direction, because of a German roundup ahead; or Polish schoolboys warning passengers in a bus of an approaching German patrol in the vicinity.[6] These were some of the more instinctive displays of local animosity.

Although laughter was a rare commodity among the suffering Poles, malicious humor was some consolation that produced temporary relief and reduced mental turmoil. Poles made amusing alterations to German words: the name of a senior SS officer stationed in Warsaw was Moder, but he was always referred to as *Morder* (murderer); "Hitler" was changed to *Hycler* (dog-shooter); on walls the slogan *Deutschland siegt an allen Fronten* (Germany is victorious on all fronts) became *Deutschland liegt an allen Fronten* (Germany is prostrate on all fronts.)[7]

In the fall of 1942, when the Germans requisitioned all of Poland's furs and wool for the Eastern Front, large posters appeared displaying a gaunt, gloomy soldier wrapped in a very feminine mink coat with a silver fox muff protecting his hands. The caption read: "Now I am so warm, dying for our Fuehrer will be a pleasure."[8] One Varsovian slur emphasized the abhorrence of Warsaw residents for the Germans. When applying for travel passes within Poland, authorities asked a man whose name was Schmidt if he were German. "No," he replied, "I'm Polish." Then when asked where both he and his parents were born, he answered "Berlin." "Then you are a German?" Schmidt's retort: "Look, if a hen lays an egg in a pig sty, does that necessarily make her a pig?"[9]

Although work strikes did not take place because of the ruthlessness that would result from such activity,10 demonstrations and various boycotts developed as equally virulent forms of obstruction. On September 1, 1940, the first anniversary of the German invasion, the Poles in Warsaw left all the cafés and restaurants between two and four o'clock and refused to buy German newspapers. Instead, they went to church. At one time during the war, Polish Underground authorities put out a notice advising Poles to stop buying German newspapers on Fridays. Poles responded so well to this directive that the Germans had to severely limit the Friday edition of their newspaper. Those Polish subscribers, buyers, and advertisers who disobeyed the boycott by catering to the Germans were often exposed to stigmatization by their neighbors. Unbeknownst to a subscriber, "an invisible hand might place a card on his back on which was written: 'This pig patronizes German trash.' On his house the next day, an inscription might appear in indelible paint: 'A fool lives here; a stupid vile Pole who obeys the German gangsters instead of his own leaders.'"[11]

On November 11, 1941, Polish Independence Day, the Poles in Warsaw observed a street boycott in which Underground units laid flowers on memorials and wrote pro-Polish and anti-German slogans on walls.[12] For the German authorities, demonstrations were both irritating and nerve-racking provocations, and officials often had difficulty deciding how severely to respond. Just how sensitive to this type of activity they felt showed when, the following month, new general legislation decreed long penal sentences and even the death penalty for persons, including those under sixteen years of age, who committed any of a large numbers of vaguely defined crimes, such as making anti-German statements, provoking authorities, or simply harboring a hostile mentality toward Germany.[13]

Among the people, a common front rapidly developed as the result of the dozens of mass killings, especially in western Poland, and the deportations from those same western lands. This increased the bitterness of the citizenry against the Polish prewar government, which was held responsible for the defeat, and incited their hatred of the Germans, which inevitably led to more violent activity by Polish patriots.[14] Barns, cellars, and attics across the land became vast armories of rebuilt weaponry. After the six years of World War I, from 1914 to 1918, followed by the 1920 to 1921 campaign against the Red Army by an earlier generation of Poles, the country had become an arsenal whose stores were now being reconditioned for use by a younger, but no less determined, generation. Every barn, every attic, and every cellar had its weapons and ammunition.[15]

The Boy Scout Underground, known as the Grey Ranks, also played an important role in the Resistance. The younger boys acted in noncombative roles as couriers and some gathered intelligence. Writing patriotic and anti-German graffiti on public buildings was also usually the work of the Scouts. Older Scouts delivered clandestine newspapers and took part in "minor sabotage" activities. From the very beginning of the occupation, young people prevented the Germans from moving about easily by effectively planting homemade tire-puncturing devices on the roads or by slashing the tires of military and police vehicles. On one occasion in Poznań two Scouts hung an enormous Polish flag on the tower of the German security service headquarters. As a result, several German auxiliary policemen were sent to the Eastern Front in disgrace for failing to maintain proper vigilance.[16]

For most people passive or nonmilitant resistance might be nothing more than providing faulty or slow service, conscious or unconscious evasions of obedience to certain orders or decrees, or little more than just the spreading of rumors.[17] Those who witnessed resistance activities for the most part simply remained silent and stayed out of the way.

Despite the resilience and determination to carry on in the face of overwhelming opposition, the occupation had a terribly demoralizing impact on many of the Polish people.

> *The terror campaign against the Jews and the Poles increasingly deadened basic instincts of horror and pity because pain and tragedy had become so commonplace. . . . The stress of living in a society where a person could never be certain whether he would survive until the next day wore heavily on the face of the Poles who appeared to be in a constant state of fatigue. For those who labored in the Underground, the stress was so intense that those who did not possess the physical or emotional resources to cope with it committed suicide.[18]*

Nevertheless, the majority of the Polish people viewed survival as the overriding concern. The German occupation set in motion an economic crisis that had lasting and significant effects on all segments of the Polish population. The Germans commandeered all industry and most all of the vast landed family estates and turned them over to German administrators. Even more important changes affected the average working man and his family—both the white-collar and blue-collar segments of the urban population. These men had an especially difficult time earning money because the Polish administrative apparatus no longer existed, having been replaced by one that employed only Germans. Industrial wages were so out of line with the true cost of living that a week's salary bought food for only one day. These conditions drove masses of people into illegal activities.[19]

The organization of clandestine groups throughout the country was largely attributable to the hunger for news on which the personal lives of almost every family in Poland depended. The need was so strong that not even the introduction of the death penalty for the illegal possession of radio receivers deterred people from wanting to know what was happening outside of Poland. With the utmost caution, people set up clandestine listening centers with illegal wireless sets in cellars and portions of attics to hear the London broadcasts. Those who did not have access to radios received news bulletins distributed by those who did. These became the nucleus of clandestine newspapers that began to proliferate throughout the country. As early as October 1939, the first Underground paper, *Poland Alive* (about which we will learn more later) began to circulate in Warsaw.[20]

The principal source of information for news that came from outside of Poland and broadcast in Polish came from the BBC in London. Poles who had kept radio receivers hidden or who had ones constructed in Underground workshops received the news and passed it on to others. This was the case until late in 1942, when Stefan Korboński, who headed the Directorate of Civil Resistance, received a secret telegram from London that was known only to the Supreme Commander of the Polish forces. The message stated that a clandestine Allied radio station called SWIT that operated near London was seeking to convey the impression that the station was operating from within occupied Poland. SWIT was primarily an instrument of civil resistance that provided up-to-date reports from the Underground, news from the German press, and German decrees from inside Poland. These were being sent to London on a daily basis and then transmitted back to Poland, where the Polish people heard them. There were two main reasons for this: first, those in the outside world would place greater assurance on reports if they believed they came from inside Poland; and second, its anti-German propaganda would confuse and harass the Germans.[21] It was not until much later that the Polish people knew about the secret of SWIT.

People working for the Underground gathered information and sensational news items in Poland on a daily basis at Underground meeting places; they then sent this information to England, which broadcast it as if from Poland over SWIT. The Polish people and the world heard news and an accompanying commentary. In one instance, SWIT took advantage of a special opportunity involving a daily Polish newspaper published by the Germans, *Nowy Kurier Warszawski*. It was filled with propaganda that SWIT refuted. The newspaper appeared at one o'clock in the afternoon, but the Underground was able to get page proofs of the paper by eight o'clock that same morning, after which the contents were then radioed to London so that they could be used as the background for a rebuttal commentary that evening, and heard by thousands of Poles inside Poland only a few hours after the daily newspaper had appeared on the street. If someone were to ask, "Since the preparation and sending of a telegram took several hours, how could SWIT quote from the current issue of *Nowy Kurier Warszawski*?" Korbonski's response was simply "In the Polish Underground nothing was impossible."[22] Most everyone believed that the reporting that came from SWIT *must* come from inside Poland; how else could it report events in Poland just a few hours after they happened?

Besides keeping the people of Poland aware of developments elsewhere in the world, the SWIT conspiracy had a way of intimidating the Germans, especially those Germans who were guilty of atrocities in Poland. For example, SWIT, reporting that the Germans had publicly announced that they had taken forty more hostages, raised the number to one hundred. "The Gestapo has recently embarked upon a new wave of terror. In reprisal for this kind of terror, additional retaliatory measures will be taken by the Underground." SWIT then broadcasted the death sentences that had been carried out against Gestapo agents by the Directorate of Civil Resistance. At times SWIT listed the specific names of those Germans responsible for atrocities and made threats against them. Since the Germans also listened to the announcements, some of those same Germans "made frantic efforts to be transferred to the Reich." In this way SWIT was a good weapon in the battle against the German occupiers.[23]

An equally effective weapon utilized by the civilian Resistance against the Germans was an operation known as Action N,—*N* for *Niemcy*—the Polish word for the Germans. It was a widespread distribution network launched in Warsaw as a form of "black propaganda" designed to demoralize German soldiers and officials living in Poland and uplift Polish morale.[24] Initially it took the form of a leaflet that gave the false impression it was the voice of the German opposition, produced and circulated by a German anti-Nazi military Underground organization within the *Wehrmacht,* and that it had been brought back from the Eastern Front. The leaflet foretold a speedy defeat for Germany and a quick return home of the German soldiers. It was printed in Gothic type and full of typical army slang provided by Poles who spoke German and who had picked up the jargon in the

German army during World War I.

The Resistance smuggled a number of the leaflets across the border into Germany through the intermediary of a sympathetic locomotive engineer. Resisting Poles also copied and used various transit permits, furlough passes, and work permits stolen from the German-controlled Warsaw-East railway headquarters to facilitate crossing the closed and well-guarded border into the western lands.[25] One mininewspaper, *Der Hammer*, purported to represent an Underground organization of German social democrats. *Der Frontkampfer*, allegedly put out by frontline German troops, agitated against party bigwigs who were referred to as *Etappenschweine*, i.e., "pigs with gold braid." These papers carried sensational news about a split in the German high command and about dissension between Hitler and his party and the old-line generals, many of whom had fallen from Hitler's favor or been liquidated. The publication also claimed that the war had already been lost by Hitler who had no idea of military strategy, and that the frontline German soldiers were suffering casualties for no good reason other than to protect the party and the Gestapo.[26]

One leaflet that carried the name of Rudolf Hess, Hitler's deputy leader of the Nazi Party, claimed to be printed by the NSDAP-*Erneuerungsbewegung*, the German Underground opposition group within the party. The leaflet began with a greeting "Heil Hess," and was intended for party members. Hess was shown as the leader of those who realized the hopelessness of Germany and wanted to plead with Great Britain for a separate peace. At this time, Hess's covert flight to England was still a mystery to most of the German people.[27] From the deceptive leaflets, those party members from within the opposition learned that Hess was successful in negotiating favorable terms with the British for a cease-fire arrangement. It added that only Hitler, some party bosses, and the Gestapo opposed ending the war and a nonpunitive peace, all to protect themselves.

In addition to those pamphlets sent to prominent people in Germany, resisting Poles placed other forms of demoralizing material in Poland in front of hospitals, in railroad stations, and in public squares, which housed special boxes into which the Germans were asked to deposit books and magazines for the soldiers at the front. The N leaflets were placed in German magazines "courtesy of the German field post."[28]

Tadeusz Żenczykowski, covert name Kowalik, headed the quick expansion of Action N as a form of psychological warfare against the Germans and employed more than seven hundred people. It was divided into four sections: the distribution and organization of the network of agents; research and intelligence; the editorial office; and sabotage through forgeries of official German documents, letters, orders, and instructions. Kowalik was the head of the entire department.[29] Between July and September 1942, it published a number of different items: three different issues for soldiers, two issues for citizens of the Reich and the annexed western lands, four different issues for the Germans in the east, and several pamphlets aimed at destroying German confidence in the Nazi Party.[30]

It was not long before a much wider distribution of Underground N literature was in mass circulation, and made its way into the incorporated western territories of Poznań, Łódź, Gdańsk, East Prussia, and finally into Upper Silesia, which became the gateway into the Reich itself. Couriers who were recruited from among the railway men and who dispersed the subversive material carried documents that were partly counterfeit and partly stolen.[31]

In the crowded railway car the loud snoring of sleeping soldiers resounded. We placed our literary cargo in the soldiers' knapsacks, which were lying on the floor. The sleeping Germans did not suspect that there were several hundred thousand pamphlets and leaflets, every one of which would reach its target like a bullet, causing bloodless but painful damage. Soldiers in barracks would find in their lavatories issues of the military Underground paper Der Frontkampfer. It would be read with great interest because it was not an insignificant experience to have tangible evidence that in the Fatherland— even in the Wehrmacht—people were beginning to rebel against war, against the Fuehrer, against party bosses, and against the Gestapo with their comfortable lives.[32]

A soldier who would not believe what came from the enemy, even from the BBC broadcasts, would believe what came from his own people—people who, at the risk of their own lives, published these pamphlets somewhere in Cologne or Frankfurt. They were carried to places in Berlin, Dresden, Hamburg, and Munich, and from there the material was mailed by way of the local German post to selected addresses in the Reich.

Another form of psychological warfare consisted of demoralizing anonymous letters sent to prominent German officials "that contained at least a grain of truth about various commercial frauds, illicit love affairs, etc. This sometimes led to quarrels and sometimes fights broke out among the Germans."[33] N cells were also organized in the Baltic ports of Gdynia and Gdańsk, where pamphlets also made their way into German munitions ships and Swedish cargo ships headed to Finland and Sweden.[34]

Because of the rule of terror that prevailed throughout all occupied Poland, conditions were bound to produce an uncompromising resistance that would draw from a broad cross-section of the population.

Polish society moved underground, but without any formal leadership recognized by the government-in-exile. Toward the end of September 1939, the four major Polish political parties in the German-controlled part of the country—the Christian Democratic Labor Party, the Socialist Party, the Peasant Party, and liberal elements of the Nationalist Party—organized a clandestine resistance movement. But for the citizenry at large, there was no longer any single political leadership. Those individuals not affiliated with any specific groups consulted with friends or sought advice from well-known and respected personalities whenever they had to make decisions that involved some form of recognition of the German occupiers. Frequently, seeking advice was a preliminary step to creating the more permanent bond of an organized Underground. Under the conditions of occupation, this created the threat of complete disorganization and irresponsibility in Polish political life.[35] Nevertheless, if Polish society were to survive under the occupation, it had to resolve the authority vacuum created by the failed prewar Polish government. In short, it had to replace lost authority.

CHAPTER SIX
The Underground State

Clandestine resistance represented nothing less than the Polish nation in existence as a national entity as in prewar days. But it was something else as well—an emergent democracy; in occupied Poland political parties were more powerful, more emancipated, and more active than in independent Poland which had been a dictatorship. Polish resistance had cohesion and strength unparalleled in Europe.

—Polish Society under German Occupation 1939–1944,
Jan Tomasz Gross

To the vast majority of the Polish people, the prewar government, which had presided over the disastrous September campaign, had become totally discredited. The people felt that the government had failed and that its subsequent absence was no hindrance in continuing the struggle. After managing to evade capture, its leaders fled to Romania. By the end of September 1939, a highly positioned member of the former Polish Ministry of the Interior and a respected member of the Underground plainly outlined the underlying conditions

and the only hope for an efficacious struggle against the enemy—
and equally important—an official continuation of the Polish state.
He stated,

> *Our purpose is to maintain the continuity of the Polish state*
> *which, merely by accident, had to descend into the Under-*
> *ground. The Polish state continues its existence unchanged,*
> *except in form. Since we are in it, we must reproduce all the*
> *offices and institutions of a state. It must have authority over*
> *our people and make it impossible for a traitor to arise in*
> *Poland. We will not permit any competition on Polish terri-*
> *tory. The presence of a German regime in Poland is artificial*
> *and fortuitous. The government must defend us and our rights*
> *during the war and be responsible to us.[1]*

By early October 1939, to preserve that national continuity, a
government-in-exile convened in Angers, France, designated by the
French government as the seat of the Polish government. Władysław
Sikorski, who served as chief of staff to the Polish armed forces in
the years immediately following World War I, assumed the dual position of prime minister and commander in chief of the Polish Army.
Sikorski was a highly respected leader who favored a broad democratic
reform of future Poland[2] and immediately won the recognition of the
Allied governments.

In February 1940, a deliberating body called the Political
Consultative Committee (PKP) held its first meeting.[3] It was com-
prised of the three major parties: the National Democratic Party, the
Socialist Party, and the Peasant Party. It also included the Union for
Armed Struggle, as the Underground army was called. The National
Democratic Party was politically strong, gathering recruits from all

classes and sections of the country. Based on the basic teachings of Catholicism, it believed in the principles of individual rights and the tenets of a liberal economy. The Socialist Party believed that the means of production should be kept under government control. It advocated a planned national economy, a division of land among the peasants, and, politically, a parliamentary democracy. The Peasant Party favored reuniting the peasants with the land of their forefathers and the rebuilding of Poland's economic structure. It was the youngest of the major parties. In earlier centuries, the Polish peasants had remained politically passive and uninformed, living a life without any influence on national affairs. The Peasant Party now sought to bring them to a full consciousness of their rights and the role they were being called upon to play. A fourth party, the Christian Democratic Labor Party, was based chiefly on the papal encyclicals and the Catholic faith in general as the chief aim and major determinant of the content of its program.

These four political parties represented the vast majority of the Polish nation in the Underground State.[4] Each party conducted, on its own initiative, many of its activities within the framework of the Underground. They had the right to engage in autonomous propaganda, political and social activity, and resistance to the occupying power.[5]

The PKP was established to deal with all problems of a political, social, economic, and military nature, as well as with the ethical principles to be observed during the occupation. Everything that life under an enemy occupation involved came within the purview of PKP, whose decisions were circulated throughout the country by means of the networks established by the party organizations. At that meeting, leaders defined its aim as the "restoration of the independence of the country by means of an armed struggle against the two occupying powers."[6] Supporters unanimously agreed that the struggle in Poland would continue underground, and that it would be a part of the general war against Hitler, a part that the Allies would be bound to recognize and appreciate. Moreover, it stipulated unqualified obedience to the government-in-exile.[7]

The Sikorski government recognized that the PKP spoke for the country, and that it represented for the time being the executive organ of the exiled government in Poland.[8] Emissaries from the government-in-exile made their way through Hungary to meet secretly with the PKP, and were able to give the government's appraisal of the international situation, political reports, and other detailed information while collecting information about the Underground.[9]

After the fall of France in June 1940, the government-in-exile refused to share in the French capitulation and moved to London, where, along with large numbers of Poles who had left their homeland, a Polish army-in-exile was forming. Many joined the Free Polish forces and later served especially well in other theaters of war, while in occupied Poland the foundations of an underground state were being laid.

During the first half of 1941, the Underground in Poland was an assemblage of large and small political and military organizations. Almost every prewar political party that continued its activity in the Underground began by setting up its own private "army."[10] It was of fundamental importance to the emergence of the Underground Polish State that potential leadership existed among the politicians of those parties that had been kept from power in the 1930s. Those who held power in that earlier time believed it absolutely necessity that the structure of Polish politics be essentially the same as those "strong" regimes on its eastern and western borders; there was no place in Poland for parliamentary democracy. Those other parties, in turn, reacted by refusing to participate in the electoral process.

Ironically, while the Underground was a continuation of the Polish nation, it broke away from this prewar tradition and returned to the still older traditions of Polish parliamentary democracy. Having more power and freedom, the political parties in the Underground were able to increase their activity far beyond anything that had been possible in prewar Poland.[11] They had large memberships, considerable resources, ingenuity, and the necessary skills for planning effective stratagems against the Germans. The possibility of organized action was in no way impaired.[12]

There were several reasons for the emergence of so many Underground organizations in Poland shortly after the September capitulation. There was very little damage to life and property during the brief duration of hostilities. The country was left defeated, but not exhausted, and remained in control of its considerable resources. The only institution destroyed by the German onslaught was the central government; everything else—the outlawed political, professional, and voluntary associations—still existed. The infrastructure of the country, although somewhat diminished, had survived.[13]

The new government-in-exile was aware of the necessity of giving guidance to the population living under the occupation. What Poles needed was a source of authority—one unequivocally recognized as such—that would be familiar with all contemporary developments in Poland and that could immediately communicate its directives. This ideal, unfortunately, was never achieved because of the conditions of life during the occupation. A plurality of interests and opinions made effective centralization difficult. Hence, the essential need for a decentralized Underground.[14]

A typical cell of an Underground organization consisted of a group of no more than three to five members. In theory, only one person from such a group maintained contacts with the outside. If a member of the group were arrested, other members could be located and helped to change the group's whereabouts for a time, so that no one else would be caught. Personal relationships among members mattered more than official appointments and rank. Yet people in faraway centers did not really know local conditions of other groups and therefore could not make good judgments about what courses of action they should pursue and how to coordinate actions across those distances. For example, London could not understand what was going on in Poland, Warsaw was ignorant of the realities of life in the countryside, etc.[15]

One principal issue that needed resolving was how best to bring political order to the Underground's confusing political situation. In December 1940, because of the political divisiveness among the four major parties, leaders finally decided to authorize a single Government Plenipotentiary to transact business in Poland on behalf of the government-in-exile. However, it was not until September 1942 that the political squabbling between the various parties ended with the appointment of an agreeably acceptable delegate for the job.[16]

In December 1942, the government delegate established the Directorate of Civil Resistance (DCR). Situated in Warsaw, it was headed by Stefan Korboński, who issued various instructions, directives, and warnings through Underground newspapers, the BBC, and a network of clandestine radio stations that informed the West, including the Polish radio station SWIT.[17] Those who comprised the Directorate of Civil Resistance were a closely knit, well-organized body whose members were outstanding scientists, jurists, priests, and social workers. It consisted of a number of different departments whose tasks were indicated by their names: the Departments of Justice, Sabotage, and Diversion; Registration of German Crimes, Radio Information, Armaments; and Chemicals and Legalization. In addition, the Directorate of Civil Resistance included a delegate of the Union for Armed

Struggle (ZWZ), which later gave rise to the *Armia Krajowa*—AK (Home Army), to subordinate resistance activities to the plans of the Western Allies.[18]

The entire directorate team met regularly in some concealed locale, while each department had its own hideouts, all of which were offered for use by brave Warsaw families in what was always a cordial atmosphere, but also one of grave earnestness and vigilance. One of the family members would usually take up a sentry position either outside in the street or inside from a window in anticipation of a sudden appearance of the Gestapo; the lookout gave those inside the time to disperse. Other hideouts were of various kinds. One was a laundry where people who had business to conduct in a particular department passed through a humid backroom full of steam; another was be a monastery where the silent guide, a cassocked monk, directed the Underground member through a maze of corridors, genuflecting in front of every little altar en route to the department in question.[19]

The directorate had to deal immediately with a critically important concern, namely drafting rules governing civil resistance for Poles living under the occupation. Basic instructions included offering resistance to the Germans always and everywhere, remaining inflexible, sabotaging all decrees and laws likely to harm the Polish nation or profit the Germans, never registering as *Volkdeutsche*, never engaging in intercourse with Germans, and obeying the Underground authorities.[20] Many unforeseen circumstances arose that these rules did not obviously cover, such as whether a Pole should work in a factory whose management had been taken over by the Germans, or how a Pole should respond when offered a social invitation by a German, or whether a Pole was free to enter a restaurant reserved for Germans, etc. The directorate drafted a commission that issued rules for every section of Polish society, including as farmers, workers, civil servants, railway men, women, and young people. Certain specific professions were given definite instructions; doctors, for example, were authorized to issue false medical reports to help a Pole avoid forced labor for the Germans; and judges were forbidden in all circumstances to send legal cases from Polish to German courts.[21]

As soon as they distributed the rules and instructions governing civil resistance throughout the country, the DCR used its executive power to ensure and strengthen the rules. In view of the Poles' inflexible and unyielding attitude about the Germans, this was unnecessary for many, but the DCR did it to prevent the violation of those rules and to try and sentence traitors, collaborationists, and others who failed to follow the prescribed attitude toward the occupiers and who could not justify their conduct when asked to do so. For this reason, the DCR established a system of Underground courts of justice.

A resolution passed by the Committee for Home Affairs in April 1940 provided the legal basis for these special courts: "Special Courts are competent to pass sentences on oppressors, traitors, spies, and agents provocateurs . . . ." and were conducted in accordance with the Polish Penal Code of 1932 and by the decrees of the competent Underground authorities, especially the Directorate of Civil Resistance. A public prosecutor would review an indictment, and a counsel for the defense took part ex officio before a bench of three judges, one of whom was the presiding magistrate. Three kinds of verdicts might arise: not guilty, remission of the case to the proper court after the war, and capital punishment. Court procedures included the admittance of material evidence such as witness depositions, photographs, and reports from Underground authorities. No appeals were allowed, but the district government delegate had to approve each sentence.[22]

Anyone who had attempted to actively aid the enemy and who could be shown without doubt to have harmed Underground activities or personnel received a capital punishment sentence. The tribunals also had the power to pass death sentences on exceptionally vicious

German office holders. These sentences admitted no appeal and the courts invariably carried them out.[23] Sentences were carried out in the following way:

> *The team carrying out the sentence consisted as a rule of three men. One did the shooting while the other two covered him, no matter whether the execution was carried out at home, where the cover had to terrorize the household, or in the street, where the Germans might have interfered. The execution team never bothered about the behavior of passersby. The latter, especially in Warsaw, realizing the Underground was striking, hurried on, pretending not to have noticed anything. Executioners read out to the condemned the sentence which always began with the formula: 'In the name of the Polish Republic...' whether the execution was being carried out in a house or even in the street.[24]*

The Underground carried out the first death sentences in Warsaw. The first to be shot was an officer of the Blue Police, a Polish collaborationist auxiliary paramilitary police force created by the German government, for the part he played in a German police court that had sentenced Poles to death. He was executed in the street; a number of people waiting for the tram observed it. The other death sentence involved a Polish official of the German Labor Board who pursued Poles who avoided deportation to Germany as forced laborers. He was shot in his home while on his knees begging for mercy.[25]

Members of the Underground were always being warned of impending danger from disguised secret Gestapo agents. This was one of the duties of Underground counterintelligence. One such pair was notorious in Warsaw. A supposedly blind man used to play an accordion at street corners. His companion was a woman who sang to his accompaniment. Whenever and wherever they appeared, arrests would follow shortly after in that same vicinity. Both were sentenced to death as Gestapo agents by the Underground tribunal and then executed.[26] The Underground press and the DCR gave the greatest possible publicity to the execution of these sentences, seeing to it that the names of those executed were publicly placarded on large red posters that began with the words, "In the name of the Polish Republic . . ." and ended with the Directorate of Civil Resistance's signature.[27]

Less serious forms of improper behavior constituting punishable offenses involved prohibited intercourse with the Germans; frequenting German theatres, cinemas, or gambling casinos; and collaborating with German businesses such as with German propaganda periodicals.

Infractions of the rules of civil resistance involved another method of procedural administration, for which the penalties were head shaving, as a form of social ostracism, and flogging. The former punishment was applied to women found consorting with Germans; flogging was extremely rare. It was usually applied in villages for such offenses as attendance at a German festival or misappropriation of Polish property. However, one such case involved the manager of a Polish theater in Warsaw who was flogged for deliberately showing obscene films encouraged by the German Department of Propaganda, whose work included attempting to lower moral standards for the purpose of demoralizing the Polish youth.[28]

Throughout the course of the occupation, Polish public opinion regarded the Underground courts of justice as what they in fact were: the legal organs of justice of the Polish Underground State empowered to promulgate sentences "In the Name of the Polish Republic."[29]

In this way and in the face of an unrelenting hatred that was institutionalized toward the occupying power, the Polish people gained an orderly government protected by the rule of law. This all-inclusive coalition that would share the responsibility for the work and policies of the Underground State continued and strengthened unity.

Thus the continuity of the Polish state remained unimpaired, the will of the nation to sacrifice continued undiminished, and the adamant unyielding attitude toward the German occupant was maintained at all costs.

CHAPTER SEVEN
The Underground Army

Adversity was the challenge on which Polish resisters thrived.
For they belonged to a hard school that had little in common with the
sort of comfortable assumptions on which most British or American
soldiers could rely. They had no home base to which they could safely
withdraw. They could not count on technical superiority or on cautious
methodical strategy. Theirs was the chosen path of risk, loneliness,
sacrifice, and ridicule, even from one's own . . . . They had been taught
to value spiritual mastery over everything.

—NORMAN DAVIES, RISING '44: THE BATTLE FOR WARSAW

From the very beginning of the occupation, scores of unsolicited partisan groups of Poles in the countryside banded together in the woods, while numerous conspiratorial units formed spontaneously in small towns and villages. Taking their orders from no one, their sole tasks were to harass, distract, and demoralize the German and Soviet forces at sudden, unexpected times and places whenever possible.

On September 27, 1939, the day before the Warsaw capitulation, an organized military resistance emerged. Dispersed pockets of resisters led by a staff of high-ranking army officers gathered together to form the clandestine "Polish Victory Service" (SZP), whose main purpose was to send a maximum number of surviving Polish soldiers abroad where they prepared for the decisive struggle alongside the Allies, as well to continue the fight under cover. In November the new government-in-exile created the most important component of the Underground conspiracy, the Union of Armed Struggle (ZWZ), to subordinate resistance activities to the plans of the Western Allies.[1] The ZWZ was a military branch of the regular Polish armed forces organized as a domestic army whose special task was to fight the enemy on home ground by any and all means of clandestine warfare.

A poster proclaiming "Long Live the Polish Army.

In the winter of 1939 to 1940 a number of Polish military units in the German Zone refused to join the clandestine movement. Refusing to lay down their arms, they fought several pitched battles in the open with several hundred Polish cavalrymen before being defeated by superior German forces. It was not until nine months later, after continuous fighting in the field, that those who survived subordinated themselves to the Resistance. Several similar units fighting in the Soviet Zone went into the forests and the marshes where they fought off units of the Red Army for many months.[2]

Once the Union of Armed Struggle was established, everyone believed that a national uprising was the ultimate goal. One of ZWZ's earliest instructions made this point:

Once the armed uprising erupts, by orders of the Government, the Area Commanders have the right to issue military orders to all military personnel in their territories, and they devolve this right onto the Union's organs that are subordinate to them.

Those "younger brothers and sisters of men who had fought in the September Campaign, and who, if they had not been killed or held in German or Soviet prison camps, flocked to the colors in their thousands."[3] They owed undivided allegiance to the government-in-exile abroad, and took their orders from commander-in-chief of the Polish Armed Forces, Władysław Sikorski, and his regional commanders, who had all the rights and prerogatives of army commanders with regard to the population of a war zone. In fact, the commander in chief was authorized to call a partial or total mobilization of all Poles the moment the government-in-exile, acting in concert with the other Allied governments, gave the order for an open, universal uprising against the German occupants.

Authorized leaders could issue military edicts to guide the

behavior of the population and to requisition men for necessary war work. Each soldier had all the rights and duties of a frontline combatant, including counting as double all time spent in combat toward all benefits, such as veterans' pensions, priority rights, and civil service.[4] By 1941, the Union of Armed Struggle emerged as the strongest of all the secret military groups across Poland. The following year it was renamed the *Armia Krajowa* (AK) or the Home Army, and put under the command of General Stefan Rowecki (code-named Grot) until his arrest by the Gestapo in 1943.[5]

The Home Army was not a regular army that lived in barracks or followed strict military discipline; it was a revolutionary, insurgent organization that was not able to move its formations at will from one end of the country to the other. Essentially, participants were divided into three categories. The first and largest group was comprised of people who led double lives. They were civilians who lived in their native towns and villages, and in no obvious way differed from any other person on the street. They were confined to their own jobs in factories, offices, railways, etc. Nevertheless, each of them was in touch with his direct superior, from whom he received orders and tasks to fulfill, often involving espionage—for example intelligence, sabotage, or diversion—and that he carried out where he had access through his employment. He would then return to "normal" life after he completed his assignment.

The second category of members comprised what might be termed professional conspirators, i.e., those who worked full-time for the Underground, or at least had to be available at any time during the day or night for work in the staff or for other numerous branches, intelligence, liaison, etc. They neither had time for any occupation outside the conspiracy, nor a mode of life that would limit their availability. They lived under false identities, with forged documents and labor permits.

The third group consisted of those who had broken totally with their former ways of life and set out to live as soldiers of the partisan units. They lived mainly in the forests, wore uniforms, and fought the Germans in the open.[6]

Throughout all of occupied Europe, the establishment of a resistance organization was founded upon a system of volunteers, whether they were individual volunteers or partisan groups of volunteers, whose willingness to receive and obey orders was not based on any obligation owed to a state or any established authority. Rather,

> *It was based upon a sense of loyalty to comrades, or loyalty towards the common cause to which one had consecrated one's strength and life. Every Resistance authority had to work under the pure democratic law that they must win their authority by their words and deeds, day by day, situation by situation. Directives, not concrete and unassailable commands were the rule, and the Resistance groups could usually be trusted to obey directives, with the addition of their own independent initiative.[7]*

The AK required its members to obey the orders of their immediate superiors, take classes in military theory, and, if possible, having practical training in the art of warfare.[8] Members were trained in guerrilla tactics, from how to overpower a sentry to how to place dynamite under a railroad track. When they needed nitrate for explosives, they stole it from German-controlled fertilizer factories. By mid-1943, the Home Army numbered more than four thousand women in addition to the forty thousand men in uniform under arms. People from all walks of life took part. Clerks, railway workers, artisans, factory workers, and students all took up arms against the Germans. Their weapons were transported right in the heart of Warsaw, concealed in barrels, coal carts, or camouflaged under an assortment of old quilts or beneath the straw of a hay wagon. Forays took place against numerous military objectives; for example, the army destroyed fuel dumps and military warehouses, burned factories and military food storage houses, damaged or destroyed military transports, derailed trains, and ambushed convoys. By the beginning of 1944, the AK was the largest Underground army in all of occupied Europe.[9]

Although the Home Army's principal goal was to prepare the country for an eventual uprising against the Germans, the military leadership also conducted sabotage, diversionary, and reprisal operations to hamper German war potential and lower the enemy's morale. Because illegal assembly and the possession of arms were punishable by instant death, those engaged in active resistance needed to take the utmost caution. There was also the danger that the AK might lose the support of the people and even encourage those who were tempted to collaborate with the enemy because of German reprisals resulting from AK operations.

In fact, the resistance army discouraged many large-scale military activities against the Germans, as they brought massive retribution down on innocent civilians. One of the most notorious German practices was the principle of "collective responsibility," which entailed the slaughter of hundreds of innocent men and women for each act of defiance or resistance.[10]

In retaliation, Polish attacks were directed against selected Gestapo men, SS officers, and German civilians who were involved in the persecution and murder of innocent civilians. The aim of the Resistance was to have a restraining influence. One could usually expect the killing of a number of innocent people in retaliation for the killing of a high-ranking SS officer or official, but one could also expect some other German official to be reluctant to step into his shoes for fear of being assassinated.[11]

The Home Army (AK) eventually encompassed numerous groups with varying political positions. In 1941 and 1942, the Peasant Battalions, which had been active in rural areas and formed to oppose the German deportation and pacification programs, joined the Home Army. Other groups included the National Armed Forces (NSZ), that remained outside the AK umbrella until 1944 and the National Military Organization (NOW), which merged with the AK in 1942 and fought both Nazis and Communists. The smaller, more loosely Communist-fighting squads took exception while the Soviet Communists were still allied to the German forces.

By the winter of 1940 to 1941, when Nazi-Soviet relations worsened, small, unorganized Communist groups active in the territory of the Government General made some military preparations, but the groups did not join the mainstream Polish Resistance. They refrained from any sabotage activity until well after the outbreak of the Soviet-German split in June 1941.[12]

After the German attack on the Soviet Union on June 22, 1941, a dramatic reversal took place in Polish-Soviet relations. The two governments, under strong British pressure, negotiated a treaty. It provided for a resumption of diplomatic relations between the two nations and for the Soviet Union to renounce the territorial changes in Poland provided for under the 1939 treaty with Germany.

The treaty also provided for the establishment of a Polish army in the Soviet Union under a Polish commander, provided for mutual support against Germany, and promised amnesty to Poles who had been detained earlier in the Soviet Union.[13]

The Communists in Poland now shared with the Allied nations a desire to defeat the Germans. Now known as the People's Guard

(GL), whose character was completely different from the actions of the Home Army, they directed their attacks blindly against all Germans and uprooted the greatest number of people, disorganized normal life, and created the greatest anarchy. For example, they threw grenades at a German military column on the street. In October 1942 the GL bombed a German café in response to the public execution of fifty of their members. They had also thrown grenades through the windows of a military hospital, killing several wounded soldiers. At the same time they accused the Home Army of doing nothing. These occurrences provoked the most severe repressions by mass German retaliation against the Poles.[14]

As early as March 1940, Polish railroad workers undertook some of the most dangerous tasks without expecting any benefits from their wartime exploits after the war. Not only did the Underground rely on them to distribute resistance literature, as mentioned earlier, but it depended on them to help the intelligence and sabotage programs succeed, since many of the major targets to be sabotaged were trains, railroad bridges, and related rail installations.[15]

One such tactic involved a person on the train slowing it down without touching the emergency brake to allow for an escape from the train or to facilitate an ambush by AK forces at some given point between designated stops. A steam pipe ran under all of the carriages, and one only had to turn off the stopcock, located between each pair of carriages, in order to apply the brakes; then, just before others were to jump off or just after others were to jump on, the facilitator simply had to move the stopcock back to its former position to resume the movement of the train.[16]

Polish scientists also played a role in these kinds of Underground offensives. Acting in conjunction with railway workers, one group of scientists designed an incendiary device that facilitators could swiftly and easily attach to tank cars loaded with Russian crude oil. The fuses were then timed by the rhythm of the rails, i.e., a certain number of thumps set off the explosion, sometimes in Poland and sometimes in Germany. Unable to determine the source of the sabotage, the Germans were unable to investigate. Underground members also disabled locomotives by applying an abrasive to the lubricating system.[17]

In 1941, the Union for Revenge, created by General Rowecki, undertook a wide-ranging series of operations. In addition to the AK members who made inoperative a large number of locomotives used by the Germans, experts in bacteriology and toxicology participated in what came to be known as bacterial sabotage, with impressive results. "The Poles became so proficient in administering typhoid fever microbes that during the first four months of 1943, its use was so successful that it resulted in affecting more than 600 Germans."[18]

The highly regarded Polish Underground courier Jan Karski, who survived incarceration by both the Nazis and Soviets and who repeatedly crossed Nazi-occupied Europe to bring intelligence to the government-in-exile and the Allies, spoke of a desperation that led to this form of extreme retribution by some Poles:

> *The people who did not live under German domination will never be able to gauge the strength of this hatred and will find it difficult to understand that every moral law, convention, or restriction on impulses simply disappeared. Nothing remained but the desperation of an animal caught in a trap. We fought back by every conceivable means in a naked struggle to survive against an enemy determined to destroy us. Poland snarled and clawed back at its oppressors like a wounded cat.[19]*

Karski speaks of one Pole who frequented bars to enter into a conversation with a German soldier and drink with him. At the appropriate time, he would drop a louse from a box containing lice or other typhoid-bearing germs either behind his drinking partner's collar or simply into his drink. He would also introduce them to girls who had venereal diseases. To other Poles, he soon became known as the "walking germ."[20]

As the result of the unification of the various Underground military organizations, the AK finally emerged as an umbrella organization for a national military force of more than 350,000 soldiers. The AK single-handedly liberated numerous places from German control. The following is a list of confirmed Union of Armed Combat (ZWZ) and Home Army (AK) sabotage-diversionary actions inflicted upon the Germans from January 1, 1941 to June 30, 1944.[21]

Damaged locomotives 6,930

Delayed repairs to locomotives 803

Derailed transports 732

Transports set on fire 443

Damage to railway wagons 19,058

Blown up railway bridges 38

Disruptions to electrical power in Warsaw 638

Army vehicles damaged or destroyed 4,326

Aircraft damaged 28

Fuel tanks destroyed 1,167

Tons of gasoline destroyed 4,674

Blocked oil wells 5

Military stores burned down 130

Production in factories disrupted 7

Defective parts for aircraft engines produced 4,710

Defective cannon barrels produced 203

Defective artillery shells produced 92,000

Defective aircraft radios produced 107

Defective condensers produced 70,000

Defective electro-industrial facilities. 1,700

Important factory machinery damaged 2,872

Various acts of sabotage performed 25,145

Assassinations of Germans 5,733

This summary list gives only the more characteristic acts of sabotage and suggests only half the picture of the scope of the Home Army activities.

The Home Army's own production of secretly manufactured armaments reached its climax in 1943 and 1944, when entire stocks of hand grenades, mines, flamethrowers, and a great part of the machine guns, as well as many other arms and war material, were being made ready for the uprising that was soon to take place. Its equipment included:

5 mechanical workshops fitted with 44 machine tools

2 machine carbine-barrel workshops

2 assembling workshops of machine carbine with complete equipment for serial assembling

4 hand-grenade filling workshops

3 test-firing ranges

3 nitro high-explosive plants

1 pyrotechnic and chemical plant

2 research and control laboratories

1 flamethrower assembling workshop

2 flamethrower experimental proof ranges

1 design, drawing, and blue print office[22]

Sabotage activity was not the exclusive province of the Home Army. In mid-1943 the Directorate of Civil Resistance initiated a plan intended to adversely affect the German war economy. The Underground Peasant Movement, and in particular its armed forces—the peasant battalions that had now joined the Home Army—carried out the plan. The groups received special instructions to sabotage the quota deliveries of foodstuffs such as meat, dairy products, and grain that Polish farmers were required to surrender. The slogan was that the goods were to be delivered "as little, as late, and as bad as possible." Conversely, the peasants were urged to supply the cities that were filled with hungry masses with foodstuffs at low prices. For this, the slogan was "as little as possible for the enemy, and all that is available to the population of the cities." The effort sought to frustrate, damage, or destroy whatever was of economic value to the Germans to maintain their war economy.[23] The Germans tried to maintain deliveries by reprisals, by burning villages, and by murdering peasants, but the sabotage was so extensive that the Germans were left helpless. Resistance groups held up trains and let loose the quota cattle being transported to Germany. They launched armed raids on wagons carrying quota grain to German warehouses, opening the stores in transit and pouring them out.

Armed squads of the peasant battalions also raided, seized, and burned files and documents from village offices concerning delivery quotas, putting the German authorities at a loss as to who made their quota deliveries. According to Korboński, who headed the civil Resistance,

The successful sabotage of delivery quotas, though less spectacular than fighting the enemy arms in hand, represented

a substantial Polish contribution to the struggle against Germany, though it has never been fully appreciated. If a balance sheet could be drawn up it would be found that it was worth at least several divisions fighting at the front.[23]

CHAPTER EIGHT
Poland and the SOE

The long sobs
of the violins
wounds my heart
with monotonous languor

—French poet Paul Verlaine's poem used as
code words by the BBC to signal the Resistance to begin
destroying rail lines, communications, and other German
targets to pave the way for liberation prior to D-Day.

Unlike the various Underground organizations that emerged in German-occupied Poland and that later unified under one national military force, a separate, clandestine organization emerged in July 1940 in Great Britain of which the Poles were initially an integral part. After the German occupation of Austria and Czechoslovakia and the invasion of Poland, Denmark, Norway, Holland, Belgium, and then France, Winston Churchill created a secret Department of Ungentlemanly Warfare called the Special Operations Executive (SOE). As it was to be an unorthodox fighting service made up of unconventional warriors, it was removed from the control of the military and placed under a civilian head. Its purpose was, in the prime minister's words, "to set Europe ablaze" by coordinating local acts of subversion, sabotage, and even assassination by the people in those same oppressed countries who must be the direct participants of acts of chaos and disorder. The goal was to cause maximum disruption to enemy efficiency by forcing personnel to guard vulnerable points. This also would keep the enemy preoccupied by immobilizing thousands of troops who might otherwise be employed in some other theater of operations.

The SOE was comprised of sections that included individuals from all of the occupied countries of Europe, but the Polish section differed from the others in one fundamental respect. The secret agents who were sent to those other countries remained under the SOE's instructions. Their radio links were with London; they sent in reports to London and returned there after completing their mission. Conversely, all the agents, couriers, and parachutists who traveled from Britain to Poland, most all of whom were Poles, came, as soon as they landed on Polish soil, under the authority of and reported to the Polish authorities in the homeland.[1] The Poles were eager to regain what they had lost from the Germans and the Soviets, and the British recognized their potential from the start. When the first evacuees arrived from Dunkirk, the Poles had already fought the enemy in their own homeland and in France, making them the most experienced troops facing the aggressor. Thus Poland was put high on the list of SOE priorities.

Before the collapse of France, occupied Poland and its exile-government in Paris met no insurmountable difficulties in establishing connections. Great numbers of Poles were able to escape to the West where they joined the Free Polish Forces. The British government had a special political responsibility towards Poland arising from the fact that, in the spring of 1939, Britain had signed a military pact with the

Polish government and then declared war on Germany after the invasion of Poland. In addition, a large number of Free Polish Forces who had made their way to Britain served on Western Allied fronts, and this augmented the British feeling of a special responsibility toward the Poles. And even though the Germans did not treat all the inhabitants of the occupied countries with the same degree of severity, the occupiers were hated everywhere; and nowhere was that vituperation more strongly felt than in the hearts of Poles.

The Polish Command in London set up the Sixth (Intelligence) Bureau, which had the duty, in close cooperation with the Polish section of the SOE, of maintaining and developing intelligence and communications with Poland, training operatives, obtaining supplies, and arranging for the delivery of supplies and personnel.[2] This was the limit of its authority in Polish affairs. Within the Polish section was a subsection entitled EU/P, which maintained liaison between the SOE and the Polish government in London regarding the mining and industrial area in and around Lille and St. Étienne in northern France, with its colony of about a half million Poles.[3] The Polish government-in-exile recruited Polish expatriates in large numbers, but the SOE's Polish directorate was responsible for recruiting those expatriates who were individuals of exceptional caliber in order to turn them into agents, and drop them into France and Poland to work for the SOE.[4]

Among the Polish troops in Britain were officers and NCOs whose combat experience both in Poland during the September Campaign and in France qualified them to select suitable candidates as agents who would be sent back into their native lands on specific subversion missions. In addition, there were many young people who had grown up in independent Poland who were inspired by high ideals.[5] Instructors were also dropped back into Poland to train acceptable individuals at clandestine Polish training schools where—apart from parachute jumping—they would be instructed in signals training, sabotage technique, intelligence, propaganda, and other aspects of Underground warfare. A total of 579 instructors were trained, and 345 of them reached Poland before the end of October 1944.[6]

At the beginning of 1941 the first Polish candidates enrolled in the SOE introductory course. Those selected were both male and female volunteers who were intelligent and in perfect physical condition, with plenty of initiative, self-reliance, and discipline, and who were capable of arduous infantry training. They had to be able to take risks, keep secrets, and be not only tough, but brutal at times. At least half of those who volunteered were rejected as unsuitable.[7] The entire training program was kept classified in the darkest secrecy. Applicants went through a variety of tests and courses. They were taught to handle demolitions, to deal with various forms of sabotage, and to make parachute drops by night; they became skilled at firing pistols and other hand weapons, and had to know Morse code and the arts of unarmed combat and silent killing.[8]

Every applicant who was selected and trained for operations in Poland took the same oath as had the members of the Home Army Underground forces who took their orders from the Polish government in London; and as long as he or she remained in Poland, each was a soldier of that army. Political couriers took a somewhat different oath, and as soon as they arrived in Poland became subject to the authority of the political Underground *Delegatura,* headed by the delegate appointed by London.[9]

Now that the supreme authority of the Polish State was located in London, and, as such, was responsible for the nation's policies and overall military effort, it was vital to find some quick means of sending men and supplies into Poland. The difficulties, however, were formidable. Flying was limited by the season of the year. In the summer months, the short nights precluded flying. This left spring, autumn, and winter, but in the cold weather, iced-up planes kept flights grounded. Other challenges arose as well. In order to allow for necessary detours to avoid German air defenses, airplanes needed to endure a two-thousand-mile round-trip and complete the journey within the hours of darkness to allow for the best possible chance of success. These criteria proved difficult to meet. In December 1940, the SOE planned a flight on a slow, cumbersome twin-engine Whitley aircraft to drop agents into Poland; however, it was cancelled when authorities realized that the aircraft's range was not adequate to make a successful round-trip.[10]

Another SOE flight was scheduled to leave on the moonlit night of February 15, 1941, with the aim of establishing an advance guard and thereby proving that authorities abroad could maintain liaison with the home country.[11] After two false starts, a Whitley aircraft was modified to carry a special auxiliary fuel tank for the trip, which would take eleven to fourteen hours, depending upon the weather. Even so, the Whitley had to turn back after covering only 850 miles; the plane dropped three Polish parachutists, two officers, and a political courier 60 miles in advance of the planned target because the pilot, who was under orders to carry out the drop at all costs, could not find the drop zone. As a result, the men landed in German territory close to the prewar Polish frontier, which had been annexed to Germany after September 1939. Although the party lost all of its equipment, they met some Polish sympathizers who helped them reach the Home Army high command in Warsaw. Nevertheless, this was the first connection with occupied Europe and given the time involved in making the flight and the wintry weather, it was considered a notable feat of navigation and endurance. One redeeming feature of the flight was that

> *this first SOE landing from the air in occupied Polish territory had a tremendous effect on the population's morale and the development of the Resistance movement . . . Polish hearts*

beat faster and hopes rose higher—the Western Allies were at last making their presence felt.[12]

In reality the mission showed the difficulty of supplying the Polish Home Army. And once the dark winter nights yielded to long summer evenings, flights across occupied Europe became terribly exposed. Thus the British Air Ministry was unwilling or reluctant to loan aircraft and very few additional operations took place in 1941. The six months of short nights were ruled out, but twenty flights were planned for the winter of 1941 to 1942, and of these, twelve were carried out, but only nine successfully.[13] It was only in 1942 that the Polish government gained three four-engine Halifax bombers with greater range and load capacity. They operated with the British Special 138 Squadron, which had the task of supporting the SOE's actions.

Not all airdrops were successful. As the fortunes of war would have it, unexpected hair-raising situations arose, some resulting in terrible misfortune. For example,

One group of Polish parachutists landed where a German division was billeted, another on a police station; on one night a navigator mistook the lights of a railway station for those of the drop zone. Men were landed in trees, in icy waves of river, or on the roof of a peasant's hut. Sometimes the parachutes failed to open; on other nights the heavy containers dropped from too low an altitude and fell on sleeping villages with fatal results.[14]

Nevertheless, that first heavy Whitley aircraft that made its way across Germany set the stage for the later night flights and the secret drops of supplies and people, a need that increased day by day.

While SOE efforts were being made to obtain and adapt aircraft for the long journeys across continental Europe, the Poles—along with the Dutch, Belgians, Danes, Norwegians, Czechs, and free French, all of whom were in German-occupied countries and were Britain's allies—had another problem. They lacked equipment. After the fall of France, Britain was the only source of supplies and equipment in the West for the Polish forces. Materials had to travel by air to Poland via the Polish section of the SOE, to which the Sixth Bureau submitted its requirements in the form of money and equipment. But unfortunately Britain did not have the equipment to spare. British war preparations were complete in only a few specifically defined areas and its industry was just beginning to develop more rapidly its large-scale military production. Raw materials were running low and could only be replaced by cargoes moving in slow convoy by long, roundabout routes swarming with German submarines.[15]

In April 1941, Polish Premier Sikorski visited the United States and met with President Roosevelt to discuss supplies needed in occupied Poland: war material and irregular warfare equipment, printing machinery, duplicators, typewriters, cameras for intelligence purposes, and wireless and medical supplies. The Americans readily agreed to make supplies available. Initially, the materials were purchased on the open market; later, specified articles came under Lend-Lease. As a result of this new American bill, the United States could send large supplies to countries at war with Germany without asking those countries for payment. They would settle their debts after the war, with the proviso that the United States would take into account all that they received from their debtors, such as services during the war, etc.[16]

In July 1941, several weeks after Hitler's invasion of the Soviet Union, the German armies had advanced over the eastern Polish territories that Russia had occupied. The Poles saw this as an opportunity to infiltrate saboteurs and agents into the newly German-occupied territory. By the end of the year, they worked out a plan to harass the Germans' extended communication lines that facilitated the provision of supplies to the Eastern Front. The assignment was given to a large-scale organization known as Fan, which was responsible to the Home Army command in Warsaw for all subversive operations in the eastern territories.[17] Because of the highly clandestine nature of Fan, the Home Army forbade Fan members from contacting anyone in any of the local Home Army networks.

In the early spring of 1942, an SOE parachutist, Captain Alfred Paczkowski (code-named Wania) set up headquarters at Brest-Litovsk where he, with the help of a dozen or more local residents who knew the area well, began to create a subversive network to attack German rail communications. In the autumn an additional thirty-two SOE agents parachuted into Brest—where Wania and his men conducted a series of successful operations that included blowing up railroad tracks, destroying locomotives, and derailing transports—to meet with Fan members.[18]

While on their way to carry out another raid, Wania, who broke his leg crossing a frozen river, his SOE deputy, and another soldier were captured by the Germans and taken to a prison in Pinsk, some 210 miles from Warsaw. When news of the capture and imprisonment reached Warsaw, the Fan commander ordered an SOE officer, Jan Piwnik, code-named Ponury, to rescue the three men. With two other SOE parachutists and three capable Home Army soldiers, he left for Pinsk. In addition to drawing sixty thousand marks from official funds to use as bribe if necessary, Fan arranged for the use of a car and two lorries.[19]

On January 2, 1943, after obtaining arms to recruit additional members for the group, Ponury took arms, explosives, and the uniform of an NCO in the German SS and arrived at Brest, where he established a hiding place on the outskirts of town as his base of operations. He made contact with a warden at the prison who was a member of the Home Army. Ponury got a layout of the prison area and learned that the Pinsk garrison consisted of 3,500 men. He also learned that he wouldn't be able to bribe his way into the prison. He and his group decided to carry out the rescue on January 18. Sixteen soldiers divided into three parties of four plus two patrols of two men each. Because of the likelihood of German reprisals after the rescue, the men posed as Soviet partisans and planned to speak Russian or German during the raid; those who knew neither language were to remain silent. They made arrangements to cut the telephone connections before the attack, and to conduct a reconnaissance and issue arms a few hours before the rescue.[20]

At exactly 5:00 p.m., a small, camouflaged Opel drove up to the prison gate. In the car were Ponury and another agent dressed in the German SS uniform; the uniformed man leaned out and shouted to the guard, who promptly opened the gate. Once inside the prison, two members took control of the sentry box, and two other groups who had ladders scaled the outer wall and went to the administrative office, where they got the keys to the cells. Several German guards resisted, but Ponury's men shot them with Sten guns. Soon all the groups joined forces; some occupied offices and others stood over the prison guards. Ponury went to the prisoners' section and opened the cells. Altogether, they set more than forty men free. They located Wania, his deputy, and the Home Army prisoner and took them to the waiting car outside the prison, and they sped off in the darkness. The break into the Pinsk prison and the release of the men, among them the Fan sector commander, was a classic example of the tactics of a small commando group led by well-trained and selected SOE parachutists.[21]

Before his untimely death in July 1943, Commander-in-Chief Sikorski created an elite special-operations group of the Home Army known as *Cichociemni,* the "Dark and Silent Ones." It was a highly secret organization of volunteers whose purpose was covert operations behind enemy lines in Poland. Originally more than 2,400 volunteers secretly left their regular army units for specialized training designed by the Sixth Bureau and the SOE. Conducted mainly in Scotland, it included training in covert operations, topography, cryptography, sharpshooting, judo, and assuming new identities. Six hundred five completed the training, and of those, 344 secretly parachuted into Poland as covert agents of the Home Army. Once attached to special clandestine units of the AK, they coordinated airdrops, served as instructors in secret military schools, and conducted sabotage operations, partisan warfare, and assassinations.[22]

Besides the Poles who dedicated themselves to the struggle inside Poland, others who were no less patriotic took part in Underground activities independently of the official organizations and in association with Poland's allies. Some were people of unusual distinction who sooner or later found themselves in the ranks of the SOE. One of the longest-serving and most capable of all SOE agents was Krystyna Skarbek, or as she was later known, Christina Granville. The daughter of a Polish count, she became an outstandingly courageous and remarkably resourceful covert intelligence agent. After the invasion of her Polish homeland, and determined to help her now-occupied country, she fled to London where she was accepted by the British Secret Intelligence Service (SIS). Her ability and inclination to take risks, along with being an expert skier and an active sportswoman, made her an ideal candidate for spying. She was given an alias as a journalist and sent to Budapest, where she served as a courier. She made six skiing excursions across the snow-covered Tatra Mountains that separated Hungary and Poland, smuggling Polish propaganda leaflets to the Polish Underground forces to help lift the morale of the Resistance. As a courier, Skarbek not only survived as a spy; she flourished. To her, danger was a stimulus. She also organized a system of Polish couriers who took intelligence reports, especially those dealing with new German weapons made by Poles in German munitions factories, from Warsaw to Budapest and then to London.

Krystyna Granville Skarbek, an undercover spy with the Special Operations Executive (SOE) who had numerous exploits in Poland, Hungary and France. Because of her contribution to the liberation of the France, she was awarded the Croix de Guerre, and in England, she was made an officer to the Order of the British Empire for her work in conjunction with the British authorities during the war.

Hungary was still neutral in 1940, but was increasingly pro-German; under pressure from Germany, it joined the Axis Powers. Budapest became both Skarbek's base and her home. There she met a former Polish officer, Andrzej Kowerski (also known as Andrew Kennedy), whom she helped organize escape routes for Polish officers and well-trained pilots who came from Poland. Kennedy's activities, and to a lesser extent Skarbek's, were discovered by German surveillance experts in Budapest, who found grounds for arresting them. But by convincing a Hungarian doctor that she had an advanced stage of tuberculosis and was about to die, she was released. With the help of the British Ambassador to Budapest, she escaped with Kennedy and together they went to Cairo, which was British territory and a war-free zone. She remained there for two years.

In April 1944, the SOE contacted her, and because of her fluency in French and English and her knowledge of some Italian, she joined the SOE and went to work with a team operating in France. In July Skarbek parachuted into southeastern France, where she worked with a network that linked Italian partisans with members of the French Resistance in the French Alps.

In August, she was assigned to work in a new network as the assistant to Francis Cammaerts, probably the most experienced and highly regarded SOE agent in France during the war. The work was in the Vercors Mountains, a rough region in the south of France that consisted of high limestone plateaus and deep caves and gorges, and that was a stronghold of the French Resistance. On August 13, just two days before the Allies landed in southern France, the Germans arrested Cammaerts and another agent at a roadblock. Skarbek, after learning that they had been arrested and would be executed, made a plan for their release. She went to the Gestapo headquarters and introduced herself as British General Bernard Montgomery's niece. After arguing and bargaining with the Gestapo, she told him that she was a

British parachutist who worked for the SOE and that the Allies would soon arrive. She said that she had been in constant wireless contact with British forces, and to prove her point, she produced several useless crystals. She also offered the Germans two million French francs for the men's release, which the SOE agreed to forward to her and which were air dropped the following day. As a result, the Germans freed the two agents.

In September 1944, she made contact with Allied forces, filed an official report in Avignon of her mission, and returned to England. Nicknamed the Queen of the European Underground by friends, Krystyna Skarbek received the Order of the British Empire, the George Medal, and the French Croix de Guerre. After the war she worked as an ocean liner stewardess and on June 15, 1952, a man who had been obsessed with her stabbed her to death in a hotel; she was forty-four. The former chief of staff of the Polish Armed Forces and Colin Gubbins, the director of the British SOE, attended her funeral.[23]

In September 1943, the Poles received three long-promised Liberator bombers from the Americans, which they adapted for night sorties over Poland. The Polish command was under direct orders of the Polish section of SOE in London. The aircraft flew over neutral Sweden from Britain and back, a journey that was over 1,100 miles each way, on trips that took over fourteen and sixteen hours respectively, and in which the planes were required to use their last drops of fuel. Matters were made worse by a huge German antiaircraft, artillery, and fighter barrier west of Berlin, from north Denmark to Bavaria, that aircraft bound from England with supplies for Poland could not penetrate.[24]

Given these circumstances, the Polish base moved to Brindisi in southern Italy. More than five months lapsed between the last flight with parachutists from England in October 1943 and the first one from Brindisi in April 1944. But even in Brindisi, from which the routes were shorter, the weather resulted in a limited number of flights. The incessant storms, snow, heavy rain, and fog precluded flights in the Mediterranean and the Balkans at the turn of the year. An additional concern was the Brindisi airfield, with its single runway that was highly dangerous for bombers when a side wind blew. The severe winter was followed by a fine spring. The nights were long and the backlog of supplies was enormous, so pilots made special efforts over a very short period. Fifty-eight sorties flew to Poland in April and seventy-two in May.[25]

In spite of the shorter routes and an increased number of aircraft, improved technique, and additional drop zones, the amount of supplies that reached Poland was still far too small and far short of what was promised and expected.

There were two main reasons for this shortage of supplies and equipment. Poland, as the most distant allied country, presented especially difficult problems. Because Poland was not a strategic theater of operations in the overall conduct of the war, the Western Allies directed their attention principally to France, Belgium, and Holland. They were aware of the Home Army's existence, however, and sent them a bare minimum of supplies for diversionary purposes. But the Poles did not respond favorably when the Allies refused their requests for additional materials. Those outside of Poland believed that, since the Soviet Union was beating the Germans, the lend-lease supplies that they were receiving on a large scale were sufficient for the Eastern Front; from the Poles' viewpoint, they were victim of the Allies' lack of foresight.

The second reason was both political and moral. When the Soviet Union joined with the West—after having two years earlier aided Hitler in dismembering Poland—the British showed less and less interest in their Polish allies. Indeed, both the British and the Americans went on to regard Poland as part of the Russian sphere, not as a country to be included in the allied invasion plans or in any other theater of operations.[26]

The following supply figures show that the Allies excluded Poland from their operational plans. Throughout the course of the war, supplies dropped into Poland from the West amounted to 600 tons. Greece, a country one-third the size of Poland, received 5,796.; France and Yugoslavia received 10,000 tons each. Poland, of course, was farther off, and the flights were dangerous, requiring specially adapted aircraft; and Greece and Yugoslavia could be supplied by sea. Nevertheless, the difference in figures is highly significant and disappointing.[27] Nevertheless, given the technical difficulties in supplying Poland, and being at such a far distance from the West, the SOE Polish section carried out a difficult task extremely well.

By the summer of 1942, when Germany had completed the occupation of most all of continental Europe, four hundred million people lay under the yoke of German rule. In Poland alone there were 27,500,000 Poles, of which more than 5,500,000 were killed. And as statistics show, the largest number of Polish losses during the war included not military insurgents, but civilians. But it was not the fact that they were killed, but rather the inhuman way in which innocent civilians were treated by the occupying forces, that created such deep feelings of vengeance and retaliation and that gave the people such a strong inclination to fight back. And those who were inclined to fight back were only able to do so by the initiative of the SOE, which provided the equipment and the training.

Because the work of the Home Army was mainly diversionary—keeping the German divisions away from areas where they could have been more effective—the SOE provided the men and materials for them to continue to act.

> *They landed with weapons and materials for making weapons. They brought plans, orders, couriers, and large amounts of money for financing the Underground. (SOE's grant to the Polish Section for its first year of operation in 1941–42 was 600,000 pounds.) Above all, they brought the knowledge that the Underground had allies, that it was not fighting alone.*[28]

These were the SOE Polish Section's key contributions. Given the general feeling of the Western Allies and the diversionary nature of the Home Army, no other known organization could have supported the Poles in this way. If assisting the Polish Resistance had been left to the British Royal Air Force alone, it could not have happened. Rather, it came from the Polish SOE and the Sixth Bureau, which worked out a plan that met that need.

Moreover, it is worth noting that at the start of the war, the United States had no organized secret service or special operations department. What they learned, they learned from the SOE. From its beginning in 1940 as a novice organization, the SOE quickly developed into a blossoming force that not only served the war effort well but within two years accepted officers of the U.S. Office of Strategic Services (OSS) at specialized training schools in Great Britain and in Toronto, Canada. Soon after, these officers conducted special operations of their own in conjunction with the British in various theaters of war.

CHAPTER NINE
Women in the Polish Resistance

The deepest tenderness a woman can show to a man,
is to help him to do his duty.

—DINAH MARIA MULOCK (1826–1887) ENGLISH NOVELIST

The Poles, as a strongly united people, did more than any other nation in Nazi-occupied Europe to come together under what were impossible circumstances. Nothing illustrates this more vividly than the role that women played in the Resistance. It is no overstatement to say that without women, the Home Army could not have existed. In occupied Poland, thirty-five thousand to forty thousand women took the Polish Soldiers' oath to protect the constitution.[1] In April 1938, the Polish Sejm, the lower house of Parliament, passed a statute that granted women the right to serve in auxiliary detachments that included antiaircraft, sentry, and communications units, as well as other services "necessary for defense purposes." A year later these detachments became known as the Women's Auxiliary Army Service of the 1st Bureau of the Polish Victory Service (SWP), placed under the command of Maria Wittekówna.[2] At the start of 1940, the commander of the Union of Armed Struggle (ZWZ), Colonel Stefan Rowecki, declared that the women in Poland were carrying out the same types of military service as the men, and thus decreed that the term "Women's Service in Poland" be used. In April 1942 the Women's Service in Poland was officially raised to the rank of Women's Military Service. A special presidential decree on October 27, 1943 proclaimed that women soldiers had the same rights and obligations as men. In the following year the commander of the Polish Home Army, Tadeusz Bór-Komorowski, allocated military ranks to women, including those of both noncommissioned and commissioned officers.[3]

Yet before the decree that formalized the status of women, and even before there was an official Home Army designation for an organized resistance, Polish women participated in isolated incidents of Underground activity, since most Poles believed that the only alternative to extermination was to fight. So until the Resistance began to organize, individual acts of resistance were not uncommon.

One such case of early, unorganized resistance involved a young eighteen-year-old Polish countess, Elżbieta (Bisia) Krasicka, who took an active role in a resistance at the very beginning of hostilities before the organized Resistance had actually begun to form. After being forced from the feudal magnificence of the family's castle in Lesko on the eastern bluff of the San River, in what had become the Russian occupation zone, the Krasicki family moved to a friend's hunting lodge some distance away in territory under German occupation.

As was the case for so many Poles, the Krasickis' love of country took precedence over anything else, including family. *Amor Patriae Nostra Lex*: Love of Country is Our Law. When called to fight for Poland, no one hesitated. Everyone went: girls, boys, sixteen and seventeen, younger; it did not matter. They were raised to accept as a given that if Poland calls, you go.

Bisia Krasicka was awarded the Gold Cross of Merit with Sword by the Polish government-in-exile "for deeds of bravery not connected with direct combat and for merit demonstrated in perilous circumstances." She also received the Cross of Valor "for having demonstrated deeds of valor and courage on the fields of battle."

During that earlier period, Bisia Krasicka took it upon herself to lead Polish exiles, especially Polish officers who were in hiding, on numerous excursions through the surrounding countryside and wooded areas toward the Czech border, where many would continue the fight with the Allied forces in the West. The western exodus of Poles began spontaneously. First to go were the officers, followed by enlisted men who refused to remain in Poland during the occupation. By the time France had entered the war in the early summer of

1940, fighting was at a standstill and many went to France to fight on other fronts. Under the leadership of General Władysław Sikorski, the Polish premier of the exiled government, Krasika's brother Stas was among more than one hundred thousand Poles who fought in other theaters of war during the European conflict.

In early 1942 at the age of twenty, Krasicka was sworn in as an official member of the Home Army (AK) after taking a solemn oath to defend her country even at the risk of her life. It was a pledge of secrecy:

> *Before God Almighty and Mary the Blessed Virgin, Queen of the Polish Crown, I pledge allegiance to my Motherland, the Republic of Poland. I pledge to steadfastly guard her honor, and to fight for her liberation with all my strength, even to the extent of sacrificing my own life if that is needed. I pledge unconditional obedience to the President of Poland, the Commander-in-Chief of the Republic, and the Home Army Commander whom he appointed. I pledge to resolutely keep secret whatever may happen to me. So help me God!*

She was then advised that her duty was to fight; her only compensation was that she would be born in freedom, and that every form of treason would be punishable by death.

One of Krasicka's first assignments involved transporting arms and ammunition through German-occupied territory, an extremely dangerous task that meant almost certain death. While driving a wagon full of hay concealing a captured German machine gun and ammunition, she was stopped at a German checkpoint. Having an I.D. card and a hidden loaded pistol, Krasicka was asked by one of the soldiers what was beneath the hay in the wagon. She turned to him and replied with a smile, "A machine gun." The German laughed and then motioned her to proceed on her journey.

In addition to transporting arms, Krasicka assisted partisans from Warsaw in blowing up a bridge during Operation Tempest in the spring of 1944 before the Warsaw Uprising. This was part of a plan to show the Allies that the Polish government-in-exile was able to coordinate efforts across the country before the Russians could install their own puppet government. Krasicka received two military decorations for her service in the Resistance. The government-in-exile awarded her the Gold Cross of Merit with Swords for deeds of bravery and valor not connected with direct combat, and for merit demonstrated in perilous circumstances. She received the Cross of Valor for demonstrated deeds of courage on the field of battle. She also received third award: a memorial medal given to all members of a special AK operational unit to which she was attached in 1944.[4]

As part of the so-called Secret Polish (Underground) State that formed after German and Soviet troops attacked Poland in 1939, women were active in all areas of resistance. They taught and were students in secretly continued higher education courses, as we learned in an earlier chapter. As messengers and couriers, women ensured communication between the secret Resistance cells within the country and abroad. They were responsible for coding and decoding messages, establishing contacts with Polish prisoner-of-war camps, and dealing with the medical department. They played vital roles as field nurses and in organizing first-aid posts in villages and, during Operation Tempest, in field hospitals. They were responsible for watching places endangered by German surveillance and for guarding clandestine meetings and radio stations. They also assisted in the transport of money, weapons, and printed material. Women arranged contacts with those in concentration camps, intelligence units, and in planned diversion and sabotage. Women underwent paramedical and military administration. They were also responsible for operational liaisons. In addition, women provided logistical support to partisan detachments in the field during the difficult conditions of autumn and winter, sewing warm clothes and knitting scarves and socks. More than four thousand Underground Girl Scouts, sixteen years of age and older, were dispersed among 250 different locations working in communications and also as medics.[5]

There were girls like Marzenna Maria Schejbal who, after reciting the oath to Poland's Black Madonna and sporting a white-and-red AK armband, acted as messenger, nurse, stretcher bearer, forager for medical supplies, and jack-of-all trades for the Resistance forces. Many women volunteered their services spontaneously and never appeared in official records. Girls as young as thirteen begged to work as helpers.[6] A fourteen-year-old girl singlehandedly attacked and burned two German tanks, and a girl of eighteen blew up the door of a German police stronghold, enabling her unit to get inside the building. Seventeen-year-old Danuta Siedzikówna (code-named Inka) was sworn in as a Home Army soldier in December 1943 and, after acquiring medical skills, became a medical orderly. After the Soviets took over Poland, she was known to have said, just before the Polish Communist Secret Police executed her in 1946, "I am sad that I have to die. Tell my grandma that I conducted myself with dignity."[7]

Many unrecognized participants performed courageous acts; one such woman was Irena Kwiastkowska, known as Black Barbara, a courier during the fighting in Old Town who had other messengers under her command. She would walk down the street with classified papers hidden in her sleeve pretending to be an innocent young lady out for a stroll. When she passed some SS men, she would say to herself, "You bloody bastards. You think you are so strong and I am so weak, but my work will eventually defeat you. That was my satisfaction."[8]

According to Lt. Jan Karski, who for four years served as liaison officer between the political and military authorities and as official courier between the secret state in Poland and the Polish government in London, the workers in the Underground whose lives were most in constant danger, even though the circumstances in which they operated were far less dramatic, were the liaison women. Their chief function was to facilitate contacts between Underground workers. They were vital links in Underground operations and in many ways more exposed than the contacts they helped bring together. The Resistance insisted that a liaison woman never be out of sight—literally. She had to reside where they could find her quickly and was not allowed to change her name or her address without permission. So long as she remained active, she could not go into hiding or get lost to her Resistance superiors. Doing otherwise would have meant a breakdown in the contacts between the members and branches of the Underground. Consequently, a special observer always watched her and her apartment. If the Gestapo were to arrest her, she would be unable to betray other members, even under torture, since within a few hours, all those in contact with her would have changed their names and addresses.[9] And the Gestapo often caught liaison women:

> *The average "life" of a liaison woman did not exceed a few months. They were invariably caught by the Gestapo, usually in incriminating circumstances, and treated with bestial cruelty in the Nazi jails. Most of them carried poison and were under orders to use it without hesitation when the need arose. It was almost impossible to get them out of jail and the Underground could not take the risk of their succumbing to torture. It can be said that of all the workers in the Underground their lot was the most severe, their sacrifices the greatest, and their contribution the least rewarded. They were overworked and*

doomed. They neither held high rank nor received any great honors for their heroism.[10]

Who would have suspected "Babcza," the old lady, her head covered with a brightly flowered babushka, selling apples from a cart of being a secret liaison for the Underground Resistance? One pocket of her apron held coins for making change, but the other pocket held cryptic messages that she passed to young men who uttered the correct coded words.

Another woman of about fifty had taught French in one of the Warsaw high schools before the war. She joined the Underground as a liaison woman early in the occupation. On one occasion, the Gestapo caught her and her husband in their own apartment. Both suffered unspeakable tortures. Her husband died during the initial "examination." The woman survived two interrogations, but had to be carried back to her cell after the second one. The following morning, authorities found her hanging from a beam in the ceiling of her cell. When she committed this terrible act without anyone hearing a single sound, her doctor explained that "her determination to die had been so inexorable and her indifference to pain so steadfast that she had passed away without a groan, without kicking her legs against the wall in the last spasm before death."[11]

Another dangerous job undertaken mainly by women was that of distributing the Underground newspapers, one more task that meant certain death if caught by the Gestapo. One girl did nothing but distribute illegal newspapers for over three years. She delivered to 120 different addresses, which averaged out to about forty a day. She hoped that after the war she could get a job where she could remain at the same spot and have people come to her. She said she wanted to be a matron in a ladies' restroom.[12]

Women undertook many functions of high authority and

responsibility. During the course of the war, Maria Wittekówna was made head of liaison and communication in the Home Army staff and headquarters. In 1942, Wanda Gertz (code-named Lena), one of the first women to join the Resistance, organized and commanded a Women's Sabotage Officers' School. The school had 120 women instructors and dealt with women commando units specializing in diversionary actions and sabotage, including the theft of weapons manuals, which were translated and combined with instructions on how to build simplified models. In combat, the elite Women's Diversion and Sabotage (DYSK) unit manufactured explosives and other armaments during the Warsaw Uprising. They were active in sabotaging rail lines, bridges, eliminating members of the Gestapo, and intelligence gathering. The Germans later captured Lena and held her as a prisoner of war until April 1945 when she was liberated by American forces.[13]

A particularly legendary figure in the Home Army was Elżbieta Zawacka (code-named Zo), a former high school teacher and later university professor who was one of only two women later promoted to brigadier general of the Polish Army. During the September 1939 campaign she fought in the defense of Lwów, and in the following month she joined the Silesian branch of the Union of Armed Struggle. In late 1940 she was moved to Warsaw and began her mission as a courier. Her regular route ran from Warsaw through Berlin and Sweden; she used false documents and carried secret reports about Nazi atrocities and the Resistance to London. On one such trip in February 1943 she risked her life crossing the borders of Nazi-occupied Poland across Germany, France, and Spain to Gibraltar, where she was airlifted to Poland's government-in-exile in London. She was appointed an emissary in the Department of Foreign Communications of the Home Army High Command. She successfully made nearly one hundred trips between Poland and England transporting Underground messages, money, and men.

Elzbieta Zawacka, served as an Underground courier between the Home Army Resistance and the Polish Government-in-Exile. She fought in the Warsaw Uprising and was later relocated in Krakow where she continued her courier activities between Poland and England. In 1951 she was arrested and tortured by the Polish Communist secret police for treason and espionage. After her release from prison several years later, she resumed her teaching position as a university professor.

Zo was the only known female member of the elite special-operations group *Cichociemni*, the "Dark and Silent Ones," a highly secret organization of volunteers who carried on covert operations behind enemy lines in Poland. In September 1943, as an agent of the SOE, she was the only female covert agent dropped by parachute into Poland, where she brought orders and instructions from London to the Home Army. She later took part in the Warsaw Uprising.

In 1951, the newly imposed Communist authorities falsely accused Zo of espionage and treason. The secret security forces tortured her, gave her a ten-year prison term, but released her in 1955. For her strong and intransigent service during the occupation, she received the Polish Order of the White Eagle, in addition to the *Virtuti Militari* and the Cross of Valor. She was later a cofounder of the World Association of Home Army Ex-Servicemen.[14]

Even though the liaison women and other women in the Underground who were actively exposed to danger suffered more than the majority of others of their sex, it would be a serious omission to fail to mention those wives, mothers, and daughters of the men in the Resistance who, even though they did not actively participate themselves, lived daily lives of misery or, at best, undiminished anxiety. Since they did not actively take part in Resistance activities, they had no way of determining the extent of danger or of sensing its approach. Yet they were always ready to accept it and, for that reason, never knew a moment's peace.

> *It was a generally accepted rule that the wives of at least the leaders register with the Underground and live under assumed names. If she lived under her true name and her husband was arrested, she would also be taken. Very often, although she had taken no part in her husband's work, she would be tortured and the attempt would be made to pry loose from her*

secrets they were unable to get from the husband. Many died involuntarily as they simply knew nothing.

The worst part of it was that most of them were temperamentally unsuited to this kind of existence, but were forced to share the lives of their husbands.[15]

CHAPTER TEN
The Jews and the Warsaw Ghetto Uprising

I feel a great need to greet all those Christians and Jews who have come to this square to commemorate the Uprising in the Warsaw Ghetto fifty years ago and the crimes perpetrated against the Jewish people during the last World War. How could we not be with you, dear Jewish brothers and sisters, to recall in prayer and meditation, such a tragic anniversary? Be sure of this: You are not alone in bearing the pain of this memory; we pray and watch with you, under the gaze of God, the holy and just one, rich in mercy and pardon.

—ADDRESS BY POPE JOHN PAUL II IN ST. PETER'S SQUARE
APRIL 18, 1993

From the very beginning of the occupation, German policy toward the Jewish population in Poland was a steady and systematic movement towards the extermination of more than three million souls. Within a month after the end of the September campaign, Germany issued the first anti-Jewish decrees, the very first of which was that all Jews over the age of ten were required to wear armbands and sew a Star of David on their breast pockets. A decree that introduced compulsory labor for Jews between the ages of fourteen and sixty followed. In January 1940, Jews were restricted to their places of residence and deprived of their freedom of movement; German authorities confiscated all radios. Germans soon took over Jewish enterprises, except for small stores in Jewish neighborhoods. Signs that said *Nicht Arisch*—not Aryan—marked those stores and shops. Additional decrees followed concerning the handling of money. All Jews were required to deposit their money in blocked bank accounts. The banks could release no more than 250 złotys per week to the holder of the account, thereby making it impossible for Jews to engage in business in the open, especially with non-Jews. As time went on Jewish property and resources dwindled and, owing to a lack of food and other basic requirements necessary to exist, Jews began to realize that they faced a slow death.

On the eve of the invasion, the Jewish population in Warsaw was 337,000, about 29 percent of the city's population. Within a short time, German authorities proposed segregated Jewish districts, and on October 12, 1940, Yom Kippur, the Jewish Day of Atonement, German authorities announced a formal decree establishing a ghetto. To create the ghetto, the Germans moved 113,000 gentile residents out; and they herded an additional 138,000 Jewish residents into a sixteen-block area that comprised 2.4 percent of the city's land area.[1] Located in the worst run-down sections of the city, the ghetto clearly could not accommodate the growing number of residents who were destined to occupy the area. The population in the ghetto also included Jews brought in from the surrounding countryside and smaller towns within the General Government. The rest of the Jews had already been living there. The houses were indescribably overcrowded with as many as fifteen people to a room.

**Jewish Civilian Population being led into the
Warsaw Ghetto by German troops.**

On November 14, 1940, the Warsaw ghetto was closed and the inhabitants barricaded behind eight-foot-high walls topped with barbed wire. German sentries took position at the few entrances and any Jew found outside its confines was shot on the spot. Those in the ghetto struggled to survive on a food ration of four-and-a-half pounds of bread per month and nothing else. This was about 25 percent of the ration for non-Jewish Poles and only 8 percent of the nutritional value of the food that the Germans received for their official ration coupons. But food was passed into the ghetto in unusual ways: through the cellars of adjoining houses, through the underground canals, i.e. sewers, and through camouflaged openings that were torn in the ghetto walls at night. Smuggling occurred at ghetto gates by the help of Germans and other Poles who accepted bribery in exchange for necessary food. Children and women also participated on a somewhat smaller scale. But all the smuggling of food was far too insufficient, and as a result, overcrowded conditions, appalling misery, poor sanitary conditions, want, and hunger resulted in widespread ill health and frequent epidemics. This in turn quickly led to the loss of numerous lives. When the ghetto was sealed off in November, there were already 445 deaths in the ghetto. In August the number increased to 5,560. Then the monthly figure fluctuated between 4,000 and 5,000 for as long as the ghetto existed.[2] Jan Nowak, a Polish courier in the Resistance, witnessed a scene that grew to be a commonplace occurrence within the ghetto:

> *I remember vividly the corpses covered with newspapers lying on the ghetto sidewalks as one saw them when it was still possible to ride through the Jewish district in a "transit" streetcar. These were mostly people who had died of starvation or typhus. The bodies were collected twice a day, like garbage, by the street-cleaning department.[3]*

Signs soon appeared at the entrance gates of the ghetto with the inscription "Spotted Typhus: entry and exit forbidden." By the spring of 1941 thousands had been brought into the ghetto, and with the number of inhabitants who were densely packed into its confines, the ghetto grew to well over four hundred fifty thousand.

Throughout the summer and fall, the first stage of total extermination focused on the Polish and Russian Jews living in the newly invaded territory after the German attack on Russia. The second stage was directed against Jews in the General Government region and in those parts of Poland incorporated into Germany. The number of victims was enormous. These were not sporadic pogroms: it was mass slaughter.[4] Indeed, mass killings occurred all over eastern Poland.

The winter of 1941 to 1942 began with the liquidation of the Jews in those Polish territories annexed by the Reich. The Jews were told that they were being "resettled" in the east, where work, food, and living accommodations would be far better. Thus many Jews voluntarily left the ghetto believing that they were being transferred to agricultural employment. Many of the Jews were transported in specially adapted closed trucks in which they were gassed by exhaust fumes and killed by carbon monoxide poisoning. German authorities left the bodies in the forest, in mass graves that had already been prepared for them.[5] In the General Government, ghettos were "cleaned out" by force and many thousands were killed. Those who survived were transported to extermination camps in Beltzek, Majdanek, Treblinka, Sobibór, and other localities. This continued throughout 1942 as the rate of extermination decreased. Of the 450,000 human beings who inhabited the ghetto at the end of 1941, between 240,000 and 300,000 were deported and met their deaths at the extermination camps in the summer of 1942.[6] Those remaining in the ghetto slowly starved.

The terror that the Germans launched during those days was the final horror that the Jews could bear. The constant escalation of repression had lost its power to terrorize; people stopped being afraid because they saw that they had nothing more to lose.[7] The Jews could no longer resign themselves to passivity and submissiveness.

In mid-September 1942, a three-month period of relative quiet that followed the deportations enabled the Jews to prepare for battle once they heard that the deportations were part of an extermination process. A newly created Jewish Coordinating Committee set up the Jewish Fighting Organization (ZOB), which sent delegates to the Aryan side of the city to establish contact with the Polish Underground movement and acquire arms. Two hundred twenty men, each armed with a handgun, hand grenades, and Molotov cocktails, i.e. gasoline incendiaries, initially comprised the ZOB.[8] The insurgents had little of their own, but units of the mainstream Home Army on the Aryan side of the city provided more weapons, ammunition, and supplies. An additional body comprised of former officers and non-commissioned officers of the 1939 September Campaign joined with a Zionist Revisionist group to form an additional force, the Jewish Military Organization (ZZW). In October 1942, the ZZW consisted of 150 trained men, but by the beginning of 1943 the number raised to 400.[9] Moreover, couriers helped establish contact with the ghettos in other large towns.

The Germans' January 18, 1943 liquidation attempt led to the first instance of armed insurgency within the ghetto. The Germans had suddenly entered the ghetto, intent upon a further deportation. Within a few hours, some six hundred Jews were shot and five thousand others rounded up. One of the Jews who chronicled the event referred to the fight as "the unsuspecting Monday."[10] The SS and units of the military police that had entered and surrounded the ghetto stopped workers. Their labor cards did not save them from deportation. Although the ZOB had not yet prepared a plan of armed opposition and the German action took the Jews by surprise, individual ZOB groups took up fighting posts and began to fight spontaneously.[11] One such group attached itself to a long procession of workers being marched to the embarkation point. At a given signal the insurgents sprang out of line and opened fire. A short battle followed, with a number of Germans killed and wounded while others fled. Some of the Jewish workers escaped, but most of the ZOB insurgents were killed.[12] Those who survived tried to barricade themselves in a nearby house, but the Germans set fire to the building. Additional clashes took place inside buildings and in streets around the ghetto's shopping area where Jews suffered additional losses. After the frontal clashes stopped that first day, the Jews obtained additional weapons from individual German soldiers killed while roaming the area. The battle was finally decided after three days, when German reinforcements were brought in.[13] Deportations halted and the Germans left the Jews in peace. Of the eight thousand planned for liquidation, three thousand were saved as a result of the insurgency.[14]

This first armed action made a tremendous impression on those still living in the ghetto. "The fighters were regarded as saviors and were universally acclaimed."[15] The Polish Underground press devoted front-page articles and commentary to the January ghetto uprising. One such paper, *Gwardzista*, wrote on February 5, 1943:

> *The population is resisting with desperate courage, using the few firearms and grenades they have plundered from the Germans together with boiling water, blunt instruments, hatchets, and the like. In besieged houses, the Jews pour kerosene or gasoline down the steps and set them aflame the moment the Germans enter. Groups of fighters hide out in deserted buildings and take the Germans by surprise. . . . The battles in the ghetto are the first demonstrations of defense of the Jewish population. The Jews have awoken from apathy in a demonstration of resistance worthy of emulation.[16]*

The ZOB learned much from the January battles. The organization strengthened considerably and its ranks grew each day. Appointed commanders organized members well and the groups had well-prepared operational plans. In addition, the fighters also learned a good deal about combat tactics from the engagement. Another important lesson was the imperative of keeping mobilized units concentrated together and ready for action at a moment's notice, especially if the Germans attacked before the ZOB could assemble its fighters from across the housing blocks. The ZOB thus devised a deployment plan based on a system of mobilized units; these would be stationed near a designated place serving as a combat position and weapons store. These lessons helped the ZOB commanders to draw from the January experience in planning their course of action for the upcoming April uprising.[17]

In the spring of 1943, the Germans began the annihilation of what remained of the Jews in both the ghettos and the labor camps. The plan was to complete the deportation action within three days. On the eve of Passover, the Jewish festival of freedom, the Germans initiated the final stage of their campaign to rid all trace of the Jewish community of Warsaw. This time, however, the penetration of German troops in the ghetto did not come as a surprise, for throughout the month of April, rumors of another deportation action prompted the Jews "every day, and even a number of times each day, to stop what they were doing and dash for shelter."[18] The least suspicion of heightened activity among the enemy forces was sufficient to alarm the entire population and engender a state of alert. During this last stage of liquidation not only were the ZOB and ZZW prepared for armed resistance, but so were hundreds of other people within the ghetto.

On April 18, 1943, the ghetto received reports—including authoritative reports from the Aryan side—of the massing of troops in Warsaw and that the Germans were evidently about to initiate the decisive deportation action in the ghetto. Ghetto residents manned lookout posts in buildings throughout the ghetto while ZOB runners dashed from house to house, alerting the population to expect deportation the next morning.[19]

Toward evening, German guards strengthened gates around the ghetto. At 2:00 a.m. on April 19, additional soldiers surrounded the entire ghetto. When ZOB observation posts noticed movement at 2:30 a.m., leaders ordered a state of alert. Fighters took up arms and ammunition, as well as baskets with Molotov cocktails and hand grenades; they then assumed battle positions protected by sandbags. By 4:00 a.m., the population had barricaded all bunkers, i.e., dugout hiding places. Everyone was in a state of full readiness awaiting the enemy's next move.[20] The ZOB had twenty-two fighting groups located in three separate parts of the ghetto consisting of seven hundred men. In their ranks were a small number of both heavy and light machine guns, a limited supply of ammunition, a large number of pistols of various types, and a large quantity of hand grenades, Molotov cocktails, and explosives.[21]

The German forces were first put under the command of SS commander *Oberführer* Ferdinand von Sammern-Frankenegg, but because of his failure to contain the insurrection, SS *Brigadeführer* Jürgen Stroop soon replaced him. The German troops and arms consisted of five reserve battalions of SS panzer grenadiers, two police battalions, eight light antiaircraft guns, a howitzer, a French-made tank, two armored cars, a reserve battalion, and a reserve armored train detachment, both of which were teams of demolition experts.[22]

On April 19 at 6:00 a.m., several thousand German troops began entering the central part of the ghetto, followed by tanks, armored cars, guns, and finally several hundred Waffen-SS on bicycles. An eyewitness and member of the ZOB described the situation:

> *And suddenly it seemed to me that we are very weak. What can we do against a well-equipped army, against tanks, armored cars, having only a revolver in one's fist, or at best a hand grenade? Still, we are not disheartened. We are waiting for our executioners to settle our accounts with them.*[23]

The German forces penetrated the ghetto in two columns. The first armed clash occurred on a street where two ZOB combat squads, singing boisterously, met a German column moving up the center of the road. The Germans were completely taken by surprise. The fire—especially the hand grenades—inflicted injury on the enemy and sowed so much havoc in its ranks that the Germans retreated and dispersed, leaving casualties lying on the street.[24] After restoring order in their ranks, the Germans, supported by a flamethrower, attacked. For two hours they failed to break down Jewish resistance. German artillery finally wore the Jews down and they were ultimately forced to retreat, having suffered heavy casualties. Before withdrawing, however, they took up defensive positions and set fire to the German factories and workshops in the ghetto that were engaged in German war production. In retaliation the Germans murdered all the patients and staff of a Jewish hospital.[25]

An attempted German counterattack met a sporadic response from the Jews who enjoyed a clear advantage: the Germans were forced to hug the wall of nearby buildings and sought shelter in the entrances. They could not operate without exposing themselves. While the Jews were concealed in their positions, the Germans were easy targets. This second battle ended in a German retreat, with no casualties on the Jewish side.[26]

On the afternoon of April 19, the Germans attacked a point defended by the ZZW, an assault that was renewed several times, but each time the ZZW resisted. At 8:00 p.m., the Germans broke off the attack and withdrew to the areas separating the three parts of the ghetto or to their barracks. The Jews, despite numerous losses, had held their principal positions. Fighting was chaotic in the early stages, but gradually assumed the character of an organized and coordinated struggle. Jewish morale was high and fighters prepared with even greater determination for what was to come.

A symbolic event took place when two boys climbed up on the roof of a building at Muranowski Square and raised two flags: the Polish red and white and the Jewish white and blue. Their appearance made a deep impression on the Polish population, especially on the youth, and it became a recognized sign of common aims and unity in battle.[27]

Thus on the first day of the battle, it was the Jewish insurgents who opened fire and surprised the enemy. The Germans were forced to withdraw from the ghetto after the first clash, and German Commander von Sammern lost his advantage when he realized the strength of the Jewish resistance and failed to contain the revolt. When *Brigadeführer* Jürgen Stroop took over as German commander of the operation, he proceeded cautiously, adopting tactics of house-to-house fighting. Yet he, too, was forced into a difficult and drawn-out battle in Muranowski Square.[28]

On April 20, the Germans made a loudspeaker appeal to the Jews in Muranowski Square to lay down their arms or they would raze the ghetto to the ground. The Jews answered by continuing to fight. The Germans increased pressure on the Jewish fighters with tanks and armored cars that rained intense fire on the insurgents. As the battle grew more heated, the Jewish situation deteriorated, a problem exacerbated by the break in communications with the main ZOB organization. The Germans then began to set fire to the buildings on Muranowski Street, forcing the Jews to leave one building and move to a neighboring one under a hail of German machine-gun fire. In the afternoon, the Germans set up field cannons on the square and heavy machine guns on the roofs. Shelling continued without respite. The Germans tightened the siege by turning off the electricity, water, and gas on every street, and by bringing in police dogs to uncover bunkers, shelters, and hiding places.[29]

On the third day of the uprising, April 21, the German changed their tactics. For the most part, the Jewish fighters were unable to hold on to the stationary positions on the upper floors of the buildings because of heavy artillery, explosions, and fires set by the Germans.

At the same time, the Germans no longer came out in large groups, which, for the Jews, had proved to be easy targets. Instead, they broke up into small bands that roamed throughout the ghetto, forcing the Jews to change their strategy. Small mobile squads that lay in ambush made subsequent assaults on the Germans. Smaller armed clashes of lesser intensity broke out in other areas of the ghetto, with Jewish insurgents firing and tossing hand grenades and Molotov cocktails from alleys, windows, and street corners.

The numerous individual areas of Jewish resistance necessitated the Germans' use of incendiary bombs dropped by planes, sending buildings up in flames that engulfed entire districts. The intensity of the flames, heat, and smoke drove the Jews out into the streets, where Germans finished the work of destruction with automatic weapons and small gunfire. Sometimes the Jews remained in the burning buildings so long that, because of the heat and fearing death in the flames, they eventually preferred to jump out of windows after first having thrown mattresses into the streets. An elaborate system of passages through lofts, cellars, and courtyards allowed Jews to regroup, but in many instances, fires made such movement impossible. It almost seems fair to say that the Jews were being beaten by the flames and not the Germans. But of course, the defending fighters were easy prey to the Germans.

The population used a large number of camouflaged underground shelters prepared before the uprising, some of which were capable of containing several hundred persons, up to a point. But when the heat on the surface increased, the shelters became unbearable and the people were forced up to street level. As one ZOB fighter described the situation,

The condition in the shelters is dreadful and hopeless. There is a severe lack of air, water, and food. Days go by, it is now

the tenth day of the action [April 28]. The ghetto is burned down. Everywhere there are carbonized bodies in the streets, courtyards, and cellars. People were burned alive. In the face of this terrible situation and unable to continue the fight, we are forced, because of the grave shortage of ammunition, water, and food, and because of the inability to meet the enemy who is not within the ghetto, performing his work of destruction from outside, to consider whether or not to lead the people out to the woods, in order to continue the fight further.[30]

The only means of escape from the shelters was through the sewers, but the Germans forced many Jews to the surface of the street by dropping smoke candles or gas grenades; the candles and grenades caused many of them to run together in the sewers into the center of the Jewish residential quarter, where Germans pulled them up and out through the manholes.[31]

The German use of fire to drive the defenders out of hiding made it impossible for the ZOB to organize a clear line of defense, as it had done in the first days of resistance. In the central ghetto and in what was called the Brushmakers' Area, where a number of German "shops" and factories were located, small pockets of resistance formed. Individual fighting groups sought cover behind the closest wall or ruin and fought from there. These fighters used arms and ammunition captured from the Germans.[32]

On May 8, the Jews suffered a great loss. The Germans had discovered and then surrounded the location of the so-called inner party command, the ZOB bunker at Mila 18, which housed the headquarters of the commander of the united Jewish Fighting Organization. As the result of smoke candles and explosive charges placed in key areas, the Germans captured and killed the ZZW deputy commander; of the 200 Jews who were in the bunker, 140 were killed and 60 were captured. Despite these losses, individual ZOB groups kept up stubborn resistance, but the organization as a whole was losing strength. The casualties; lack of ammunition, water, and food; loss of bunkers; exhaustion; and heat from the fires took their toll on the defending Jews' resilience.

As Jewish resistance decreased, the Germans intensified their clean-up operation. The suppression of the uprising officially ended on May 16, 1943, with the destruction of the Great Synagogue of Warsaw. Fighters and Jews who did not fight were captured and sent to the embarkation point where every few days trains left for Treblinka.[33] On May 16, German Commander Stroop reported that the Warsaw residential quarter no longer existed and that the overall number of captured or definitely killed Jews was 56,065.[34]

The battle in the Warsaw ghetto was not the only act of Jewish military resistance against the Germans. Besides the fighting in Warsaw, the ZOB resisted the Germans in several other ghettos when the Jews discovered that the deportations were being resumed. In June 1943, the ZOB fought a one-day battle in Częstochowa. In the Będzin Ghetto in July during the liquidation, the ZOB fought a two-day battle, and in August a seven-day battle raged in Białystok. German action was also forestalled in the Sobibor and Treblinka extermination camps, where the inmates rose up in October 1943 and several hundred prisoners regained their freedom.[35]

Thus from the moment they decided to resist the German violence, the Jews were determined to pursue their aim. They prepared for the moment of final reckoning stubbornly in the face of insurmountable opposition. They did so with a sense of self-sacrifice, deeply convinced that they would be defeated. Their fight was not in defense of their lives, but in defense of human dignity and they were, to the very end, faithful to the call. Those who went to their deaths will go down in Polish history as a legend, and those who survived will always be revered as national heroes.

One of the great tragedies that took place in Poland during the Second World War was the systematic and eventual extermination of Polish Jews by the German occupying power. Terms such as "crimes against humanity," "genocide," and "holocaust" only partly convey the horror of these events. Some have asked why Poles extended so little help to the Polish Jews in their time of distress during the Jewish Ghetto Uprising of 1943. This question can only be asked by those who have no conception of what life was like in occupied Poland during the war years. The harsh reality of life for the rest of Poland's population was that everybody was preoccupied with the constant struggle for survival. Many had to focus on the utmost importance of finding work and obtaining enough food and other necessities of life. Conditions in Poland bore little resemblance to the comparatively quiescent conditions in occupied Norway, Holland, or France. Poland was the only country in occupied Europe where giving any kind of help to the Jews resulted in prompt execution of the person involved, as well as that of his or her family. The non-Jewish Polish population lived in constant fear of being arrested and sent to concentration camps, assigned to forced labor in Germany, or taken as a hostage for public execution by a firing squad or hanging. People also feared this for the entire family of anyone found sheltering or assisting the Jews in any fashion.[36] Thus it is as irrelevant to ask why the Poles did little to help the Jews as it is to inquire why the Jews did nothing to assist the Poles.

Nonetheless, there were Poles who did what they could to help the Jews. In the summer of 1942, when the liquidation of the Warsaw Ghetto began, Zofia Kossak-Szczucka, a well-known author before the war, published a leaflet entitled *Protest*. Printed in five thousand copies, it described the conditions in the ghetto in graphic terms, as well as the horrible circumstances of the deportations that were then taking place. "All will perish," she wrote. "Poor and rich, old, women, men, youngsters, infants, Catholics dying with the name of Jesus and Mary together with Jews. Their only guilt is that they were born in to the Jewish nation condemned to extermination by Hitler."[37]

A most remarkable woman, Irena Sendler, a Polish Catholic social worker, helped create over three thousand false documents to help Jewish families prior to serving in the Polish Underground in German-occupied Warsaw. Together with Kossak-Szczucka, she founded the Provisional Committee to Aid Jews, which in December of 1942 became the Relief Council for Jews in Poland, code-named Zegota, which provided help for many Jews. They organized financial aid, forged identity documents, and tendered medical care for the Jews in hiding on the "Aryan side" of the ghetto wall. One service an unknown number of Zegota volunteers provided was the placement of some 2,500 Jewish children smuggled out of the Warsaw ghetto in ambulances and coffins and into Polish foster families, orphanages, and convents run by Catholic nuns. Sendler and others forged documents in order to give the children new identities so that they could be reunited with their families after the war. The documents were placed in jars and buried underneath an apple tree in a neighbor's yard. In 1943 the Gestapo arrested, tortured, and imprisoned Sendler. A bribe to one of her jailors saved her from a death sentence, and she escaped. Throughout the course of the war, Germans pursued her, but she always managed to avoid being caught. The exact number of those who helped Sendler save the lives of Jewish children has never been determined, but according to a number of reports, it seems quite certain that the Poles did more than those in any of the other occupied countries in Europe.

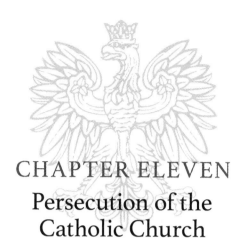

CHAPTER ELEVEN
Persecution of the Catholic Church

The Polish nation lost three million of its largest Catholic citizenry, most of whom died at the hands of the Nazis. Among the last few refugees of bigotry in the United States are the anti-Catholicism and the anti-Polonism. Since most Poles are Catholics, they have been especially vulnerable.

—Dr. Richard C. Lukas, Forgotten Holocaust: The Poles under German Occupation 1939–1944

Throughout the course of Polish history no single institution was more identifiable as the historic custodian of the national culture—as the symbol and bulwark of national unity—than the Catholic Church. This was especially true during periods of oppression. For the Germans, the extermination of Polish society necessarily meant the destruction of the Church. Before the war, the Church flourished, owning in excess of a million acres of land, in addition to refectories and convents, hospitals and orphanages, small industrial farms and small craft industries. More than 20 million Roman Catholics worshiped in 5,100 parishes served by 11,300 priests.[1]

In the autumn of 1939, the Germans began an unmitigated reign of terror began at once. Officials immediately introduced antireligious legislation in occupied regions, and Soviets began atheistic indoctrination in the Soviet-controlled zone once the country was divided between the two foreign powers. The barbarity against the Church was especially prominent in the provinces of Poznania, Pomerania, and Silesia, and in the regions of Włocławek, Łódź, and Kalisz. It was in those annexed provinces called Wartheland that included portions of Warsaw and Częstochowa, and containing 4.6 million inhabitants—that part of Poland annexed outright by Germany—in which the persecution was being most severely borne by the Catholics.[2]

In early October, Pius XII, in the inaugural encyclical of his pontificate, *Summi Pontificatus*, was especially concerned about the victims of Poland. In these official and solemn expressions of solicitude the Pontiff declared,

> *The blood of countless people, even noncombatants, gives rise to a harrowing funereal lament, especially over Poland, a dearly beloved country because of its glorious attainments indelibly inscribed in the annals of history. Poland has a right to the world's human and fraternal sympathy, and confident in the powerful intercession of Mary who is the auxilium christianorum, it awaits the hour of its resurrection in justice and peace.[3]*

The Nazi plan for Christianity in Poland was set forth in a document dated March 14, 1940. The annexed provinces were selected as a kind of testing ground for experimenting with a new form of "state-church" relations arranged for the National Socialist state. In a thirteen-point plan, the Germans proposed to reduce the churches to the status of corporations under private law. Religious associations would be permitted, but not churches. Only adults could become members of the associations; there would be no youth groups. The minimum age for marriage was fixed at twenty-eight for men and twenty-five for women. Germans and Poles could not meet together, and Catholics could have no relations with the Holy See.[4]

The plan to refashion the religious pattern of the Wartheland also involved exceptionally severe measures against the clergy. Only in Poland were those clergy of Episcopal rank arrested and imprisoned. Two bishops were in exile and efforts by the Holy See to secure the return to their diocese were rejected in Berlin. They were driven into the General Government (Central Poland, not formerly annexed to the Reich). Germans either shot or removed in one way or another fifty priests in the area. They either imprisoned or treated inhumanely hundreds of the clergy from the outset. One humiliation suffered by these men consisted in forcibly being made to press their heads into the ground and cry out, "We are Polish pigs." Many of the priests were forced into the General Government while larger numbers were sent to concentration camps. Both diocesan priests and those belonging to religious orders shared the same fate. Religious sisters were also interned in special camps.[5]

When the German authorities announced the formation of the "Roman Catholic Church of German Nationality in the Reich District Wartheland," the Church now faced government control of its finances, Gestapo regulation of worship times, and radical alteration of the church status throughout the region. By the fall of that year, German authorities had imprisoned, deported, or expelled more than half of the two thousand prewar clergy in Wartheland, and the arrests continued. German officials incarcerated at least seven hundred priests at Dachau, and interned more than four hundred nuns in a special camp at Bojanowo.[6]

During the first year and a half of the war, it is known for certain that thirty-five priests were shot, but the real number of victims whose names cannot be known amounts to more than a hundred. More than twenty are known to have died in prison. German authorities, especially the Gestapo, behaved ferociously toward the Catholic clergy, who lived under a nightmare of terror and continual provocation. They maltreated and tortured a hundred priests; another hundred suffered in concentration camps; German commands drove hundreds of others into the General Government. Those who were permitted to stay were subjected to numerous humiliations, and were paralyzed in the exercise of their pastoral duties and all of their rights. Some were seized at night in pajamas, brutally beaten, and submitted to other tortures. They were entirely at the mercy of the Gestapo, without possibility of appeal.[7]

It was common to see priests in labor squads forced to work on roads and bridges, loading coal trucks, or even pulling down synagogues. The intention of the German authorities was to humiliate and ridicule the priests in the eyes of the population by forcing them to perform hard labor in public places.[8]

In one diocese some five thousand men were so crammed in a stable where there was no room for anyone to sit down on the floor. A corner of the building was assigned to the needs of nature. The parish pastor was forced to carry away the human excrement with his own hands and in sight of the large number of prisoners. When another priest asked to take the pastor's place, their captors brutally flogged him with a whip. In another parish German authorities dragged some three hundred families from their homes without warning and transferred them to a factory. A number of the people were arrested in the street on their way back from church, including several priests. One priest was forcibly taken from his room in the rectory without warning while he was undressing and locked up in prison wearing only his pajamas. Finally they were all deported in sealed coaches to central Poland. There was no possibility of calculating the number of parishes deprived of their priests.[9]

> *Everything was deliberately planned with the aim of completely destroying the Church in one of the most religious countries in the whole world. After so many centuries passed in the service of the Church, Poland witnessed the establishment of a paganism so godless, so immoral, atrocious, and inhuman, that it could only be accepted by morbid-minded individuals who have lost all human dignity and blinded by hatred of the cross of Christ.[10]*

The general practice of the German authorities was to keep silent about everything that took place in the "incorporated" territory and to deal only with the Government General, where the terror suffered by the Catholic Church and the Polish population was "not quite" so ruthless as in western Poland. There were no mass purges like those in the annexed provinces, but neither was there was any reluctance in disposing of troublesome clerics. The Germans dissolved all Catholic associations in the Government General and closed down all Catholic educational institutions; they sent Catholic professors and teachers to concentration camps. They also rendered the Catholic press impotent.[11]

Polish police tried to justify granting permission to Poles to enter churches by explaining to the German authorities that the only reason they went to church was to socialize with their fellow countrymen and to express their patriotic aspirations. But the Nazi Party forbade any antistate expressions that it did not respect. The Papal Nuncio in Berlin, Cesare Orsenigo, reported that those Poles who were sent to work in Germany were refused permission to enter any churches, even on Sundays, for services intended for Germans, and not allowed to make confession in Polish. In fact, any German priest who agreed to give them religious consolation risked months of prison and possibly being sent to Dachau. Orsenigo stated,

> It is not the religiosity of the Poles that they want to suppress; it is the Catholic religion, the Protestant religion, without distinction. It is not so much the apolitical sense that is lacking in Polish religious sentiment, it is rather the anti-religious spirit that casts a shadow over the National Socialist policy of the ruling party and transforms a movement based on a new orientation of nations into a determined anti-Christian war.[12]

In January 1940, Vatican Radio, on instructions from Pope Pius XII, broadcast a vigorous denunciation of German behavior in Poland in several foreign languages, including German. The announcement said, *inter alia,*

> that the religious, political, and economic conditions have thrown this noble nation especially in the regions occupied by the Germans, into a state of terror, dejection, and it may even be said, of barbarity, much like that imposed on Spain by the Communists in 1936. . . . and that the Germans use the same methods as the Soviets—perhaps even worse ones.[13]

Polish Cardinal Primate Augustus Hlond was in Rome at the time, and was perhaps the first member of the Sacred College to ask Pius XII for papal intervention. In his first report to the Pope, he gave the following account of the general situation in the "incorporated" territories:

After the incorporation of the two archdioceses, Gniezno and Poznań, the extermination of all things Polish began. This was simply a well-planned procedure, a cardinal point of German policy according to Hitler's Mein Kampf. It now goes forward without interruption, and alas! It is stamped with sadistic perversity.

In the city of Poznań the deportation was carried out with excess inhumanity. To make sure that no one escaped, a decree was drawn up and published. It forbade Jews and Poles, under severe penalties, to be out of their homes between seven thirty at night and six o'clock the next morning. During this time and at any hour and without any warning, the Gestapo would swoop down upon one group of dwellings night after night on average of 500–1500 people. No one could sleep from fear and dread.

No one now even undresses for the time allowed to leave the house has been reduced to a few minutes, and those not ready to depart at once must leave with whatever clothing they happen to have on.

Once out on the street under the looming menace of the Gestapo, the members of each household wait—at times for hours—for a motor bus to take them away. There were times this winter with the thermometer at 15 degrees and more below zero, when these pitiable groups of women and children, the aged and the sick, have been forced to stand in the open air for as long as four hours. The silence of the frosty night is only broken by their doleful cries and moans.

Their immediate destination is the horrible camp in the suburb of Główna: wooden barracks, unheated with a concrete floor; there is not even a mattress in the place and they sleep on straw infested with vermin, stinking and not changed

for weeks at a time. There are no toilets and no hot water.
The food is bad. Exceptions are made for no one, neither for
the sick nor the dying, nor for infants, nor for the aged, nor
for pregnant mothers. Sickness strikes down a great number,
deaths are frequent, but no doctors and no priests are admit-
ted, except as prisoners.[14]

Cardinal Hlond, in his final observations closing his second report to the pope, gave the following account of the overall state of the Church in the western provinces of Poland:

The cathedrals have been closed; one has been made into a
garage. Five bishops' palaces have been invaded, and one of
them has been turned into an inn, the bishop's chapel serv-
ing as a ballroom. In the chapel of the primate's palace at
Poznań the police have put a dog kennel. All the seminary
students have been dispersed and the seminaries occupied by
Nazi authorities.

In many districts the life of the church has been com-
pletely crushed, the clergy having been almost all expelled;
the Catholic churches and cemeteries are in the hands of the
invaders. Catholic worship hardly exists anymore; the word
of God is not preached, the sacraments are not administered,
even to the dying. In certain localities confession is forbidden.
The Catholic Press has been destroyed. Charitable associations
and works have likewise been dissolved.

Monasteries and convents have been methodically sup-
pressed, as well as their flourishing works of education,
publicity, social welfare, and care of the sick. Everything has
been deliberately planned with the aim of completely destroy-
ing the Church and its vitality in one of the most religious

countries in the whole world. The above enumerated terrible proceedings have now continued in their intransigence and impiety for seven months."[15]

Cardinal Hlond waited in vain for German authorization to return to Poland, since he was declared an enemy of the Reich because of his statements over Vatican Radio concerning the true state of affairs in Poland. He was also refused permission to send a papal delegate to Poland. In fact, throughout the war, Polish Catholics were denied the "presence" of the Pope through a personal representative who could convey the Holy Father's concern for their condition. Poland was now sealed off in the face of Nazi intransigence and ruthlessness as the agony of Catholic Poland began in earnest.[16]

In March 1940, Pius granted an audience to Joachim von Ribbentrop, the German foreign minister and the only high-ranking Nazi to make any effort to visit the Vatican. At that meeting the Pope came to the defense of the Jews in both Germany and Poland. When Ribbentrop criticized the Pope for siding with the Allies, the Holy Father began reading from a long list of German atrocities. "The *New York Times* reported that the Pontiff, in the burning words he spoke to Herr Ribbentrop . . . came to the defense of Jews in Germany and Poland." Ribbentrop did not satisfy the Pope's request for assurances of better treatment.[17]

Additional protests made by the Papal Nuncio Orsenigo in Berlin, on behalf of the Pope "went to Ribbentrop on August 28, September 2, September 13, and September 29." Unaware of this, Catholic Poles thought the church was indifferent to their fate.[18]

When Cardinal Hlond gave a report describing the increasing discontent within certain Polish circles, the Vatican took the matter seriously. On September 3, 1941, Luigi Cardinal Maglione, the Pope's secretary of state, rejected the premise that the Pope was silent on the fate of the Polish Catholics. He pointed out that during the present year, 1941, the Pope had spoken out three times: first in an Easter message; then in a message to the United States on the occasion of a Eucharistic congress in St. Paul, Minnesota; and finally in a message of 29 June, for the feasts of saints Peter and Paul.[19]

> *One of the agonies Pius XII was to suffer throughout the war was that his countless protests against the outrages inflicted on the innocent were not heard by those on whose behalf he spoke or brought about reprisals on them. . . . All that the Pope had was the moral authority of his voice, and he had to use it in such a way that he did not worsen the matters he condemned.*[20]

Polish exiles were especially insistent that the Holy Father condemn the sacrileges being committed by the German invaders. But even voices from within Poland made the same request. But there were other voices—from other Poles—who begged the pope not to incite the Germans into further violence. "The Pope was whip lashed between the desire to condemn eloquently and the prudence urged on him by those under the oppressors' heel."[21] Letters that were sent to Archbishop Sapieha to be distributed to the clergy were deemed too risky and were retained. Hence, even the pastoral voice of the pope failed to reach his priests, let alone the Polish people.[22]

There was some basis for the fear that a public protest might make things even worse for the Poles. In Holland, for example, when both Catholic and Protestant bishops sent a telegram of protest against the deportation of Dutch Jews, the Germans retaliated by seizing and deporting all Catholic non-Aryans that they could find.[23]

The Germans wanted to prevent a papal representative from witnessing or obtaining information about what was happening in Poland at all costs. Consequently, since no one was allowed to go to Poland and see things for himself, there was no way to publicly demonstrate the Pope's interest in the Polish people. Moreover, there was no way to get detailed reports about the reasons for detention of individual prisoners or about their treatment, condition, health, or individual needs. Prisoners were obliged under threat of the severest penalties not to divulge what took place in the camps. It is noteworthy that Polish bishops, in correspondence, never mentioned the concentration camps in Poland—names such as Auschwitz, Treblinka, Sobibor, and Belzec. The Vatican had access to more information about the concentration camps in Germany, such as Dachau and Sachsenhausen.[24] However, it was not until after the war that the Holy See found out that 1,474 Polish priests and hundreds from other occupied countries were confined at Dachau, and that some 120 Polish priests were subjected to criminal medical experiments. A Carmelite priest from Kraków died from typhus he contracted while voluntarily attending to the camp sick. One died with a log tied to his shoulders on Good Friday. Another priest, who was beaten for refusing to grind rosary beads into the ground with his foot, drowned in feces.[25] At Auschwitz, a Franciscan priest bearing the number 16670 stepped boldly out of line on one occasion, walked toward the camp commandant, and said, "I would like to die in the place of one of these men," all of whom were condemned to die in a "starvation bunker." The man whose life he exchanged for his own was the father of a family. On that day, number 16670 became an individual person bearing the name Maximilian Kolbe.[26]

Germans also executed priests executed in reprisal for the Polish army's resistance. Convents kept printing presses and served as distribution centers for the Underground press. Depositories for money that was sent from abroad were also kept secret. The clergy provided people pursued by the Gestapo with false baptismal records, many of which were produced for Jewish babies and small children whom the Underground secretly removed from the Nazi-built ghettos in the General Government area and placed with Catholic families and in religious convents. In remote areas, priests often concealed Underground agents moving from one part of the country to another. Priests also made strong references in their sermons to the resurrection of Poland. One young priest survived a Gestapo interrogation and worked Underground throughout the course of the war. His nom de guerre during his clandestine ministry in Warsaw was Sister Cecelia, as in "Where is Sister Cecelia saying Mass today?"[27]

Priests could also pay a heavy price for simply carrying out clerical activities and responsibilities, such as leading a procession around their churches without permission; one priest was so severely beaten after hearing confessions in the penitents' own language that he later died in jail.

The Germans forbade participation in Catholic youth groups and the price of defiance was high, especially when the groups were involved with the Resistance. One young Catholic Resistance courier, Wanda Półtawska, spent several years as a medical guinea pig in the Ravensbruck concentration camp, where medical personnel injected diseased bacilli into her bone marrow.[28]

In April 1943, Vatican Secretary of State Luigi Maglione asked Papal Nuncio Orsenigo for verification of all such incidents, but the head of the camp refused. The wall of silence surrounding the concentration camps in Germany—and even more in Poland—was not only erected against the Holy See. The International Committee of the Red Cross was also prevented from visiting the camps and determining the truth through its own observers.[29]

Some detractors who maintain that the papacy was on friendly terms with the Germans falsely claim that the Pope's anti-Communism led him to support Hitler as a buttress against the Russians. In 1942 the Pope stated that the "Communist danger does exist, but at this time the Nazi danger is more serious." He also concurred with the American bishops in support of lend-lease for the Soviets, and he explicitly refused to bless the Nazi invasion of Russia.[30] Clearly, support for Stalinist Russia seemed far less foolish during the 1940s when the Soviets were an ally than it may have been during the height of the Cold War.

In late 1942, Pope Pius sent three letters of support to bishops in German-occupied Poland. The bishops thanked the Pontiff, but said they could not publish his words or read them aloud, because that would lead to more persecution of Jews and of Catholics.[31]

> *We leave it to the pastors, according to each location, the care of evaluating if, and in what measure, the danger of reprisals and pressure, as well as perhaps other circumstances due to the length and psychology of war, warrant restraint—despite the reasons for intervening—so as to avoid greater evils. This is one of the reasons for which We ourselves are imposing limits in Our declarations.[32]*

It was believed that every move of the Holy See had to be carefully weighed so that it would not result in an effect that was contrary to the one desired. In the words of Secretary of State Luigi Cardinal Maglione:

This prudent caution was based upon the earlier unfortunate experiences that the Holy See has already had. How many times, instead of helping those for whom, with the best of intentions, it was hoped some good might be done, its direct intervention has proved further repression and persecution.[33]

This point was further underscored by Marcus Melchior, the chief rabbi of Denmark and a Holocaust survivor, who argued that "if the Pope had spoken out publicly, Hitler would probably have massacred more than six million Jews and perhaps ten times ten million Catholics, if he had the power to do so." Author and professor Margherita Marchione believes that provocation from the Holy See "would have resulted in violent retaliation, the loss of many more Jewish lives, especially those then under the protection of the Church, and an intensification of the persecution of Catholics." Robert M. W. Kempner, the deputy U.S. counsel during the Nuremberg trials, relied upon his experience when saying, "Every propaganda move of the Catholic Church against Hitler's Reich would have been not only 'provoking suicide,' . . . but would have hastened the execution of still more Jews and priests."[32] And late in 1942, Archbishop Sapieha of Kraków and two other Polish bishops, after having experienced the Nazis' savage reprisals, begged Pius not to publish his letters about conditions in Poland.[34]

In March 1943, Cardinal Maglione sent a final note to Foreign Minister Ribbentrop, which was a most severe indictment of the entire antireligious campaign precipitated by the Nazi occupation. But within the next two years, in the face of continuous death and violence, Hitler's intransigence was such that there was no reason for the Holy See to hope for a favorable change in Berlin.[35]

In those five years beginning in 1939, both the church and state in Poland were indelibly marked by the suffering and sacrifice of more than 2 million Catholics, which included innumerable laity; 3,646 priests imprisoned in concentration camps, of which 2,647 were killed; and 1,117 nuns imprisoned, of whom 238 were executed and 25 died from other causes, all of whose lives formulated an edifying and unforgettable chapter in the historical record of the Polish people.[36]

CHAPTER TWELVE
Resistance through Culture

It was a constant effort to sustain life and culture in the face of death and barbarism, to testify to the superiority of spiritual values over material ones, while one's very physical existence was continually threatened and degraded in daily life by coercion, torture, and extermination.

—Kazimierz Braun (1936–)
A History of Polish Theater 1939–1989

Cultivation to the mind is as necessary as food to the body.

—Cicero (106 BC–43 BC)
Roman statesman, philosopher, and writer

Since the Germans established a policy of eradicating Poland as a state and exterminating the Polish people as a nation, not only did they target for destruction the Catholic Church as the repository of moral values and ethical standards so alien to Nazi ideology, but they also furiously attacked the country's culturally prominent and educated classes: scholars, writers, politicians, physicians, teachers, landowners, businessmen, and professionals. The Germans were not content to maintain control over the external conduct and affairs of their subjugated Slavic neighbor. They intended to bring about the construction of a racial "New Order," establishing a cultural transformation that would bring about a change in the human substance of the nation. They closed all universities, libraries, theaters, concert halls, museums, radio stations, and even secondary schools in what was a de-Polonization of the cultural elite. Estimated losses included library and private book collections of over twenty-two million volumes from thirty-seven thousand libraries. Everything that was of value to the nation's cultural heritage—language, literature, history, folklore, customs, and identity—was in danger of annihilation.

In May 1940, Reichsführer Heinrich Himmler, who next to Hitler was one of the most powerful men in Nazi Germany, issued a memorandum, stating that "the sole purpose of this schooling is to teach simple arithmetic and how to write one's name; and the doctrine that it is divine law to obey the Germans . . . I do not regard knowledge of reading as desirable."[1] Governor General Hans Frank announced that "the Poles do not need universities or secondary schools; the Polish lands are to be changed into an intellectual desert."[2]

In the annexed provinces, German authorities closed those elementary schools where Polish was used as the language of instruction, whereas in the General Government area they allowed a certain number to remain open. Nevertheless, the ultimate goal was the obliteration of *all* traces of the former Polish culture throughout the entire country. Himmler defined this goal in what he called his maxims on the treatment of alien tribes in the East:

Over the next ten years the population of the General Government will consist of a residue of inferior people . . . This population will be at our disposal as a leaderless labor force, supplying Germany year by year with seasonal laborers and with workers for special undertakings (road-building, quarries, house-building).[3]

During the interwar years, the rebirth of an independent Poland achieved a number of cultural accomplishments. Illiteracy was drastically reduced. Polish intellectual life, especially in philosophy and mathematics, increased dramatically. In 1920 schools of higher learning enjoyed wide autonomy. State universities opened in Warsaw, Kraków, Lwów, Poznań, and Wilno. The arts experienced an acceleration of creativity. Literary groups of poetry and avant-garde artists were active, and scientific centers opened up where important research was conducted in physics and chemistry. Musical and dramatic theater productions expanded, and cinematography developed rapidly.[4]

So the Underground was concerned not only with carrying out sabotage, diversion, propaganda, and other forms of obstruction and demoralization associated with the war, but also with preserving and developing those cultural achievements in education, academic research, the publication of books, the protection of cultural relics and memorabilia, and live theatrical productions, all of which had now to exist as Underground activities; in short, Poland had to sustain and defend almost all of the elements of normal national life.

It is not difficult to visualize how partisan units operated or how saboteurs attacked German factories or created a train derailment. It is much more difficult to imagine how clandestine schools or theatrical presentations formed and operated underground; how small groups of students attended classes and lectures in private flats and homes or how groups of actors produced plays in private residences and cellars. All of these activities were carried out in secret—in all the occupied cities, in the forest refuges of the partisans, in émigré groups in London, and even in concentration camps. These activities were especially difficult and dangerous because the Germans penetrated so much of Polish society with the help of collaborators, some of whom were Polish and who were prepared to betray their own people.[5]

As early as October 1939, in response to the German closure and censorship of Polish schools, resistance among teachers led to the creation of large-scale Underground educational activities, most notably the Secret Teaching Organization (TON).[6] In the autumn of 1941, TON worked in coordination with the newly established Underground's State Department of Culture and Education. Classes were either held under the cover of officially permitted activities or in private homes.[7]

Pupils met secretly in groups of three to six, for different ostensible reasons: to play chess, for social visits, or to learn a trade. Any common purpose could serve as a pretext. Teachers were always at risk because of the youthful curiosity of their students, who might want to know the teacher's true identity, where he or she taught school before the war, etc. The imprudent word of a parent or student could, and sometimes did, mean the torture and death of the teacher.[8] By 1942, about 1.5 million students took part in Underground primary education. In the next two years nearly 6,000 teachers held Underground classes for more than 90,000 secondary-school students in the cities of Warsaw, Kraków, Radom, and Lublin.[9]

Overall, during that period in the General Government, one out of every three children received some sort of education from Underground organizations.[10] In Warsaw there were over 70 Underground schools, 2,000 teachers, and 21,000 students.[11] For a high school student to receive a graduation diploma, the applicant had to pass final tests in five subjects, covering the material of a twelve-year course in each subject. Three of the subjects required both oral and written examinations. Written and oral examinations were required in Polish, English, and Latin; physics and mathematics were to be written. These examinations were almost of the same standard and specification as before the war.[12]

One person whose family risked arrest by opening their apartment to clandestine instruction described the atmosphere of the times in a personal memoir:

> One of the meetings we had arranged was due to take place in an hour. The chairs were all arranged in the room for about thirty people. Then the Gestapo arrived. They were asking about somebody whom we probably knew and they saw all the chairs. My mother said we were preparing for a party. This seemed to satisfy them and they left. But that was a very close thing. . . . If the Gestapo had arrived when there were people there . . . I would not be speaking today.[13]

The absence of Polish Jewish students was notable. Compared to prewar classes, they were confined by the Germans to ghettos; however, there was underground Jewish education in the ghettos that was often organized with support from Polish organizations like TON.[14]

Institutions of higher education were no less defiant in their efforts of self-preservation reconstituting underground. Throughout Poland, many universities continued classes throughout the war. Beginning in November 1940, despite the difficulties of access to libraries or laboratories, 150 scientific books dealing with all subjects taught were written, printed, and distributed. Students wrote literary, medical, legal, and scientific doctoral theses. Students studied everything except German.[15] And entrance to the clandestine universities was free. Especially noteworthy was the extensive program of medical studies located in Warsaw, where clandestine teaching departments set up in hospitals. The State Institute of Hygiene housed secret classes. Some four thousand students enrolled in medical and pharmacy classes. A somewhat less extensive program in legal studies was situated in a secret law school in Warsaw comprised of some six hundred students.[16]

In 1942 the Jagiellonian University in Kraków operated clandestinely with five faculties, including all the departments that had been in operation before the war. During the three years of its existence, 136 professors risked instant death by teaching 800 students, often at night in private homes. Providing textbooks to the students was a problem for the educational authorities until they decided to print facsimiles of prewar textbooks so that in the event of discovery by the Germans, they would look as though they had been dated before the occupation.[17]

Jagiellonian University issued 468 master's and 62 doctoral degrees and employed over 100 professors and teachers. Underground Warsaw University educated 3,700 students and issued 64 master's and 7 doctoral degrees. Warsaw Polytechnic educated 3,000 students and issued 186 engineering degrees.[18]

Although Polish Underground State patronage was not a major policy priority during the occupation, it was practiced on a daily basis, together with spontaneous private sponsorships of scientific, literary, and artistic works. Since most artists, academics, and writers were unable to officially continue their professions and provide for their families, aristocrats and landowners gave broad material support, opening their manor houses as sanctuaries for people of science and culture. These "lodgers" received upkeep and a place and condition in which they were able to continue their work.[19]

After the partition of Poland between Germany and the Soviet Union in September 1939, all Polish public cultural institutions, including all theaters, were either demolished by bombing and shelling, as was the National Theater in Warsaw, or closed down or taken over by the occupying powers.[20] In March 1940, the Germans issued a decree stipulating that all theatrical artists in the annexed territories must register in the German work offices. If obeyed, the decree would have given the Germans total control of the artists, incorporating them as useful propagandists. In response, the Actors Union unanimously passed a motion by forbidding actors and actresses to perform on public stages under German control, thereby boycotting all public performances. Their vote was a formal rejection of the occupation, "thereby giving testimony to their civic awareness and maintaining the Polish theater's dignity throughout the war." For those actors who did boycott official German-controlled productions, the Clandestine Theater Company provided financial support.[21] Since they could not perform in German-controlled theaters, a number of actors and actresses became singers or gave recitations at coffee houses.

Nevertheless, during the war, close to two hundred clandestine theatrical productions took place in Poland, primarily in Warsaw and Kraków, with shows presented in various underground locations. In addition, thousands of shorter, more modest drama and comedy performances took place all over the country. These included one-person shows, puppetry, play readings, and poetry recitals, and were prepared by professionals, students from Underground acting schools, and amateurs, together with writers, scholars, and teachers. Most productions were held in private homes, others in artists' studios, and parish or convent halls; they took place even in cellars, shops, garages, factories, and churches. Twenty to fifty people usually attended performances. Underground acting schools emerged.

In the five years of German occupation, the Gestapo failed to enter a single theatrical performance, despite the fact that the performances occurred on numerous occasions. This was likely due to the fact that productions followed a strict clandestine routine. People received invitations only by word of mouth, those putting on the shows blacked out all windows, lookouts took up their posts, and people came and left individually. Performers limited the lengths of their shows, since both actors and spectators had to return home before curfew.[22]

Theatrical activism that came to be known as the Rhapsodic Theater became a broader form of Polish cultural Underground resistance. It started in a third-floor apartment at 10 Felicjanek Street, in Kraków, but to avoid arousing the suspicion of the Gestapo, performances and rehearsals moved around clandestinely to different sites.[23] Those who took part in this new form of artistic expression in clandestine plays and dramatic poetry readings were young actors, actresses, and authors who were determined to foil the German attempt to stamp out Polish culture. Their intention was not a matter of filling time that would otherwise have been lost to boredom; these young actors saw themselves as involved in the Resistance, a movement whose purpose was clearly "to save our culture from the occupation and to help restore the nation's soul, which was a precondition to its political resurrection."[24]

The Rhapsodic Theater was designed to carry on an old Polish tradition, namely "the artistic recitation of poetry or poetic prose with restrained acting, minimal stage accessories, and simple stylized costumes."[25] The basic means of expression was *the word*, and the main idea was to pronounce every vowel and every word with the greatest precision, without slurring, swallowing, or exaggerating, so that the general effect was attractive and natural.[26]

One of the most notable of those young actors whose life was forged largely by the Rhapsodic Theater was the man who was later to become Pope John Paul II, Karol Wojtyła. It was in theatrical activism that, under the rigorous formation of theater director Mieczysław

Kotlarczyk, Wojtyła sharpened his articulation, timing, and sense of connection with an audience. "As one who could calmly continue a clandestine performance of the epic poem, *Pan Tadeusz*, one of the greatest masterpieces of Polish literature, while Nazi megaphones blasted their propaganda through the streets below, he would likely be able to handle publicly in virtually any dramatic situation."[27]

> *Wojtyła believed that the power of drama lay in the spoken and received word, not in theatrics. . . . and whose literary instincts had already inclined him to the view that "the word" could alter what the world of power thought were unalterable facts, if that word were proclaimed clearly, honestly, and forcefully enough.*[28]

In the spring of 1940, Wojtyła wrote his first and second plays, which were biblically inspired dramas. The narrative of the first, *Job*, followed the biblical story "with Job's circumstances representing Poland's suffering under the Nazi jackboot—an adaptation of nineteenth-century Polish Romanticism and its identification of dismembered Poland as the suffering 'Christ of nations.'" The next play, *Jeremiah*, followed another biblical theme and continued the young playwright's examination of the *why* of Poland's suffering.[29]

In 1940, once it had become evident that Nazism was attempting to eradicate Poland from the map of history, the Rhapsodic Theater was allied to a broader movement of cultural resistance known as UNIA [Union], which was formed by the merger of three preexisting Underground organizations, one of which Karol Wojtyła was a member.

> *The aim of the organization was to apply Christian moral principles and Catholic social doctrine to public life at a time*

when there was, officially, no "public life" for Poles. It expressed a vision of postwar Poland as a nation in which differences of ethnicity, religion, and social class would be overcome through two shared convictions: politics and economics, (both of which) should be guided by the universal moral law, the only legitimate source of public authority in their public lives. . . . The new Polish state would be embodied in the communitarian themes of Catholic social doctrine developed by Popes Leo XIII and Pius XI: support for the family as the basic unit of society; and the anti-totalitarian principle of subsidiarity in which decision-making should be left at the lowest level possible in society and self-government.[30]

People also practiced music and the visual arts underground. Another type of patron, namely artistic cooperatives, most notably those located in Warsaw and Kraków, supported clandestine concerts. German officials permitted serious Polish music only in private homes. And they officially banned the music of Polish composers, although one might infrequently hear the muted notes of a Chopin polonaise or the rhythmic sounds of Polish folk music coming from a distant apartment. German authorities permitted light, frivolous music in Polish cabarets.

All Polish sports activities were suspended and the sports fields reserved for the Germans. One of the basic aims of German policy was the demoralization and degradation of the Polish youth so as to destroy the moral strength of the nation. To this end, Germans made alcohol easily accessible to the Poles, and intended it to be the main source of pleasure and entertainment. Vodka, for example, was part of the currency Germans paid for agricultural products sold by the farmers under the German compulsory deliveries plan. In fact, Germans offered vodka to schoolchildren as a reward for collecting scrap badly needed by the German war industry.[31]

Throughout the occupation, Joseph Goebbels' Department of Education and Propaganda took control of all cinemas, and German movies, always preceded by propaganda newsreels, dominated the programs. The Underground discouraged Poles from attending, since all the profits from Polish cinemas went directly toward German war production. A famous Underground slogan declared: "Only pigs attend the movies." The few Polish films that were permitted were edited to eliminate references to Polish national symbols as well as Jewish actors and producers; and no Polish films were shown after 1943. German officials forbade all Polish cinematographic activity except for attempts at producing documentaries or news subjects.[32]

Cinema personnel—directors, actors, technicians, authors, and critics—incurred serious losses during the war on the battlefield, under bombs, and in deportation and extermination camps resulting from hunger and deprivation. Those filmmakers who survived actively recorded facts and reactions of a terrorized population under the intense bombings that took place. In September 1943, a group of filmmakers received the official title of Cinematographic Branch of the Polish Army. They followed troop movements and participated in numerous battles. In the words of one literary director, "We don't attack with guns alone, but also with a portable camera which captures on film everything that will otherwise disappear in an instant and which must remain alive in the hearts of the entire army, of the whole struggling people."[33] In their effort to obliterate all signs of Polish culture, Germans destroyed numerous works of art, monuments, and architecture. Some artists were able to record scenes of German terror, including mass arrests, deportations, and executions. In fact, visitors to museums in places such as Auschwitz and Majdanek can view authentic illustrations by prisoners who survived the war.[34]

Although German officials forcibly closed all art galleries and museums, artists and others used private homes and some cafés and restaurants that were not shut down to display visual works of art.[35] Most artists were not able to officially continue their professions. Nonetheless, private art collectors and patrons request wartime commissions. Thanks to such people, secret artwork presentations and exhibitions took place in Kraków, Warsaw, Lwów, Wilno, and Lublin. The Department of Culture and Art, authorized by the Polish Government Delegation, took charge of literature, theater, libraries, archives, monuments, museums, music, and fine arts.[36]

Some artists worked directly for the Underground State, forging money and documents in addition to creating anti-Nazi satirical posters and caricatures or Polish patriotic symbols. All of these were intended for public display and plastered or painted on walls. Many of these activities were coordinated under the Action N's Bureau of Information and Propaganda. One prominent example was a twenty-foot display of giant puppets, caricatures of Hitler and Benito Mussolini, publicly displayed in Warsaw.[37]

When a nation's people suffer to the degree that the Poles suffered, symbols of national identity not only gain in prominence but also acquire a life-and-death significance. As historian Norman Davies so vividly describes it,

> *Men and women were ready to risk all to paint the anchor-sign of "Fighting Poland" on walls and placards, tear down the new German street signs, or let a gramophone blare a recording of the banished Chopin onto the street. The simple act of wearing a white blouse over a red skirt [national colors] constituted a dangerous act of defiance. Refusing to speak German, or still better, speaking it very badly with an execrable accent, was a patriotic duty. The soul could sometimes smile even if the body was in chains.[38]*

These simple expressions of defiance by Poles of all political persuasions constituted a clarion call that the very existence of Polish civilization was at stake; that the confrontation was between barbarism and humanity; and that no cultural values or moral order that embodies the concepts of justice and freedom could be compatible with the Hitlerian social order that was being imposed on the Polish people. Cultural resistance forged that common bond, uniting in an extraordinary time ordinary men and women whose disposition to resist was of one mind with those who took up arms in defense of the principles and ideals of Western civilization.

CHAPTER THIRTEEN
The Underground Press

Four hostile newspapers are more to be feared than a thousand bayonets.

—NAPOLEON BONAPARTE, (1769–1821) EMPEROR OF FRANCE

Lack of illegal publications is for a political organization like lack of blood: an anemia which condemns an organization to oblivion.

—JÓZEF PIŁSUDSKI, (1867–1935) POLISH CHIEF OF STATE, 1918–1922

In a further effort to eradicate Polish cultural life, the German Ministry of Propaganda press system abolished all Polish-language newspapers in those western and northern provinces in Poland that were directly incorporated into the Greater German Reich, and replaced them with German titles. In the General Government region, occupying authorities replaced authentic Polish newspapers with German papers, but kept them in the Polish language. Initially, the newspapers only provided information, but before long the Germans used them to influence attitudes in Polish society. Forbidden topics included anything critical of the German regime either at home or abroad, news of the enemy, any mention of national holidays, religious issues, or any obituaries of persons executed by the Germans. As far as news and editorial commentary were concerned, censorship destroyed their credibility. This was particularly noticeable during the years from 1939 to 1941, when the legal German press could report just the German victories—the stories of which were mostly true—that the occupied Poles wanted to read least of all. These newspapers contained articles with propagandistic material written to weaken the spirit of resistance and to instill feelings of total defeat and the pointlessness of continued resistance. The Poles popularly referred to them as the "reptile press." It was estimated that in the years from 1939 to 1944 a total of fifty "reptile press" titles appeared in occupied Poland.[1]

At the very outset of the occupation, the Germans fully recognized that, with their monopoly on information and the imposition of strict censorship, they encouraged the development of an Underground press, one that proved to be one of the most effective weapons in the struggle against the occupying powers. As a result the Germans decreed that the penalty for circulating clandestine newspapers, or failing to report the receipt of a newspaper, was imprisonment; for anyone actively associated with the writing or production, the penalty was death.[2] Nevertheless, life for the Poles had to be bearable, so they necessarily began to listen and believe everything that they were forbidden to believe. Despite the fact that Poles were forbidden, under penalty of death, to own radios, a large and well-organized chain of secret radio listeners helped supply world news. People of all ages risked their lives to listen to foreign broadcasts in soundproof cellars, in small huts set up in forests, and in attics. The London

BBC, Columbia's WCBX in New York, and WRUL in Boston were major sources of information.[3] Having had long-standing experience in printing and circulating clandestine newspapers in defiance of the Tsar's secret police some thirty-five years earlier, the *Okhrana* was not all that different; it confounded the Gestapo. Just as in those earlier days under foreign rule, Poles operated small, portable hand presses in Polish towns concealed in the dingy cellars of the workers' dwellings.

> *Don't think these sheets have anything like the appearance of those that are sold in broad daylight. They are miserable squares of paper. Clumsy sheets that somehow get printed or typed. The characters are blurred, the headings thin. The ink often smudges. The people turn them out as they can. One week in one town and one week in another. They take what lies to hand. But the paper appears. The articles follow subterranean channels. . . . It isn't big, it doesn't look impressive. But every line is like a ray of gold; a ray of free thought.*[4]

At first young boys took handwritten or typewritten letters copied from radio news messages, which had been passed on as chain letters, to the basements or the huts in the woods. Kerosene lamps provided the light for the man who was the reporter, editor, publisher, and printer of the Underground paper, who would then make use of his hand press or mimeograph machine.

Before long the Polish government delegate, military organization, and staffs of the large political parties organized special press agencies. From these, Poland received accurate reports of the outside world, other military theaters of operation, and major occurrences in the other occupied countries. These press agencies had regular correspondents in neutral and Allied countries.[5] The correspondence they sent was in code and included speeches by Churchill and Roosevelt, important interviews with the members of the Polish government-in-exile, and news from the fighting fronts that was widely circulated in Poland within a few hours. The emergence of Underground publications was virtually the only source of reliable information. It served to inform the Poles of the war's progression, of the international situation, and of resolutions made by the Underground authorities. Additionally, it enhanced the sense of patriotism throughout the country by keeping up the spirit of resistance and creating a broad base of public support for the Underground.[6] In addition, it exposed the misrepresentations published in the reptile press, which interested the average Pole little more than advertisements about where one could buy secondhand children's clothes.

> *More important, the Underground press served to counteract the pressures of social division by providing information to people in various parts of the country and in several social environments about what was happening beyond the reach of their everyday experiences. It therefore contributed to breaking down the relative isolation of various groups. The press made constant efforts to draw a picture of a common fate, and therefore of a common bond, uniting Poles despite the Germans' local variation of policies and their clumsy attempts to exploit old grievances or new interests in accordance with their strategy of divide and rule.[7]*

Editorials, essays, and articles in Underground newspapers that discussed problems of ordinary everyday life under the occupation proved particularly helpful to the general populace. They provided people with guidelines about how to behave in new circumstances, which was an invaluable help to millions who otherwise might have lost their sense of civic responsibility as loyal Poles and helped the

Germans destroy the social bond that united Polish society.[8]

All the political parties had their own newspapers, and they were highly popular with their public. Before the war there was no place for parliamentary democracy in Poland or freedom of public expression; now, paradoxically, under German occupation, people with all shades of opinion felt free to express themselves. The newspapers published poems by ancient and modern Polish authors, with great influence on public opinion; children learned them by heart at school, where the curriculum emphasized the permanence of Polish culture. In addition, the Ukrainian, Byelorussian, and Jewish minorities also had their own news sheets.[9] Now that the Underground movement was a principal factor in returning Poland to democratic policies, the illegal press provided an extremely important forum for discussing the alternative political programs of different political movements and parties. (The term "illegal" refers to those publications in conflict with the German directives, not with Polish law, and is synonymous with the term "Underground.")

In the early days of the occupation political and military groups took the initiative in printing Underground newspapers. Besides those secret press services organized by the government delegate, there was the Military Press Agency of the Underground army—first, the Polish Victory Service (SZP)—later the Union for Armed Struggle (ZWZ), and finally the Polish Home Army (AK). As early as 1940, the ZWZ/AK produced no less than 250 newspapers with a total circulation of over 200,000 copies during the occupation. Its chief newspaper, the *Information Bulletin*, a popular weekly, had a circulation that ranged from 25,000 to 50,000 copies. The central authority for the Underground press was the Bureau of Information and Propaganda (BIP).

The Military Press published two army newspapers: *Insurrection* and *Polish Soldier*. Their purpose was to serve as educational material for junior officers of the Polish Home Army. They contained articles about military history as well as the operational and tactical situation on the fighting fronts. In addition to newspapers, the Home Army set up its own publishing facility, which produced two books series on morale and discipline entitled *Armed Forces of the Free Polish Republic* and *The Spirit of the Polish National Army*. Another series on the tactics and techniques of propaganda was *A Course in Propaganda*. The unit extended its scope by publishing a particularly noteworthy collection of true stories concerning resistance in the Boy Scout movement called *Stones on the Rampart*. Its wide appeal prompted a reprint and after the war editions were published in Italy and Great Britain.[10]

Unlike the French or the Dutch, the Poles did not have a legal Polish press that was expected to cooperate with the German Propaganda Ministry. And while in other European occupied countries the output of the Underground press did not increase dramatically until the last year and a half of the occupation, in Poland it increased steadily throughout the course of the war. Incomplete statistics compiled in 1947 show that in Warsaw there 18 Underground papers were published simultaneously in 1939, a number that grew progressively to a total of 650 newspaper titles by the end of the war. Another study located 137 titles in Kraków alone.[11] How many millions of copies of Underground publications were distributed during the war is impossible to assess. Some papers only had a short lifespan, others appeared at irregular intervals, and some papers merged with each other. Estimates range of a regular circulation of between 1,400 and 1,500 newspaper titles, which not only bore testimony to Polish society's undeniable will to resist and regain independence, but was also a unique phenomenon in the whole of occupied Europe.[12]

In another important role, BIP published propaganda material aimed at citizens of the Third Reich, the *Volksdeutschen* (German nationals), and functionaries of the occupying administration. The operation was code-named Action N and its purpose was to disorient and undermine German morale and counter German propaganda. I have described this at greater length in an earlier chapter. At the end of 1943 BIP also initiated Action R to counter communist and Soviet propaganda. Apart from publishing anti-Communist material, their newspapers, which were directed at both the urban and rural population, also included news about how fighting was progressing against the Germans.

Throughout the war the Underground press existed primarily in the major cities within the General Government, but press network also developed in those annexed territories incorporated into the Third Reich. Apart from the difficulties acquiring the information that went into the Underground papers, the actual printing posed considerable problems. Most of the printing houses were confiscated in 1939, and consequently there was a huge shortage of printing machines, paper, and ink. Presses stole or bought most paper from the Germans by various methods of bribery. But other kinds of paper were brought covertly to secret printing places by farmers' carts. Hidden beneath cabbage or potatoes were sheets of white, yellow, or even dark brown wrapping paper to be used as newsprint.[13] Those persons who were involved in the circulation of the Underground papers used a "three-man" method of distribution. Every man engaged in the circulation knew only "one man back and one man ahead," the man who delivered to him at a secretly specified place and the man who took the papers from him in another town. If the Gestapo discovered a paper carrier, that man could only give two names, since he did not know any more.[14]

The Germans devised a particular ruse to discourage the distribution of Underground papers. Having obtained copies of clandestine newspapers, the Germans sent them anonymously to suspected Polish readers. This tested the recipients' adherence to the German regulation that required them to report such incidents to the police. Consequently, the Poles countered this scheme by accepting clandestine newspapers only if they received them from someone they knew.[15]

On the street, those involved in the Underground circulation practiced every kind of artifice. Newsboys in Warsaw and Kraków sold the local German papers, but "No one would buy the paper unless the boy smilingly said to him: '*Today* you have extraordinary news about German victories . . . Buy it,' and handed him a copy." The passersby knew the paper was worth buying since inside the paper would be a hidden copy of the desired Underground paper. Similarly, in a grocery store while wrapping a woman customer's meat, the butcher would say to her, "Put on ice *immediately* when you get home." She would then know that the covert paper was wrapped inside the package.

Waiters in restaurants also placed papers under patrons' plates. But there were tragic reverses. While serving as a waiter in a Warsaw café, the famous Polish world-record breaker in the five-thousand-meter race and 1932 Olympic winner, Janusz Kusociński, was shot by the Gestapo. He was also known to put covert newspapers under the patrons' plates.[16]

Anyone involved in the writing, production, printing, or distribution of illegal newspapers felt, not unnaturally, tremendous psychological trepidation and anxiety, and had to control his or her imagination under the strain of sleepless nights and other moments of fear. Those living in Warsaw who were involved in the Underground press knew all too well of cases of brutal interrogations and cases of torture and death at the Gestapo headquarters at 25 Szucha Avenue and at the dreaded Pawiak Prison. One Polish patriot who was awaiting execution in a condemned cell had a priest smuggle out a simple but deeply felt message to his fellow conspirators: "Keep going if you can; you will, I know. We haven't much choice. I salute the new Poland. Goodbye." And this is a poem that was widely circulated:

> *Though I perish, though I fall,*
> *Yet life will not have been in vain*
> *For the finest part of life*
> *Is in struggle and pursuit.*[17]

These words came from a fifteen-year-old boy who had been severely tortured and was now due to be executed. Besides those who, despite the most horrible torture, refused to divulge the names of colleagues, there were those who were aware of their weaknesses and shortcomings and who took adequate precautions. One such case was that of Józef Fell, editor of the Polish Underground paper *Freedom*, who always carried a cyanide capsule with him. While he burned a used copy of the paper in his office, some smoke curled under the door just as two members of the Gestapo passed by. After noticing the wisp of smoke, the two officers forced their way into the room. Fell quickly put his cyanide pill into his mouth, but one of the officers noticed and pounded the editor on the back so that the pill fell out of his mouth. He threw himself to the floor and got in a position to lick sufficient poison in order to die.[18]

There were also occasions when not only the editor or publisher of the paper would suffer such a fate, but also the entire staff and others not directly involved. One such story is taken from the Warsaw Underground paper *Glos Polski* (Poland's Voice):

> *In a fashionable residential section of Warsaw a villa sheltered*
> *a printing shop, the editors and printers having been shad-*
> *owed by the Gestapo. When knocking at the door by the police*
> *armed with machine guns brought no response, hand grenades*

were thrown through the windows along with several blasts fired from the machine guns. Two of the men inside were killed and two women seriously wounded, both of whom died later in the hospital. A few days later, the owner of the villa, his wife, and two sons aged 15 and 17, as well as all tenants of two neighboring houses, were arrested and subsequently shot. In all, 83 persons perished as a result of the incident.[19]

Nevertheless, a newly published, unnamed clandestine paper appeared in a bold new format, a size generally considered unsuitable for public consumption, and its first editorial made it unmistakably clear that no form of German opposition would stand in the way of the resilience and resolution of the Underground press:

We have resolved to take no notice of the bloody scoundrels of Szucha Boulevard (the site of Gestapo Headquarters). We ignore the dangers of the Gestapo and pay no heed to the German Occupation. Just as the spirit of a nation cannot be killed, neither can its courage and contempt for the enemy. The only payment we ask from our readers for the risk we are taking is audacity, a wide circulation, and a bold perusal of our paper, which is being edited contrary to the rules of conspiracy.[20]

In addition to the newspapers, the clandestine press published books and pamphlets of all kinds. Besides reprints of textbooks printed before the war for underground education, there were verses of Polish classic authors and modern poets and previously mentioned military works. Moreover, besides being the political and military mouthpiece, the secret press was also a medium for religion. Many illegal newspapers printed a particularly meaningful, albeit melancholy and passionate, *Lord's Prayer*; it circulated widely in Polish schools throughout the country. It reads:

Our Father who art in Heaven, *look upon the martyred land of Poland.*

Hallowed be Thy name *in the days of our incessant despair, in these days of our powerless silence.*

Thy Kingdom come, *we pray every morning, repeating steadfastly: Thy kingdom come throughout Poland, and may in liberty and sunshine Thy Word of Peace and Love be fulfilled.*

Thy Will be done on Earth as it is in Heaven. *May it be Thy Will that humid prison cells stay empty—that forest pits cease being filled with corpses—that the whip of Satan incarnate in man stop its whiz of terror over our heads.*

Give us this day our daily bread. *Our daily bread is toil beyond any endurance. . . . It is a forced clenching of our fists and setting of our teeth in the hour that cries for bloody revenge.*

And forgive us our trespasses. *Forgive us, Oh Lord, should we be too weak to crush the beast. Strengthen our arm lest it tremble in the hour of revenge.*

And lead us not into temptation . . . *but let traitors and spies among us perish.*

But deliver us from evil. . . . *Deliver us from the evil one, from the foe of our Polish land. Save us Oh Lord, from the paths and misery of deportation, from death on land, in air and in the sea, from treason of our own.*

Amen. *Give us freedom Oh Lord! Amen.*[21]

No source within the Polish Resistance proclaimed that longing for freedom more loudly or more persistently than the clandestine Underground press. As a catalyst of Underground activity, the press was living proof that the fight had not yet ended, but rather had begun in earnest.

CHAPTER FOURTEEN
Poland Betrayed

I am persuaded that he who is capable
of being a bitter enemy can never
possess the necessary virtues that constitute a true friend.

—Sir Thomas Fitzosborne (1710–1799), English author

By mid-1943, those active in the anti-Nazi Resistance throughout Poland could sense that the hour of reckoning was coming. As the eminent historian Norman Davies eloquently stated, "Psychological horizons were slowly lifting. Before 1943, the Nazis looked invincible. From 1943 onwards, they were in retreat."[1] The German defeat in North Africa was the first sign that the war was beginning to shift in favor of the Allies. Severe German setbacks in Stalingrad and all over the Eastern Front were accompanied in the West by the Allied invasion of Sicily, which was a stepping-stone to the Italian mainland. By midyear American and British bombers conducted massive daylight and night raids against the industrial heartland of Germany with ever-increasing frequency. These were clear signs that the German war machine was no longer the leviathan that it had been when it invaded and occupied most of continental Europe in 1940 and 1941. Nevertheless, the Western powers had still not established a military presence on the continent outside Italy, while the victory of the Soviet Army on the Eastern Front was forging rapidly ahead. With this in mind the Polish government-in-exile became deeply concerned with the likelihood that its territory would not be liberated by the Western powers, but by Stalin's armies.

Early in 1943, General Rowecki elaborated a well-calculated plan in preparation for a general Polish uprising, which was to go into effect when the German collapse appeared imminent. The plan, code-named Tempest, called for an increase in sabotage and intensified diversionary activity in the rear of the retreating Germans by larger units of the Home Army. It was timed to take place as soon as Soviet troops entered Poland's prewar territory in January 1944, but before the Soviets entered the country in force. The operation did not at first include a plan for action in Warsaw. Initially it was designed to avoid fighting in major towns in favor of more rural concentrations in order to spare the defenseless population.

However, in mid-July 1943, after General Rowecki's arrest, Tadeusz Bór-Komorowski, who was now given command of the Home Army, decided to capture the capital before the Russians entered the city. Within the Polish Underground itself, there was a general feeling that Soviet Russia was and always would be Poland's enemy. This would make clear to the Russians "beyond any doubt the strength of the Polish Resistance movement faithful to the Government in London, and the will of the Polish people to remain independent."[2]

There was also serious concern over certain ethnic groups in eastern Poland whose sympathies there leaned toward the Soviets; they acted unpredictably and the Underground felt that it could not count on this much weaker Polish community along the Polish border to support a general insurgency. This concern was augmented by the break in Polish-Soviet diplomatic relations by Stalin when Commander-in-Chief Sikorski asked the International Red Cross to investigate the Katyn Forest massacre.[3] Sikorski was also a firm believer that the Soviets as well as the Germans were Poland's enemies. Polish strategic thinking was now just as concerned about the Russians' entry into Poland during a general uprising as they were about the destruction of the German occupying forces. Nevertheless, Sikorski directed the Underground to concentrate on the Germans as the principal enemy, since the Poles were in no position to resist the Soviets.[4]

Despite a series of proposed variants for a future uprising by the government-in-exile if diplomatic relations with the Soviets were not resumed, local commanders retained some latitude of judgment. General Bór-Komorowski ordered his insurgent forces, in the fight against the Germans, to "reveal themselves to incoming Russians, but to assert the existence of the Polish Republic." The Home Army commander clarified his position, insisting that "no armed action be taken against the Soviets who were in hot pursuit of the Germans, except in essential acts of self-defense, which is the right of every human being."[5]

One of General Sikorski's principal concerns regarding the Soviet Union was to avoid a Communist takeover in Poland. According to one informed source, it is possible that he would have made some concession to avoid such an occurrence, but before any decision was made, Sikorski, the prime minister and commander in chief of the Polish Armed Forces, met an untimely death on July 4, 1943, in an airplane crash off the coast of Gibraltar on a return flight from an inspection of Polish troops in the Middle East.

Despite the conflicting positions within the government-in-exile, almost everyone favored a major uprising in principle, regarding it as a legitimate means of overthrowing the German oppression.[6] Underground officials also made appeals for help to the British and

Americans. In response, the British simply said the logistical problems of intervening in the East were too great. The Americans said that, because the Eastern Front was the Soviet theater of operations, the Poles must somehow deal with the Soviet command themselves. Months passed, but nothing was ever arranged.[7]

In April 1943, less than two years after the German attack on the Soviet Union, the Soviet government established a group of Polish Communists and leftist intellectuals in Russia called the Union of Polish Patriots and dominated by the surviving remnants of the Polish Communist Party (CPP). It was introduced as the body that truly represented the Polish people. Its president was a woman named Wanda Wasilewska who, albeit of Polish origin, held the rank of colonel in the Red Army and was a member of the Presidium of the Soviet Union. The Soviet press failed to mention these two latter facts. The Soviet Union then used this as an assurance for attacking the legality of the Polish government-in-exile, and relying upon Soviet propaganda, the Communist press in England and in the United States. They attacked the legality of the Polish Government by questioning the existence of democratic values among exiled Poles.[8]

Throughout the course of 1943, the exiled Polish government was faced with mounting difficulties over which they had no control: the break in Soviet-Polish relations by Stalin over the Katyn Forest affair, the untimely death of General Sikorski, and in November and December 1943, the discussions at the Teheran Conference that foreshadowed the fate that later awaited Poland. The dispute between the Soviets and Poland revolved around two basic issues: the Soviet territorial demands and the Soviet insistence that the Soviet-sponsored Committee of National Liberation of Lublin should rule Poland. The

Polish government in London stubbornly resisted both demands, considering them irreconcilable with the idea of Poland's integrity and sovereignty. The government was backed on both issues by the non-Communist Polish Underground movement.[9] Of the two issues, that of the government was the more vital, but the emotionally charged territorial problem overshadowed it from the beginning.

As the tide of war turned in favor of the Red Army, Stalin envisioned the return of the Polish soil that he had obtained by the German-Soviet pact of 1939. The Soviet leader clung to the argument that these seized eastern lands were not technically "Polish," but rather were principally an ethnic mix of Ukrainian and Byelorussian, with Poles in the minority. And even though the Soviets had take these lands by conspiring with Hitler, Stalin saw the land grab as a Soviet fait accompli.[10]

At the Teheran Conference, Winston Churchill knew full well that the Polish government-in-exile was firmly against losing territory in the east. Nevertheless, he agreed with Stalin about rearranging Poland's borders, and told the Soviet leader that "he would like to see Poland moved westward." At that same conference, Franklin Roosevelt met privately with Stalin about the revision of Poland's borders. He told Stalin that he

> *personally agreed with the Soviet leader's views, but that he had to consider the reaction of six to seven million Americans of Polish extraction whose votes he did not wish to lose in the election of 1944. Consequently, he would not make any public statement about the Polish issue at Teheran.[11]*

Stalin now had Roosevelt's private assurance that the Polish issue would be settled in a way favorable to Soviet interests.

The Western powers, bent on capitulating to the Soviet demands, were merely looking for a suitable way to make them palatable to the Poles. The question of how to revise the frontier in favor of the Soviets despite Polish protests, and how to compensate the Poles for their losses, became one of the most crucial issues of the wartime conferences at Teheran, Yalta, and Postdam.[12]

**Prime Minister Winston Churchill,
President Franklin Roosevelt, and Premier Joseph Stalin at
the Yalta Conference.**

The Polish government-in-exile in London had counted on the support of Great Britain and the United States—in both cases in vain. While trying to preserve the appearance of mediating between the Poles and the Soviets, the Western powers would occasionally warn the Polish allies about the *changing facts of political life*. These changing facts were envisioned as early as February 1942 by the Western powers when Edward Raczyński, the then-acting foreign minister of the Polish government-in-exile, went to Washington in the hope of enlisting American support against Soviet claims on prewar Polish territory. The American position, as outlined by U.S. Assistant Secretary of State Adolf Berle, stated that "it was difficult to conceive that unlimited sovereignty of smaller states, in the prewar sense of the word, could stand in the way of the natural and inevitable political and economic expansion of a great Power."[13] Roosevelt made a far more penetrating and graphic exposition of the point in June 1944 to the Polish Prime Minister Stanisław Mikołajczyk. The president pointed out "that the Soviet Union had five times the population of Poland and could swallow up Poland if she could not reach an understanding on her terms."[14]

The British position was similar. Churchill realized the correlation of power all too well: only the Soviet Union could defeat Hitler in the east. Even though he wanted a strong independent Poland, he knew that Britain was not wedded to, nor would it fuss over, any particular border or frontier. He knew that Poland would be liberated by Soviet arms and that the Poles should be happy with whatever it got.[15]

What the Western powers did not know was that, after the entry of the Red Army into Poland in January 1944, Soviet security agencies and the NKVD were routinely arresting members of the Polish Home Army not only on the Polish territories ceded to them by Roosevelt and Churchill in Teheran, but *also on undisputed Polish territory where the AK operated against Germans and to which Soviets could claim no legal, historic, political, or moral rights whatsoever.*[16] It is now common knowledge that, in what was unquestionably Polish territory, Stalin sent political agents and partisan groups to work in collusion with the local Polish Communists to penetrate Polish civilian and military circles loyal to the Polish government-in-exile in order to undermine that government by all possible means. A pro-Communist National Council was created to collaborate with the Soviet security agencies and the Union of Polish Patriots. The National Council was so named to confuse the Polish public since the legal underground parliament was called the Council of National Unity. Both Polish and Soviet propaganda in the summer of 1944 reiterated to the Polish community that neither the Polish Home Army nor the Polish exile-government in London had any real wish to fight the Germans.[17] Bór-Komorowski bluntly refuted those charges of Communist propaganda in a report to the commander in chief on July 14:

> *Inaction on the part of the Home Army at the moment of the Soviet entry is likely to mean general passivity on the home front. The initiative for fighting the Germans is liable then to be taken by the PPR (Communists) and a considerable fraction of the less-informed citizens might join them. In that case the country is liable to move in the direction of collaboration with the Soviets and no one will be able to stop it. Also, in that case the Soviet army would not be received by the Home Army, loyal to the government and the commander-in-chief, but by their own adherents—with open arms. . . . Finally, the participation of the Home Army in the battle for Warsaw would definitely silence the lies of Soviet propaganda about the passivity of our country and our sympathies toward the Germans, and the liberation of the capital by our own soldiers should testify with unquestionable strength to the nation's will to safeguard the sovereignty of the Polish state.*[18]

The fact that it was now plain to Stalin that he did not need to take the Polish government seriously was particularly relevant to the cession of Eastern Poland by Roosevelt and Stalin at Teheran, especially in relation to the upcoming uprising in Warsaw. Giving away the seventy thousand square miles that included millions of Polish citizens also gave away the prestige, credibility, and viability of the legal Polish government.[19] It was so secret that it was not known either to Polish society as a whole or to the leaders of the Home Army.

According to General Bór-Komorowski, who regulated the conduct of the Home Army, the orders concerning Operation Tempest stipulated that the Home Army was to fight a rearguard action as the Germans withdrew under Soviet pressure by intensive sabotage activity. Tempest was to move westward with local AK units rising as the Germans retreated. Local commanders would initiate local action. On the arrival of the Red Army, all Home Army action would cease. The Poles, believing that the eastern territories were their own, would carry out Operation Tempest whenever the timing was favorable. They attacked withdrawing Germans, often collaborating with the Soviet Union against the common enemy. Home Army commanders reported with their units to Soviet officers as part of the Polish Army fighting on its own soil. The Soviet command saw the situation differently. As soon as German units retreated and fighting ceased, they arrested and disarmed the Poles.[20]

In July 1944 the Red Army, with the effective collaboration of Polish Home Army units, seized the Polish city of Wilno from the Germans. When Stalin promptly announced the liberation of that city from the Germans as the "capital of Lithuanian Soviet Socialist Republics," he ordered 24 salvo and 324 gun salutes in honor of the Soviet troops who captured the city. The Polish AK units who had also fought for the city were disarmed and arrested, and some were executed.[21] What took place in Wilno was a fair sample of what took place in all Polish eastern territories. In mid-July the Red Army hunted down, disarmed, and imprisoned more than seven thousand Home Army (AK) soldiers. The Soviets now said that eastern Poland was their land, their country, and that the Polish government-in-exile did not exist anymore, even if the Poles did not know it. As a result of this situation, Home Army soldiers asked through clandestine radio stations whether the order to reveal their identities to the Soviets and report to their Soviet commanders was still valid.[22]

The Polish General Staff in London was equally at a loss to understand why the Soviets were arresting AK members in eastern Poland, despite their joint effort with the Soviet forces against the Germans. The Poles still believed that if the AK was coordinated and commanded directly by the Supreme Allied Command, the intentions of the Poles could not be misinterpreted, misjudged, or manipulated by Soviet propaganda in Great Britain or the United States.

In January 1944 in a letter from the Allied Combined Chiefs of Staff (CCS) to Colonel Leon Mitkiewicz, the Polish representative to that body, Great Britain and the United States made it unequivocally clear that they "are not assuming any responsibility for the preparation of the general uprising of the AK, nor for its activities on the Polish territory, because this territory is not in their strategic sphere."[23] The letter pointed out that this question was basically political rather than military, a direct result of Roosevelt and Churchill's secret discussions with Stalin concerning Poland several weeks earlier at the Teheran Conference.

As the front approached Warsaw, the Home Army command grew increasingly confident that the time was at hand to put the Tempest plan into operation. By the end of July 1944 the Red Army's offensive advanced rapidly and appeared unstoppable. The Germans were showing signs of exhaustion and demoralization as their disordered retreat continued. On July 28 Moscow announced that in Central Poland, Soviet tanks and motorized infantry were advancing toward Warsaw on a fifty-mile-wide front within forty miles from the Polish capital.[24] On July 29 the Communist Union of Polish Patriots addressed a call to the Polish people of Warsaw: "Poles! The time of liberation is at hand! Poles to arms! . . . Every Polish homestead must become a stronghold in the struggle against the invader. . . . There is not a moment to lose."[25] The appeal apparently indicated that the Soviet command was about to launch an attack on Warsaw. As a result the leaders of the Home Army judged the situation ripe for the uprising to begin. The Polish government-in-exile gave General Bór-Komorowski and its home delegate, J.S. Jankowski, discretionary powers to commence armed action with the aim of liberating Warsaw, which was not only the Polish capital but also the nerve center of the Polish Underground State.

During those last days of July people heard the rumble of Soviet artillery across the Vistula River, a clear sign that the Soviet Army was advancing and the whole of the Eastern Front moving closer to Warsaw. Moscow Radio broadcasts in Polish called upon the Poles to take up arms and help the Soviet offensive by rising up against the "common enemy."

The five years of suffering inflicted upon the Polish people since their country was overrun in September 1939 had not broken their courage. A secret force of two hundred thousand Poles, forty thousand of whom were in Warsaw, had been organized and were impatiently awaiting orders to attack the Germans in open warfare.[26] The order to rise up came on July 31, with the news that the Soviet forces had reached the east bank of Warsaw on the Vistula. It is to that memorable sixty-three-day Warsaw Uprising that we now turn.

CHAPTER FIFTEEN
The Warsaw Uprising

*I do not think that in history the leaders of a people
could be so completely certain of fulfilling a nation's will. . . .
No dictator, no leader, no party, and no class had inspired this decision
to continue the struggle. The nation had done it spontaneously and
unanimously.*

—GENERAL BÓR-KOMOROWSKI,
COMMANDER OF THE HOME ARMY

Although Bór-Komorowski was in Warsaw and was the AK commander in chief for all of Poland, and it was he who issued the order
to start the uprising, he did not command the uprising. The order was
given to his subordinate, General Antoni Chruściel (nom de guerre
Monter) who initiated and implemented the order to set the time of the
uprising to commence at 1700 hours (5:00 p.m.) on Tuesday, August
1, 1944. The commanding officers decided that by beginning at that
time, the insurgents would have a few hours of daylight in which to
take over strategic German strongpoints across the city before dusk,
according to plan, which involved taking over six municipal districts

of the city, including City Center, Żoliborz, Wola, Ochota, Mokotów, and Praga, as well as some outlying areas.

General Tadeusz Bor-Komorowski, Commander-in-Chief of the Polish Home Army.

The Home Army forces of the Warsaw District were estimated at between thirty five thousand and forty thousand insurgents, of which about twenty-three thousand were combat-ready at the outset of the uprising. Women constituted about one-seventh of the force. They acted chiefly as messengers to maintain liaison and communication with isolated posts; they also worked in medical services and attended to the welfare and feeding of the soldiers. Office clerks, railway workers, artisans, factory workers, and students were all prepared to take up arms against the occupying Germans. Apart from regular insurgent units, most of the civilian population, both male and female, took part in the uprising, arranging hospitals, supplies, improvised fortifications, and essential services.

A Polish air force squadron of bombers under British command received the special assignment of providing arms and supplies to Warsaw during the uprising. However, because flight conditions were extremely hazardous, it was a task beyond the squadron's capabilities: the distance was too great for a fighter escort. Nevertheless, the Polish supreme commander in chief in England demanded that the pilots fly, regardless of weather and losses. All those planes that went to Warsaw and returned were hit, and even the parachutes inside the planes were riddled by German bullets or explosives.[1]

Polish-piloted bombers based in Italy successfully dropped by parachute about one-third of the insurgents' equipment. They consisted of the following weapons: 1,000 carbines, 1,700 pistols, 300 automatic pistols, 60 submachine guns, 7 heavy machine guns, 35 antitank guns and PIAT bazookas, and 25,000 hand grenades. In view of these statistics, the state of the insurgents' armament at the outbreak of the uprising was far too low.[2]

The amount of ammunition was no better: 35 bullets to a pistol, 300 bullets for an automatic pistol, 190 pieces of ammunition per carbine, 500 rounds of ammunition for a submachine gun, and 2,300 rounds for the heavy machine guns. Weapons were transported in the heart of Warsaw concealed in barrels, oxygen cylinders, or coal carts, or camouflaged under a cluster of quilts, or beneath straw on a hay wagon. When sector reports were forwarded to General Monter complaining about arms deficiencies, he responded, "You have to win arms from Germans, even if it means fighting with sticks and clubs. Those dissatisfied will be court-martialed."[3] Those arms taken from the Germans were mainly captured in previous engagements.

To make up for the shortage of manufactured armament, about one-third of the arms produced came from homemade weaponry constructed clandestinely in Underground arms plants situated in attics and basements. Improvised flamethrowers called Molotov cocktails, made from bottles filled with petrol, as well as homemade catapults for hurling the petrol bottles under German tank treads, were used to halt the tanks. From Underground workshops men busily produced forty thousand additional handmade grenades made by stuffing old socks with a mixture of nuts, bolts, and scraps of iron and explosives plugged with corks. Fighters in the uprising salvaged explosives from unexploded German artillery shells and bombs. They even made use of fire-brigade equipment: they adapted motor-pumps to spray gasoline and other flammable material against tanks and buildings defended by Germans.[4]

At just before five o'clock the traffic in the city was at its heaviest as people returned home from work. The trams were crowded with young boys deliberately bunched up on the front platform reserved for the German passengers, who passively just stood aside. On the sidewalks women transported concealed arms and ammunition in heavy bags and bundles to designated locations. Among the hurrying crowds of workers coming out of their offices and factories were the Home Army insurgents, with pistols, hand grenades, and Sten guns hidden under their jackets; they looked simply like normal passersby, mixing with the crowd of civilians and moving to their appointed places in small groups. One observer recalls seeing a young couple coming through a gate. The girl put her arms around the boy's neck and affectionately kissed him. Realizing that it was time for him to depart, the couple embraced one more time and the young Home

Army soldier hurriedly moved off to his assigned post.[5] Here and there a German in uniform made his way without knowing precisely what was taking place around him. German patrols were throughout the city, while armored cars moved throughout the streets; the Germans suspected an assault from the Poles at some unknown point in time. They just didn't know when.

The Underground selected most of the targeted German-occupied buildings according to a definite plan: corner houses situated at crossroads or facing railway stations, German barracks, stores, or public works departments. They chose strategic locations across the city to attack, use, and take in the first incitement.[6] To gain access to the private homes from which much of the initial fighting was to take place, the insurgents requisitioned orders signed by the proper authorities of the uprising; they handed these to the occupants of the residences, who showed no signs of resentment toward them. Conversely, civilians did all that they could to assist the soldiers and provide them with their best food.[7] After five years of German occupation, people found it hard to imagine that there would be no more gallows in the streets, that execution squads would no longer kill hostages, and that from now on the nights in the city would be peaceful. This was the day the Poles had been anxiously waiting for.[8] Once inside the homes, the insurgents, a motley crowd, brought out their concealed weapons, and put on their one visible bond—the white-and-red armbands, stamped with either the name or number of their unit and usually with the letters AK. The armband indicated that after five years of occupation they were no longer an Underground resistance movement, but now had become once again regular soldiers and free men fighting in the open.

The insurgents took up their positions at windows, in attics, and on roofs and chimneys. Sentries in the areas denied all residents in their homes access to the street for fear that the Germans might discover the final preparations. Insurgents closed entrances to blocks and barricaded them from within. Thirty minutes before zero hour they completed all preparations.[9] Before long, many civilians disappeared from the streets. Suddenly there was a strange feeling in the air: a strange secret urgency, a feeling of expectancy. And suddenly the silence shattered.

At precisely 5:00 p.m., all of Warsaw erupted as six hundred units of Home Army soldiers flung open thousands of windows; they unleashed a hail of small-arms fire, assailing passing Germans with bullets, riddling their buildings, vehicles, and marching formations from homes alongside the street. From the entrances of houses, insurgents streamed out and pressed on for the attack. Within fifteen minutes every kind of traffic came to a halt and an entire city of a million inhabitants was at war with some thirteen thousand German troops, a number that would soon amount to over twenty-one thousand.[10] Some civilians were still on the streets, a number of whom were hit in the crossfire and unable to get to their homes. A wave of explosions and bursts of automatic rifle fire set off the uprising throughout the city. In the midst of the dust and fire, white-and-red flags (not seen since 1939) were raised along the streets and fluttered from windows and rooftops to hail the great moment.[11]

Before long the red-and-white banner—the Polish flag—waved defiantly from atop the sixteen-story Prudential Building, dominating the whole center of the city. The blood of the Polish people had paid for the right to hoist it up.

German tanks sat on the corners of all the main boulevards and squares, and their shells and machine-gun fire now prevented insurgent units from crossing the streets. Heavy gunfire, machine guns, and exploding shells broke out all over. The battle had started in earnest. Now the whole city was awake and vigilant. German units dug in behind barricades and gun emplacements. On that first day at a cost of some 2,500 lives—80 percent of them from the Home

Army—insurgents captured a major German arsenal and storehouse. So, too, did they capture the main post office, the power station, and the railway office in Praga, an easterly suburb of Warsaw, and wide portions of the city.[12]

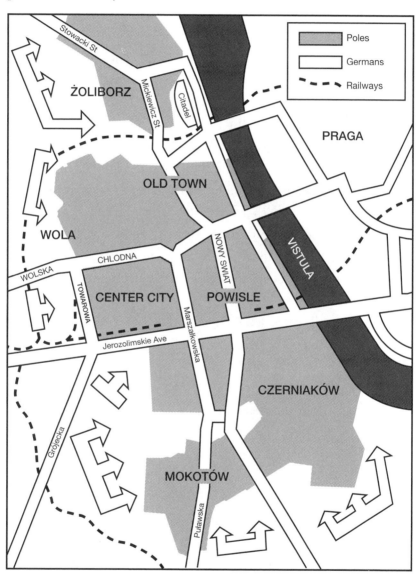

**Early August 1944 at the beginning
of the Warsaw Uprising.**

The Home Army command headquarters was relocated in the Kammler furniture factory in the western suburb of Wola, a district of working-class houses. Along with AK Commander Bór-Komorowoski were the government delegate, his secretary, and the chairman of the Council of National Unity so as to enable each of them to be in continuous contact. This was also the place where the main Home Army's network of communications strove to maintain contact between units within Warsaw and other parts of the country, as well as with the outside world. A voice-broadcasting station called Lightning in Warsaw had the greatest impact on listeners outside the city, continuing its broadcasts in Polish, English, and German.

On the day of the uprising the German owner of the factory, Lieutenant Hans Kammler, and his thirty-three workers transformed into a fighting unit—with fifteen rifles, forty grenades, and a few homemade grenades—ready to do battle.[13] The Underground command headquarters adjoined a tobacco factory that the insurgents soon discovered was occupied by a German garrison and guarded by two pillboxes. Fighting broke out when a Polish sentry at the factory gate fired two rifle shots at a German lorry that was approaching the factory on the street. The Polish sentry killed the driver and two other Germans on the lorry, at which time the nearby German pillbox immediately opened fire and sprayed the factory entrance with machine-gun fire. Germans from the nearby garrison were expected to appear on the scene momentarily. From the windows of a house adjoining the factory, German soldiers appeared in full equipment. A platoon of Poles took position at windows and gates to the factory entrance. They realized that, with their shortage of weapons, the Poles would have no way of getting them out if the Germans gained entrance into the building. Within a minute, they went to work barricading both gates, reinforcing them with barrels, handcarts, tables, planks, and furniture. Additionally, they pushed anything movable against the windows on the ground floor to provide as much cover as possible. After smashing one window, a well-aimed homemade grenade successfully silenced the German machine-gun that came from across the street.

At six o'clock a fierce exchange of fire took place in an attic that the Germans had managed to enter after gaining access from the roof and wounding the Polish spotter who had been stationed there. Two other insurgents replaced the wounded Pole and after fifteen minutes the Germans were wiped out. By eight o'clock the fighting at the factory halted. By now it was clear that the insurrection had engulfed the center of the city, but with no sign of outside relief from Soviet forces.[14]

For the first few hours the fighting was isolated to numerous small incidents. Tanks from outside supported Germans barricaded inside their buildings. Each Home Army unit fought independently, and consequently it was extremely difficult to get from one street to another. Inhabitants inside the houses began blasting holes in the walls of their cellars, gaining access to adjoining houses that ran parallel with the streets outside; thus they opened a wide, large subterranean labyrinth of underground passages. It ran through adjoining cellars and in some cases across the back courtyards of the houses. By such underground access Home Army units moved and people transported both the wounded and ammunition; the network assured personal liaison. All along the route security corps soldiers stayed on duty to keep traffic rolling, which also included numerous civilians who lived in those buildings where the catacomb-like spaces were located. Irena Orska, an Underground nurse, described conditions in the cellars in this way:

> Both sides of the narrow passages running through the laby-
> rinth were jammed with chairs, tables, and beds on which
> people had earlier been trying to sleep. Their faces were gray
> with the mould of the caves they rotted in. Their eyes were

poignant, watchful, inquiring. They were the eyes of people who had given up everything and suffered in dreadful silence, with clenched teeth and tearless hearts. Nursing women and pregnant women, old women who could hardly move or talk, children and aged men, sick and feeble, were all huddled here. Condemned to darkness, to waiting and to nothingness, they crouched alongside the damp walls, not quite alive, and not yet dead, following us, the couriers and officers of the Home Army . . . .[15]

Throughout August 2 heavy rain fell, but this did not lessen the fighting. The Home Army completed the capture of Wola in the early morning hours with the effective cooperation of the Polish Socialist Party militia, which was now a part of the Home Army. Paper-delivery boys were on the streets passing out Home Army's *Information Bulletin* carrying declarations from the military and political authorities and instructions from the civilian commissioner. All the dead, both German and Polish, were to be given temporary burial. All self-appointed courts were banned. All members of the regular German Army were to be treated as prisoners of war according to the Geneva Convention. All those accused of collaborating with the enemy and those who had declared themselves *Volksdeutsche* were to be handed over to special courts and all members of the Gestapo and all SS men were to be court-martialed and treated as war criminals.[16]

In the historic center of the city, Home Army attacks failed, their losses were high, and their fighters captured none of the principal strongpoints. But by blocking and fortifying apartment blocks, streets, and alleys, the Resistance managed to carve out three central pockets of territory in the city that they could defend from German assaults. They believed they would only have to wait a few days at most for the Red Army arrived. Thus the Poles anticipated a battle of attrition in the first few days.

On August 3, without any specific orders and on their own initiative, the inhabitants of neighboring houses put up barricades to hamper the movement of German tanks. From windows they threw out tables, divans, cupboards, chests—everything movable they possessed. Among the furniture taken from a German lodging was a pram. Residents tore up paving stones and used blocks of cement; they dug a deep trench in front of this barrier of miscellaneous objects.[17]

Wherever they could, Poles removed signs of the foreign occupying presence in the city. They took down German store signs and street names. They dragged photos of Hitler and other prominent Nazis from German offices and hung them on the outside of barricades to be disfigured by Germans firing at the barricades.[18]

The resistance to the Germans manifested itself in many ways. Here are the words "Poland Will Win," one of many slogans written along the Vistula embankment in Warsaw.

Insurgents actually did not remain behind these obstructions, since the structures attracted fire from German tanks. Instead they took positions on either side of the street, just before or just beyond the barricades, where they waited with light weapons to return the fire of German infantry or throw Molotov cocktails onto the tanks. Even children who had never built sandcastles were at war; children who had never played in a world at peace now played a grim and terrible game in a world at war. Sometimes children volunteered to approach tanks with these bottles filled with gasoline. Adults had to restrain them from running into the open and throwing them directly in front of the tanks.[19]

Although insurgents most feared mortars—these gave no warning by sound and no time to take cover before they hit—they found air raids equally terrifying. Whole apartment complexes caved in under bombings. German infantry followed up with ground attacks by over the heaps of collapsed buildings. Insurgents struggled to assist civilians and fellow soldiers buried beneath the ruins while others were simultaneously trying to stop the advancing Germans.

The uprising enraged the Nazi leaders. At the same time they saw it as a pretext for punishing Warsaw once and for all. Hitler's initial response was a demand that all German units withdraw from Warsaw and the city be bombed out of existence by the *Luftwaffe*. This proved impossible, since Polish insurgents blocked their withdrawal. Hitler, giving the same overall directive—completely destroy Warsaw—left the details of the solution up to SS Reichsführer Himmler and Chief of Staff and tank tactician General Guderian. With a plan to use heavy artillery in street fighting, Guderian was prepared to destroy the city completely and Himmler issued an order not to take any prisoners, explicitly demanding that German troops kill every Warsaw citizen, including women and children. Warsaw was to be leveled to the ground.[20]

On August 4, Warsaw witnessed the entrance of two notorious Nazi SS brigades: the Dirlewanger Regiment, of with common criminals making up 50 percent of its soldiers, and the Kaminski Brigade, which consisted of Soviet prisoners who had been freed and enlisted in German units, as well as collaborating former Ukrainian soldiers. On August 5 in Wola, in the western part of the city, German troops forced citizens out into the streets block by block and shot to death an estimated thirty-five thousand. The soldiers' brutality and lack of any humaneness resulted in horrifying atrocities that were followed by extensive looting, mass rapes of the female population, and the burning of hospitals.[21] The same pattern of murdering, looting, and raping occurred in Ochota, an adjacent western suburb of the city. Once word of the atrocities in Wola and Ochota had spread to other parts of the city, the defiance that characterized the Polish defenders was intensified, even during the next month, bringing about an even closer bond between the Home Army and the civilian population. On the fourth day of fighting, a few hundred Polish Communists responded to a PPR declaration calling on its members to join in the struggle and accept tactical orders from Home Army sector commanders. By this time the Home Army numbered some forty-six thousand men.

Meanwhile, the Poles still awaited a response from Moscow and for coordinated help of military operations. Yet Soviet-controlled broadcasts continued to be silent on the subject of the uprising. German forces now compelled Soviet troops, which according to Moscow's own communiqué had been about to capture Warsaw, on the east bank of the Vistula River. According to Soviet forces, the forces made towards Warsaw, but after a German counter-attack on July 30th, the Soviet commander issued an order on August 1 to assume a defensive position outside of Praga that same day, *an hour before the first shots of the uprising were exchanged.* German forces attacked again on August 3. In order to avoid encirclement, the Soviets withdrew, and by August 5, again took up a defensive position. The official Soviet position maintains that "Soviet troops could not proceed with the same high speed of advance, and therefore were unable to give immediate help to the insurgents."[22] During the ten days of its offensive, the Soviet Armored Army had covered 220 miles, lost 500 tanks, and was very low on fuel and ammunition and "that at the end of July, even before the Warsaw Uprising, the tempo of the offensive had greatly slowed. The German Supreme Command had by this time thrown very strong reserves against the main sectors of the Soviet advance. German resistance was strong and tenacious."[23]

On August 8, Soviet commanders recovered their offensive spirits and submitted to the Soviet supreme command an operational report with a plan for liberating Warsaw, setting August 25 as the date for the operation's commencement. Units regrouped on the assumption that they would be allowed to proceed with the "seizure of Warsaw." But permission to proceed was not forthcoming.

It seems reasonable to assume that "it was during the second week in August 1944 that Stalin decided to halt the seizure of Warsaw because the date on which the true intentions toward Warsaw were decisively revealed was August 13, when the Soviet news agency TASS issued a communication condemning the Uprising."[24] According to a former major in the Soviet Army, a member of Soviet Field Commander Marshal Konstantin Rokossovsky's personal staff, the latter received a radiogram directly from Stalin "ordering him to leave the Warsaw people to their own fate," and that later a blunt written order came: "Stop the offensive! Let the Poles feel their dependence on the actions of our Army!"[25]

After receiving the order from Stalin, Rokossovsky claimed that the uprising was a mistake, since the insurgents started it prematurely without consulting the Red Army; that the uprising should have started only when the Red Army actually entered Warsaw; and that the Poles rose up before this had occurred. Nevertheless, had Stalin wanted the liberation of Warsaw by the Soviet Army in conjunction with the Home Army uprising, he could have indicated publicly by the 9th or 10th of August that his armies would attempt the seizure of the city. Or he could have approved Rokossovsky's plan to seize Warsaw after the middle of August. As the supreme Soviet commander, Stalin alone had the power to order Rokossovsky's army forward toward Warsaw or to stop it. According to Polish historian J. K. Zawodny, the fact that Stalin did not order the army to move ahead indicates that the Soviet leader's decision concerning Warsaw was dictated not by military, but rather by political considerations, and was an element of Soviet foreign policy.[26]

In the early morning of August 5, the *Luftwaffe* attacked Wola, dropping bombs at low altitude, as low as within one hundred feet above the rooftops. Dense smoke covered the entire district. Thick columns of smoke billowed over the immediate vicinity of the Home Army command headquarters. Carrying with them what remained of their belongings, people fled their burning houses in search of safer quarters. In the afternoon, German planes dropped leaflets with the faked signature of General Bór-Komorowski announcing that the Home Army was negotiating with the Germans on the question of common action against the Soviets. But after five years of brutal occupation the Polish people were not easily misled by German lies and were not deceived by the German forgeries.

On the evening of August 6, the situation at the AK command headquarters sector grew increasingly worse. The factory was under continuous enemy machine-gun fire. Neighboring houses had already been destroyed and maintaining any liaison was now nearly impossible. As a result, command headquarters moved from Wola to another part of the city. Headquarters personnel could only make the withdrawal through the ruins of the ghetto to *Stare Miasto* or Old Town, an insurgent enclave on the banks of the Vistula River; it was a district of high, narrow, ancient houses, reminiscent of central European towns of the Middle Ages. Houses and churches huddled together, flanking the narrow streets. The new command headquarters moved into part of a school that the Germans had transformed into a hospital. Certain buildings in the adjacent area, such as the Treasury Printing Building on the river side, the town hall toward the City Center, and the Bank of Poland, served as strong defensive points in the district.[27]

The first week of the uprising ended in somewhat of a stalemate, as both the insurgents and the Germans fell short of what they expected to achieve. Both the opening assault by the insurgents and the later German counterattack fell short of their goals. Far more civilians had been killed than combatants. And neither side was willing to halt the fighting. In fact it continued with unrelenting intensity.[28]

The German strategy, although holding back the Soviet advance, kept the uprising separate from operations at the front. A cordon encircled Warsaw, strengthened by two reserve Hungarian divisions, while the Germans took measures to keep open an east-west supply line. Guards received reinforcements on the Vistula bridges and the eastern suburb of Praga, where the insurgents had been defeated and which was heavily fortified.

The Home Army strategy concentrated almost exclusively on active defense. No longer able to rely on the element of surprise and lacking heavy weapons, the insurgents could only mount local counterattacks and were constantly forced to make tactical withdrawals. Poles sustained their hopes by witnessing the German inability to strike a final knockout blow. Soviet intentions remained ominously obscure as their presence on the far side of the Vistula remained ever more ominous. "Death from surrender was seen as more likely than death in combat. So combat continued."[29]

After the loss of Wola to the Germans, the character of the fighting changed considerably, with intensified air attacks, tanks, and artillery, and the systematic burning of houses one by one. The fight for Warsaw had now split up into a series of isolated actions. Old Town had not yet been touched by fire or bombing. But air raids in other areas had forced the entire population to take shelter in the cellars beneath the old houses in the created subterranean passages. Moving from place to place was a difficult and exhausting process. Germans encircled the Old Town sector, but they had not yet entered the district. During the first week of the uprising, thousands of civilians from Wola and Ochota fled there. By August 9 German forces barred all usual routes. There was only one safe route to Old Town: through the sewers. Streets no longer had the appearance they once had before the uprising. Many were not even recognizable. Pavement was torn up and the citizenry used stones and blocks of cement to make barricades. Overturned tramcars, carts, and miscellaneous furniture were still very much in evidence. By the second week of August, there were about 170,000 people crowded into the district—approximately twice the normal population.[30]

The defenders of Old Town, Home Army insurgents, were a

mixture of incongruous elements unlike soldiers in most all other armies. Some wore German SS uniforms that they had either taken from vacated stores or from captured prisoners, but they were recognizable by their AK red-and-white armbands. Others wore Polish Army pre-1939 uniforms that they had kept. Their metal hats also varied: they were German, Polish, French, and Russian, some dating back to the previous war, and even included firemen's helmets. In addition, their blouses and tunics varied in color and design.[31]

Every day, new waves of civilian refugees from other parts of the city poured in to find refuge and relief. Nurses, soldiers, and liaison girls were on hand to assist those descending the sewers down narrow ladders of iron rods into the darkness below. Initially, the sewers were high enough to walk in, though most people had to stoop down. At first the area was dry and the stench did not seem too bad. People moved ahead in single file. After a while the area became larger, enabling people to straighten up and even walk in pairs. But as they proceeded farther through the darkened areas, conditions grew worse. The pipes became narrower and people were forced to breathe filthy air. Some got sick with nausea from the hateful stench. Eventually the sewers became so small that people had to get down on all fours and crawl ahead like monkeys on hands and knees, wrist-and ankle-deep in dirt and human excrement. People could not stop crawling for a moment because of others behind them. The sense of unbearable weariness was too much for some. Moans and cries echoed in the tunnels. Three-and-a-half hours after finally reaching the manhole in Old Town where they could ascend into daylight, one person said that if she had to go any farther, even a few more steps, and she would fall flat on her face and died there, drowned in slime. It was worse than being in a tomb.[32] Once above ground, people were led away into the cellars of the old medieval homes or to the hospital for needed relief.

It was not until August 19, toward the end of the third week, that the Germans mounted a concerted attack on Old Town that went on until September 2. By the middle of August the insurgents were holding the district in strength. The assault began when *Luftwaffe* Junkers and Stuka dive-bombers made ceaseless strikes throughout the area. At first they attacked every hour, but later the intervals between raids were reduced to fifteen minutes. Heavy artillery bombardment heaved from self-propelled artillery, tanks, mortars, and guns positioned on railway platforms accompanied the air raids. The Poles made an attempt to break out of Old Town on August 22 and establish contact with the Żoliborz sector, but they was unsuccessful. It is estimated that during the three-week battle 3,500 to 4,500 tons of shells fell on an area three-quarters of a square mile. From morning until night, Poles felt the profusion of firepower. Thousands of men and women were buried alive under the debris that had made up the seven hundred homes that had been destroyed.[33]

By the fourth week of August, General Bór-Komorowski was forced to prepare a military withdrawal to the City Center sector through the sewers, the only way left to get out of the Old Town district. To evacuate the entire detachment of 1,500 defenders would mean leaving the entire district undefended. And the manhole from which they were to evacuate was only two hundred yards from German positions and covered by their grenades and machine guns.

On the night of September 1 the 1,500 soldiers, 500 civilians, and 100 German prisoners began the 1,700-yard trek through the sewers.[34] Throughout September the sewers became the route of withdrawal for military units and civilians evacuating from overrun positions taken by the Germans. Those fleeing even transported the wounded underground and insurgents ran telephone cables through the sewers. At first the Germans did not realize that the soldiers were making use of the sewers. It was not until they accidentally came across a sewer during a tunnel excavation that they realized the Home

Army was using the sewers as a system for movement and communications. It was then that the Germans devised several cunning ruses to frustrate the uses being made of the underground tunnels. They hung hand grenades with the pins removed in the tunnels. If a man crawling along struck one of them, the grenade immediately blew him to pieces. Another method conceived by the Germans involved pouring gasoline at certain crossing places in the sewers and setting it on fire. This stream of fire would then meet a column of approaching men. Those at the head of the file might jump to the side to avoid the fire and save themselves, but others would die in the flames. Frequently the man in front of such a procession—fearing his approach to an open manhole where Germans were situated—would hold up an entire convoy. In these places Germans dropped hand grenades, mines, smoke bombs, and canisters of corrosive gas.[35] The Polish defeat in Old Town was the turning point of the uprising, even though the tenacity of those soldiers in the district to solidify their defenses for eleven days and nights against the advancing German attack enabled the other insurgent sectors in the city to last for another thirty days.

Meanwhile it was now clear to both the Americans and the British that aid from the Soviets was not forthcoming. American Ambassador Averell Harriman sent a request to Stalin's Commissar for Foreign Affairs Vyacheslav Molotov; he wanted approval from the Red Air Force for a shuttle mission of American bombers, situated at air bases in the Soviet Union, to drop arms on Warsaw for the Resistance forces, since it was impossible to intervene with long-range bombers from England. The Soviets simply ignored the fact that Warsaw was separated from the nearest Allied air bases in the West by well over 850 miles and from Italy by more than 750 miles, almost entirely over enemy-held territory. By September 1, Stalin made clear that he would not take responsibility for refusing to provide aid to the Poles in Warsaw. The moment had now come when the Polish government in London was being told to come to terms with the Communist "Polish" National Committee.[36]

On September 10, the Soviets had what first appeared to be a change of heart or a change in tactics. Soviet artillery fell upon the eastern outskirts of Warsaw accompanied by Soviet planes. From September 14 onwards the Soviet Air Force dropped supplies in bags on Warsaw, but without parachutes. The contents were American canned food and rifle ammunition, but most were smashed and of no use to the Resistance forces. The following night the Soviets dropped heavy weaponry, machine guns, and large numbers of hand grenades, again all without parachutes. The following day the Soviets occupied the Praga district, leaving the Poles the impression that they would cross the Vistula and come to their rescue, but by going no farther inland, they demonstrated their total lack of concern for the survival of Warsaw and for the lives of the non-Communist Poles who were now on the brink of defeat.[37]

On September 18, after numerous pleas from the Poles to the Americans and British to provide aid and the Soviet refusal to allow American planes to use their bases, a massive force of 110 American B-17 Flying Fortresses and three escort groups of P-51 Mustangs took off from English airfields. The planes dropped 1,284 containers of supplies with multicolored parachutes. Out of the 110 bombers, 105 arrived in Russia, where limited access to Soviet airfields was then given by Stalin.[38] This token cooperation by Stalin was designed to enable him to refute any claim that he did nothing to help the Poles.

After the Soviet occupation of Praga, Soviet activity grew less and less. All major German positions east of the Vistula had been overrun. The Germans then resumed a systematic destruction of

Warsaw. Small groups of German Stuka dive-bombers circled the capital and bombed from the air. After the earlier two-month destruction of Wola and Ochota, the Germans now concentrated on the Żoliborz and Mokotów sectors of the city, repeating the air and artillery attacks that converted the districts into masses of rubble.

Throughout Warsaw the daily food situation and sanitary conditions had become appalling. Besides hunger, there was a dire lack of water, even for the sick and wounded who poured into the hospital day and night. Doctors carried out surgical operations without anesthetics in cellars by the light of a few candles. Dressing materials were short and medical personnel used paper to stop hemorrhages. People became indifferent to everything. They had used up all their strength, and there were no more men to clear the rubble. Additionally, the Soviets still left unanswered all Polish proposals to organize a combined attack by Polish and Soviet forces on the German positions.

In mid-August and throughout early September, the German command proposed capitulation to the Polish command that included a promise of combatant status for the Home Army insurgents. But before responding, the insurgents requested further instructions from London on what action to take. On the thirty-sixth day of the uprising, in anticipation of far more bloodshed, death, and destruction, General Bór-Komorowski sent the following radio message to London:

> *The civilian population is undergoing a crisis that can have*
> *a definite impact on the insurgents' combat capacity. We are*
> *in crisis and these are the reasons: (1) the town is being bom-*
> *barded with growing intensity and complete impunity; (2)*
> *there is a general conviction that the enemy is attempting to*

destroy completely the entire territory of Warsaw, including Old Town and central Warsaw; (3) there has been an extension of fighting with no end in sight; (4) smaller and smaller rations, bordering on starvation; (5) great mortality among infants; (6) a stirring-up of the population by unfriendly elements; and (7) lack of water and electricity in all parts of the city.[39]

Both Bór-Komorowski and the delegate of the Polish government in Poland sent an additional communiqué to the Polish prime minister and commander in chief in London. It proposed three possible courses of action: after obtaining agreement from the Germans, the removal the civilians and then fight to the death; unconditional surrender; or sector-by-sector surrender as and where the Germans attacked them, which would allow further time for the Soviet Army to cross the Vistula River but would result in wholesale destruction of the city.[40] The appeals were of no avail. They received no assistance for the relief of Warsaw or instructions as to which course of action to take. As a result both Bór-Komorowski and General Monter, commander of the uprising, decided to fight on to the end. The fact that neither Roosevelt nor Churchill nor, above all, the Polish government-in-exile in London did anything to assist the Poles in a search for alternatives to end the conflict left the people, both the insurgents and the civilian population, completely alone. The ever-present questions were: Will the Soviet Army come to our assistance? How long can we hold out? Should we capitulate? The military leaders refused to surrender because they still hoped that diplomatic efforts might move the Soviet Army to come to their aid. An equal concern was the fear that both insurgents and civilians might be completely annihilated by the Germans after they surrendered.[41]

On September 26 Mokotów fell. The hopeless situation in which the insurgents found themselves prompted Bór-Komorowski to dismiss any further hope of a response from the Soviets and ordered the surrender of Żoliborz. On September 28 the Germans proposed capitulation to General Bór-Komorowski. After failing to receive any further response from Soviet commander Rokossovsky about assistance to Warsaw, the Polish AK commander agreed to a cease-fire and to capitulation. On October 2 the surrender agreement was signed at German headquarters with General Erich von dem Bach-Zelewski, who expressed praise and admiration for the courage of the Home Army.[42] The agreement also provided for the evacuation of the civilian population on October 1, 2, and 3. After two months of uninterrupted fighting, the uprising ended. In accordance with the rights of the Geneva Convention all AK soldiers were to be treated as prisoners of war.

St. Florian Church in Warsaw amidst a wilderness of ruins and mountains of rubble. It was destroyed by the Germans as they withdrew from Poland in 1944 after the Warsaw Uprising and was rebuilt and restored in 1972. It currently serves approximately one million Catholics.

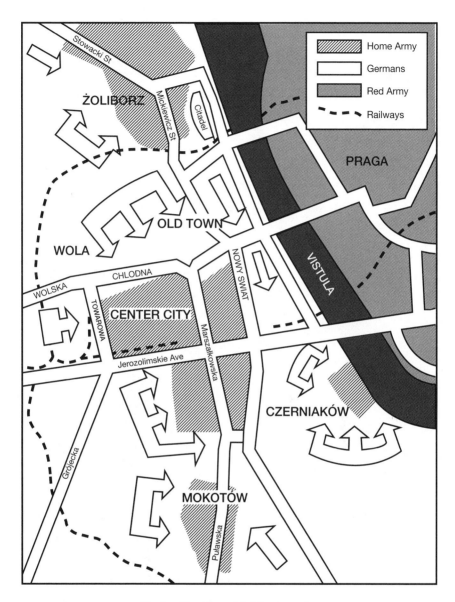

**Early October 1944 near the
ending of the Warsaw Uprising.**

Throughout the lamentable sixty-three day uprising in Warsaw, a residual community of over a million people, the loss of human life, the pain and suffering, the anguish, the psychological and emotional trauma, let alone the wasteland of physical devastation and mountains of rubble that resulted from the life-and-death struggle, can scarcely be explained or described by statistical data. But they do convey a measure of the severity of what transpired: insurgents killed in combat 10,200; missing 7,000; gravely wounded 5,000; total losses 22,200; 10,000 Germans were killed; 7,000 were missing; and 9,000 were wounded; total losses were 26,000. Civilians killed in Warsaw were between 200,000 and 250,000, and 700,000 were evacuated during and after the uprising and sent to concentration camps or to forced labor camps in the Reich.

In accordance with Hitler's orders, the city was razed, building by building. By the time of the final German withdrawal from the city, the Germans had demolished 85 percent of Warsaw: 10,455 buildings destroyed, 923 historical buildings, 25 churches, 14 libraries, 64 high schools, and 81 elementary schools.[43]

No nation in history—certainly no nation in modern history—had undergone what the Poles underwent, not only in the uprising, but also in the preceding four and a half years of German tyrannical rule. In the period immediately after the war it was assumed that Poland's fight would significantly help influence Poland's political future. The Poles came to realize that that assumption was wrong. But the principal impediment was that, both geographically and geopolitically, and for which neither they nor their allies were responsible, their country lay directly between Scylla and Charybdis—Germany to the west and Soviet Russia to the east. And as the highly regarded Polish historian and former member of the Resistance who took part in the uprising, J. K. Zawodny, stated: "In August 1944, they (the Poles)

would have been damned if they fought and damned if they didn't. In their own concept of honour and duty, they chose to fight rather than to wait passively for events to overtake them. They reaped destruction, but in their own cultural style, defending their homes and national independence."[44]

Afterthoughts on the Uprising

There can be no nobler national motive than to fight selflessly for one's freedom and independence. Remarkably, since mid-1940, Polish armed forces had been engaged in other theaters of war, having fought in the air throughout the Battle of Britain, in the Narvik ground campaign of Norway, in Tobruk in North Africa, in the Battle of the Atlantic, in Italy at Monte Cassino, in Falaise, France, after the Allied invasion of Normandy, and in the parachute landings at Arnhem in the Netherlands.[1] No other European country had made such sacrifice and support to Britain's war effort. And as General Bór-Komorowski later explained, "Fighting everywhere, we could not remain passive on our own land. The nation that wants to live in freedom could not be passive at moments when its fate is being decided."[2]

Nevertheless, from a more contemporary perspective, the dramatic events of 1944 appear quite different. According to Jan Nowak, a secret courier who, as an emissary, spoke with Winston Churchill, Anthony Eden, and other Allied leaders in support of Poland against Stalin's designs for subjugation, "the Warsaw Rising, which ended in rivers of spilled blood and the almost total destruction of the nation's capital, seemed at the time to be a wasted sacrifice; for after Teheran, Poland's independence was irretrievably lost."[3] On a practical plane, the Warsaw Uprising, taken for the most honorable motives, was a blameworthy, lightheaded enterprise that consigned the Polish nation to defeat and did nothing to enhance or strengthen the Polish political institutions in the postwar period that were established in the formative years of the Resistance. It was the inability of those institutions to survive, brought about in no small measure by political events and circumstances over which the Poles had no control, and the foreboding consequences which led to the irretrievable loss of Poland's independence for almost the next half-century.

The series of events that ultimately led to the Warsaw Uprising began shortly after the untimely death of General Sikorski in the air crash in 1943. Besides being prime minister, he was also the commander in chief of the armed forces. After his death that power was divided between two men who were both personal and political enemies: Stanisław Mikołajczyk, who became prime minister, and Kazimierz Sosnkowski, who was supreme commander-in-chief of the Polish Armed Forces. When discussions were taking place concerning the proposed uprising, Sosnkowski produced a number of recommendations, warnings, and advice, but was unable to make firm decisions and failed to provide an unambiguous strategic plan for the Home Army. In addition, he involved his subordinates in Warsaw in London's political arguments and undermined his own authority and that of the government by openly criticizing Mikołajczyk to them.

Under the circumstances, the prime minister tried to shift to Warsaw decisions about such vital matters as Poland's postwar borders, participation of Communists in the government, and the issue of the general uprising. But since most of the Poles in London opposed the prime minister's policies , he deferred to those leaders in Warsaw for support. Under these circumstances, the Underground leaders in Poland had no other recourse but to take matters into their own hands.[4] Unfortunately, neither the leaders in Warsaw nor the Polish public realized that the fate of their country had been decided when the future occupation zones were settled by the Western Allies and the Soviet Union.

The Poles in Warsaw had only one source of information: London radio. Both the BBC and Polish Radio in London focused their news coverage principally on Polish developments, which were obviously of primary interest to the audience inside occupied Poland. This created a self-centered reaction among the Poles, a kind of illusion that the attention of the whole world was focused on their country and that they had become the object of general admiration among the Allied powers. "Nothing could shake the Poles' deep-rooted faith that the Western Allies would resist any open onslaught on the independence of Poland."[5]

The one critical source of information that the Poles lacked was military intelligence, which only the Soviet command could have supplied. The plan to seize Warsaw in that short period between German withdrawal and the arrival of the Soviet Army was entirely dependent on intelligence that the Poles never received. The idea that Warsaw could have been held by the Home Army as representative of the government-in-exile, without a subsequent confrontation with the Soviets, was rejected by all previous experience. The notion that the Western powers could have afforded to take the part of the Poles in any major dispute with their Soviet allies was, to say the least, groundless.[6]

What the Poles received was Soviet propaganda radioed to Warsaw from Moscow in the form of false allegations that the Home Army was collaborating with Germany. After the Teheran Conference at a meeting with British Foreign Secretary Anthony Eden, Polish Prime Minister Mikołajczyk was told that "Stalin, on two separate occasions, had accused the Polish Home Army of fighting and killing Soviet and Communist partisans active in Poland. Not only did

Eden not reject these allegations outright; he demanded that the Poles prove them untrue."[7] In order to counter the Soviet lies, the Polish Underground leadership had to prove their loyalty to the Allies by escalating military attacks against the Germans and refraining from clashes with Soviet and Communist partisans. They realized that this was an essential precondition for obtaining Allied help in defense of Polish independence.[8] In addition to pushing the Poles to step up their partisan warfare against the Germans, Churchill and Eden pushed them to make territorial concessions to the Soviets as a demonstration of Allied goodwill, in the hope that Moscow could be brought to take a more conciliatory attitude. Nevertheless, the British had neither the will nor the means to press successfully for a Polish-Soviet compromise. Churchill simply had one single goal: the unconditional surrender of Nazi Germany.[9]

It was the fifth year of the war and Germany was already experiencing persistent Allied bombing attacks—the Americans by day and the British by night—and at the same time the Soviets were fast approaching a fifty-mile front from the east toward Warsaw. Those Germans who returned home on leave confirmed that the end was approaching. And in Warsaw,

> *Handfuls of people stood on street corners, watching with a quiet smile as trucks were loaded with wardrobes, mirrors, and rugs—the contents of German offices and private homes. They were fleeing. No one was afraid of them anymore. The posters ordering all males to report for work on fortifications were received with jeers. You could already hear Russian*

*artillery fire. Rumors of an armed uprising were greeted joy-
fully: a chance to throw oneself at one's tormentors and take
revenge.*[10]

Feeling for their own predicament, the Germans prepared for
a last-minute desperate defense of Warsaw when the Poles rose up in
armed rebellion with the expectation that the Soviets, who were now
only twenty-five miles away from Warsaw, would soon enter the city.
Although the German fighting strength was divided on the Soviet
front and in the city of Warsaw in the late summer of 1944, it still
represented a considerable force, totaling 327 divisions and brigades.[11]

When Bór-Komorowski gave the order to start the uprising, he
hoped that the Soviet Army would enter Warsaw in the first days of
August. But it was only a half-hour later after giving the command
that he learned that the Soviet tanks sighted on the other side of the
Vistula River in Praga were not part of the main body of the Soviet
Army, but part of an isolated patrol of a Soviet unit. But the couriers carrying the orders to start the uprising had already made their
way into the cellars, homes, and byways of Warsaw and could not be
recalled on short notice.[12] Given the benefit of hindsight, the highly
regarded historical analyst, Norman Davies, stated that "the stage for
tragedy was set."[13]

During the first four days of the conflict the insurgents occupied
Warsaw's city center, but failed to take some of the more principal locations such as the airport, the main central station, the Vistula bridges,
or the vital right-bank district of Praga. The command to start the
uprising came so suddenly that most of the units were either ill armed
or without weapons yet facing a well-armed Nazi war machine. Their
intention was probably no different from that of the French Resistance,
which started the gun battle in Paris as the U.S. Army approached
the city. The outcome, of course, was entirely different. For the next

fifty-nine days the Poles were on the defensive, day by day, street by street, and the Polish capital and most of the inhabitants were reduced to ashes.

The Germans directed their energies as much against the defenseless civilian population as they did against the insurgents. They set hospitals, with their nurses and patients, on fire. They commonly carried out the wholesale execution of civilians. They drove rows of civilian hostages in front of the German infantry as a shield against snipers. While 1,500 survivors carried 500 casualties on stretchers and down a manhole into the sewers, 4 containers of arms and supplies were dropped into Warsaw from miles of waste-deep sewage to safer places. In mid-September 1,800 British and American planes dropped arms and supplies, but the Germans picked up 90 percent of the containers. And under British orders, the Polish Parachute Brigade was sent to Arnhem in the Netherlands rather than to Warsaw.[14] To have continued the struggle would have meant the entire obliteration of the Warsaw inhabitants, both the insurgents and the civilian population.

All available evidence leads to the widely held belief that Stalin deliberately deceived the Poles by encouraging Warsaw to rise up while holding back his own forces in order to ensure the destruction of his political rivals in Poland by the Germans. On August 16 in Moscow, the U.S. ambassador was told that "the Soviet government did not wish to associate directly or indirectly with the adventure in Warsaw." And in a letter to Churchill and Roosevelt, Stalin denounced the leaders of the uprising as "a group of criminals."[15]

It is unequivocally clear that everything Stalin said and did, or failed to do, points to a calculated deceptiveness that, for the Poles, foreshadowed far darker days ahead.

There were, of course, military factors to be considered in the halting of the Russian offensive. In the middle of August, a plan by Stalin changed military priorities by shifting Soviet forces elsewhere. On August 30 the Russians entered the Romanian capital of Bucharest and headed for Bulgaria. While the Germans were effectively destroying the Polish Underground, the Balkans was falling into Stalin's hands. On August 2, a German panzer counterattack halted Soviet Commander Rokossovsky's intention to invade Warsaw. Then, after deliberate delays by the Soviet leader to authorize the use of Soviet airstrips by Allied planes after returning from Warsaw, Stalin finally granted permission; as an ally, Stalin felt obligated to permit their use. Beginning on September 14, the Soviet Air Force dropped supplies, but without parachutes, and the containers smashed, becoming useless. So the amount of Soviet military assistance was minimal, and much of what was of use fell into German hands. And in answer to a plea by the British War Cabinet to Moscow for aid to Warsaw, the Soviet response included a message that partially blamed the British government for failing to give them an advance warning of the Warsaw Uprising. It also made reference to a British failure to prevent the Poles from their action in connection with the Katyn Forest incident.[16]

One should also bear in mind that after an Allied Western Front had been established in Normandy and with the Soviet advances on the Eastern Front, it did not seem advisable for the British and Americans to disturb the Russians for the sake of Poland. Roosevelt seemed far more concerned with garnering favor with Stalin than helping the Poles, since he realized the importance of favorable relations with the Soviets to end the war against Germany, and even to end the war with Japan, particularly if an invasion of the Japanese home islands was necessary to end that phase of the war.

Although most historians agree that the decision to engage in the Warsaw Uprising was a tragic mistake, what was even more tragic were the bargaining negotiations at Teheran in November 1943 that were later formalized at Yalta in 1945, which granted moral legitimacy to what Joseph Stalin had acquired by sheer force: Russian domination not only of Poland but practically all of Eastern Europe, including East Germany. Norman Davies, whose two-volume work *God's Playground: a History of Poland* is regarded as probably the most authoritative study of the country, expressed it best: "To anyone who lived through the war in Poland, the diplomatic negotiations concerning the country's future possess an air of unreality. They did little to relieve the agonies of the Occupation . . . ."[17]

Street kitchens feeding those made homeless by the fighting.

It is my considered opinion that the most memorable words concerning the uprising came from one of the last radio broadcasts from Warsaw in October 1944:

> *Your heroes are the soldiers whose only weapons against tanks, planes, and guns were their revolvers and bottles filled with petrol. Your heroes are the women who tended the wounded and carried messages under fire, who cooked in bombed and ruined cellars to feed children and adults, and who soothed and comforted the dying. Heroes are the children who went on quietly playing among the smoldering ruins. These are the people of Warsaw.*
>
> *Immortal is the nation that can muster such universal heroism. For those who have died have conquered, and those who live on will fight on, will conquer, and again bear witness that Poland lives when the Poles live.*[18]

CHAPTER SIXTEEN
Tyranny Replaced

Yalta's Death Blow to Polish Hopes [The Crimea Conference] ought to spell the end of the system of unilateral action, the exclusive alliances, the spheres of influence, the balance of power, and all the other expedients that have been tried for centuries—and have always failed.

—FRANKLIN D. ROOSEVELT, (1882–1945)
32ND PRESIDENT OF THE UNITED STATES

In the summer of 1944, while the Allies advanced through France, the Red Army made solid progress on the Eastern Front. In October, since the Soviets occupied more Polish territory, Stalin wanted to create the belief among the Polish population that the Soviet occupation was not what it seemed. He did this by transforming some of the Red Army soldiers, as well as some members of the Soviet Air Force, fitting them with Polish uniforms so as to portray them as Polish soldiers and airmen. Those who were selected for this deception were taught to write and speak Polish and to provide false cover stories to the Polish people concerning the parts of Poland they came from. The

Soviet leader ordered this deception in order to create the impression that the Polish armed forces were totally loyal to the Soviet Union.[1]

With the Warsaw capitulation of the Home Army forces, which had now been left without any leadership, to the Germans, and with the subsequent Soviet advance through Poland, the Soviet government maintained an increasingly overbearing attitude concerning the Polish question throughout the remaining months of the war. The American chargé d'affaires in Moscow, George F. Kennan, described Stalin's behavior at the gates of Warsaw as "the most arrogant and unmistakable demonstration of the Soviet determination to control Eastern Europe in the postwar period."[2]

Within one week after the surrender to the Germans, and while Germans forcibly removed thousands of Warsaw civilians from their city and sent them to camps in Germany, Churchill flew to Moscow to confer with Stalin over the future of Eastern Europe. The British prime minister was also concerned with obtaining Soviet help in the final attack on Japan and also on a resolution of the Polish situation.

The Soviets were moving into Romania and Bulgaria, and while Hungary and Yugoslavia lay in the shadow of the Red Army, the two world leaders discussed the postwar Balkan arrangements, which included a rough division of the respective spheres of influence for the Soviet Union and Great Britain. Churchill proposed the so-called Percentages Agreement, which referred to proportions of an intended involvement in which Russia would have 90 percent influence in Romania, 75 percent in Bulgaria, and Britain would have 90 percent influence in Greece. Both Hungary and Yugoslavia would be equally divided at 50 percent to each of the two powers.[3] Churchill later realized that his proposal would be viewed as nothing more than a crude and callous attempt to deal with the Soviet advance into Eastern Europe if exposed to the scrutiny of the Foreign Office and diplomats all over the world,[4] even though the informal "percentages" discussion was temporary and not a legally binding agreement. Nevertheless, it was an omen of what was later to be expected from the Soviet leader concerning the future of Eastern Europe. The agreement said nothing about Poland, since the matter of the eastern frontier, "spheres of influence," and the country's postwar government had yet to be resolved. The issue was made more urgent by the fact that Poland had two completely different governments: one in exile in London, recognized by Great Britain and the United States, and one in Warsaw, recognized by the Soviet Union.

On October 13, discussions concerning Poland began. The Polish premier, Mikołajczyk, and Bolesław Bierut, acting on behalf of the Soviet-sponsored Polish Lublin Committee, were also present at the Moscow meeting. Being at the meeting with Stalin and Molotov, and fully aware of the insistence of the Soviet demand for the 1939 "Peace Boundary"—now called the Curzon Line as the demarcation line of the Polish-Soviet border—Mikołajczyk counted on the Western diplomats to help reach a compromise. The fate of several million people in Eastern Poland, an area that included the major central cultural city of Lwów (Lviv), hung in the balance. Then Bierut, who represented the Soviet-sponsored Lublin Committee, said, "it was the will of the Polish people that the city of Lwów shall belong to Russia."[5] When the Polish premier raised the issue of the Curzon Line frontier, Molotov interrupted him and told everyone at the table that Churchill and Roosevelt had already agreed to the Curzon Line border the previous year at Teheran. Not only was the Polish premier shocked at what Molotov said, but so was Churchill, who had, in an earlier talk he had had with Stalin, regarded the controversial Curzon Line as a proposal, not a firm agreement. However, in a separate private meeting with Stalin at Teheran, Roosevelt assured the Soviet dictator that Churchill's proposal would pose no problems. In fact Roosevelt never told Churchill of the private conversation that took place between the

American president and Stalin. Churchill obviously, too, felt deceived.[6]

Nevertheless, when it came to resolving the Polish issue, the British prime minister's attitude changed. After Mikołajczyk repeatedly refused to agree to the loss of Poland's eastern territories to the Soviet Union, Churchill lost his patience and told the Polish premier that "the sacrifices made by the Soviet Union in the course of the war against Germany and its efforts toward liberating Poland entitle it, in our opinion, to a Western frontier along the Curzon Line." The next day, when Mikołajczyk continued to refuse to accept the loss of Poland's eastern territories, Churchill, in fit of anger, shouted, "You are a callous people who want to wreck Europe. I shall leave you to your troubles. . . . You have no sense of responsibility . . . You do not care about Europe's future . . . You only have your own selfish interests in mind . . . .[7] A month later Mikołajczyk resigned, after holding out against acceptance of the Curzon Line and unable to obtain the help of the Western Allies in arranging a working relationship with the Soviet Union. It was now clear that the government-in-exile in London had lost the prestige and influence it previously possessed and would no longer have any power in deciding the future status of postwar Poland. A new opportunity was opened to the Lublin Committee, since nothing was done to establish a modus vivendi between the Polish pro-Soviet faction and the exiled London government.

On January 5, 1945, in anticipation of the Yalta Conference and contrary to the wishes of both the United States and Great Britain, the Soviet Union recognized the Lublin Committee as the "provisional government" of Poland. After the Teheran Conference the three key Allied leaders, Roosevelt, Stalin, and Churchill, had promised to meet again. Indeed, they agreed that the next summit would convene at

Yalta in the Crimea, which was then part of the Soviet Union. The wartime meeting took place in the Livadiya Palace in early February 1945 and was code-named Operation Argonaut. Stalin had earlier expressed concern about Roosevelt's health at Teheran, but this concern did not translate into action. The Soviet dictator refused to travel further than the Black Sea resort town in Yalta on the Crimean peninsula. And as at Teheran, Churchill and Roosevelt once again were the ones taking long and tiring trips to attend the summit. Each of the three leaders brought their own agenda to the conference. The main goal of British foreign policy at Yalta was to prevent the domination of Europe by a single power taking control of the western part of Europe. He now considered Communism much more dangerous to Europe than German imperialism, which prompted him to embark upon a vigorous anticommunist campaign both at home and abroad.[8]

Roosevelt considered the defeat of Germany his country's top priority, but the struggle with Japan in the Pacific was no less significant, hence the desire to ensure the Soviet entrance into the Pacific war. And he also required Soviet cooperation in the postwar settlement.[8]

Churchill and Roosevelt shared a basic understanding about the fate of Poland. For the Americans, Polish independence was an acid test of Soviet goodwill and an essential guarantee that the hope of a United Nations would become a reality. For the British, since Poland was the initial cause of their entry into the Second World War, the issue was not only a matter of symbolic significance, but also the last hope of withholding Soviet expansion in Eastern Europe. The Soviets, however, were determined to maintain the territorial acquisitions they had secured from the nonaggression pact with Germany in 1939, which assigned the Ukrainian and Byelorussian provinces of Poland to the Soviet Union. They also wanted control over the Polish government.[9]

On February 6, the three world leaders took up the future of the

Polish government. The Soviet leader started by saying that the,

> *Polish question was a matter of honor for the Russian people who in the past had "greatly sinned against Poland," but for them [the Russians] it was also a matter of security, not only because Poland bordered on the Soviet Union, but also because in the last thirty years, Germany had twice invaded Russia through Polish territory.*

Stalin insisted that the Polish Corridor

> *cannot be mechanically shut from outside by Russia. It could be shut from inside only by Poland. It is necessary that Poland be free, independent, and powerful. It is not only a question of honor, but of life and death for the Soviet State. That is why Russia today is against the Czarist policy of abolition of Poland. We have completely changed this inhuman policy and started a policy of friendship and independence for Poland.*[10]

Unlike the earlier Russian Empire, Stalin did not question the right of Poland to exist as an independent state, but neither would he allow Poland complete independence. His reason was not because he was trying to establish a sphere of influence on its borders, but because Germany threatened Soviet Russia through Poland. The Soviet leader was prepared to create a strong Polish state, but for purposes of security, the USSR would have to dominate the state completely.[11]

Roosevelt, who had two main concerns, devised the American strategy at Yalta: Soviet membership in the United Nations and Soviet participation in the war on Japan. In fact the president should never have spent any time agonizing over Soviet involvement in the Pacific War, because Stalin did not need any convincing. The Soviets were intent to assuage the feelings of humiliation that resulted from a long-ago defeat by Japan and the loss of privileges in Manchuria during the much earlier Russo-Japanese War. The Soviets were keen on regaining lost territories and optimistic that they could obtain more lands. Nevertheless, Roosevelt did not believe that further negotiations would do anything to advance the Western agenda and he had no desire to quarrel publicly with the Soviet Union. What he needed was a document on Poland that would satisfy his domestic constituencies, i.e., some six million Poles in the United States, but still be acceptable to Stalin. The leaders spent the last two full days of the conference, February 9 and 10, searching for a compromise that would satisfy public opinion at home and ensure future peace abroad.

The American proposal devised by Roosevelt and presented at the meeting suggested that "the present Polish Provisional Government be reorganized into a fully representative government based on all democratic forces in Poland and including democratic leaders from Poland abroad, to be termed 'The Provisional Government of National Unity.'" By using the word "reorganized," (as opposed to "enlarged" on a wider democratic basis), the Americans gave in to the Soviet demand that the new government be formed on the basis of the existing one, i.e. the Lublin government. The focus of the debate then switched from the form of the provisional government to future elections, which would now become the main issue in the diplomatic debate over Poland.[12]

British Foreign Secretary Anthony Eden expressed grave doubts; he did not believe that the Lublin government handpicked by Stalin could conduct fair elections in Poland. Now that the Western Allies had agreed to "reorganize" the existing government in Poland, arranging for observers was their only hope of keeping the vote honest. Churchill pointed out to Stalin that "the British government had no way of knowing what was going on in Poland, except through dropping brave men by parachute and bringing members of the Underground Movement out . . . and did not like getting their information that way."[13] Churchill would not allow Stalin to distract him from his main concern: the fairness of the Polish elections. The imposition of a newly reorganized government "without the freely expressed wishes of the people concerned" would mean the end of freedom and the beginning of serfdom for the people of Poland.[14] Churchill assured Stalin that he would raise no objection to the Soviet observance of elections held in other parts of Europe. "The British would welcome observers from the United States and the Soviet Union when elections were held in Greece and the same would apply in Italy."[15]

The three ministers met again in the afternoon of February 9, when Molotov produced some new proposals that came close to the American draft. "The Lublin government was to be 'reorganized on a wider democratic basis, with the inclusion of democratic leaders from Poland itself, and also from those living abroad.' Once reorganized the Lublin government would be pledged to hold free elections as soon as possible, and then we should recognize whatever government emerged."[16] U.S. Secretary of State Edward Stettinius had desired a written pledge that the three ambassadors in Warsaw should observe and report that the elections were really free and unfettered, but Molotov opposed this, as he alleged that it would offend the Poles. Subject to this and to a few minor amendments, the following declaration on Poland was agreed by the conference:

> *A new situation has been created in Poland as a result of her complete liberation by the Red Army. This calls for the establishment of a Polish Provisional Government, which can be more broadly based than was possible before the recent liberation of the western part of Poland. The Provisional Government which is now functioning in Poland should therefore*

*be reorganized on a broader democratic basis with the inclu-
sion of democratic leaders from Poland itself and from Poles
abroad. This new government should then be called the Polish
Provisional Government of National Unity.*[17]

The acceptance of Stalin's language that "instead of creating a
new Polish government, the existing provisional government should
be reorganized" created serious doubts in the mind of U.S. ambassador to Moscow, Averell Harriman, who later criticized Roosevelt for
accepting the use of that language. Churchill's physician, Lord Moran,
believed that the die had been cast, and that it was too late to worry
about Poland after the results of Teheran and the Churchill-Stalin
meeting in Moscow in the fall of 1944. And when American Admiral
William Leahy, who was not involved in the actual negotiations on
the issue, told Roosevelt, "Mr. President, this is so elastic that the
Russians can stretch it all the way from Yalta to Washington, without
ever technically breaking it," he was told, "I know, Bill, I know it. But
it's the best I can do for Poland at this time."[18] The outcome of the
Yalta agreement was largely the result of accepted Soviet demands. The
Soviet interpretation of the Curzon Line established Poland's eastern
frontier; the Soviet prearranged provisional government was to remain
in being and formed the basis of the postwar Polish government; elections were to be held, but a limited number of ministers were admitted
from London on terms dictated by the Lublin leaders.

In Poland on March 28, 1945, the Soviets showed how sincere
they really were about Polish political independence. Sixteen leading
Polish independent political and military leaders were invited to what
was allegedly a lunch hosted by senior Soviet officials a short distance
from where they were staying. In fact they were all transported some
seven hundred miles away to the Lubyanka Prison in Moscow, where
they were then imprisoned and interrogated. They were later accused

as criminals and enemies of democracy and put on trial. Of the sixteen, thirteen were sentenced to various terms in Soviet prisons.[19]

Churchill was outraged by what Stalin had done. He wrote to Roosevelt and asking him whether Poland, having lost its frontier, would now also lose her freedom. Roosevelt's only response was to stay out of disputes with Stalin as his only real concern was with matters concerning Germany.

Consequently, the democratic Polish government would never be established because the "free and unfettered elections" that had been promised by the Yalta Agreement never took place.

The Yalta Conference has often been regarded, and particularly by the peoples of the Central European nations such as Poland, Slovakia, Romania, Hungary, Bulgaria, Albania, and the Czech Republic, as the "Western betrayal," based on the belief that the Allied powers allowed the smaller, less-powerful countries to be controlled and established as Communist puppet governments by the Soviet Union. It was at the Yalta Conference that the Big Three attempted to sacrifice freedom for the sake of stability and that the decisions and concessions of Roosevelt and Churchill at that summit led to the power struggle of the ensuing Cold War for the next forty-five years.

CHAPTER SEVENTEEN
Epitaph to a Defiant Nation

Perseverance: The virtue lies in the struggle,
not in the prize.

—Richard M. Milnes (1805–1885),
English statesman

I titled this book *A Nation Defiant* with good reason. Anyone unfamiliar with Polish culture might well ask why a people, a civilian population less prepared to defend itself militarily than most other European nations and faced with a superior aggressor that much larger nations faced with irresolution, would subject itself to the suffering underwent by the Poles; suffering that not only came from two months of day-to-day and house-to-house street fighting, but also from aerial low-level dive-bombing attacks, incessant short-range artillery barrages, close-range heavy assault gunfire, and close-range skirmishes. These happened amongst buildings that, along with their inhabitants, were being reduced to ashes. And hunger, thirst, and an urge to stay alive and try to defeat every obstacle in the way accompanied all of it. According to one Polish author, the answer lies in Polish national history:

> *The insurgents, this includes the civilian population, had standards to measure up to, standards of their ancestors who for literally a thousand years bled to secure and maintain Polish independence. Their kings, their martyrs, and their soldiers were the models and the symbols of ideals against which they measured their own behavior. Within the last 300 years alone, Warsaw itself had fought against Swedes, Russians, Austrians, Germans, and the Soviet Union. Their city had a tradition and a past that they were proud of. It was the Warsaw style of behavior remembered and recounted to them by their grandfathers and fathers. They had something to live up to, or die for.*[1]

One example of defiance and civilian solidarity involved a contemplative order of nuns, the Benedictine Sisters of Perpetual Adoration of the Holy Sacrament, who opened their convent to hundreds of refugees. During the uprising they found themselves in the midst of a good deal of fighting. The Germans told them to evacuate the convent or take the consequences. Seeking the advice of a Home Army commander whose troops were billeted nearby, the prioress learned that the soldiers would be very disappointed to see the nuns leave. So she urged the other sisters to go to the chapel to pray. Within half an hour, a high explosive bomb struck the chapel, coming through its roof; a thousand people perished.[2]

Undoubtedly, the civilians were relieved when the constant wave of explosives and bombing stopped throughout the city. Nevertheless, another incident revealed how civilian resilience and resolve responded to the German call to surrender. The Polish government delegate told certain representatives of the population that the civilians were to leave Warsaw immediately, but at the same time, were not to tell the civilians that the Home Army was being put in internment camps by the Germans. But when the civilians learned nothing about the fate of the AK soldiers, they refused to leave the city. "If the AK is to stay, so will we! If the AK is to die, then we shall die together."[3]

Perhaps the strongest case of defiance was an appeal from a monitored Polish radio station in Warsaw that came from London an hour and a half before the formal signing of the official surrender. The message was barely audible:

> *Hello, Warsaw speaking. . . . We are still fighting, Warsaw. . . . Warsaw is not yet defeated. . . . This town of one million people is being wiped out. . . . We have given more than we could. . . . Give us immediate assistance! This assistance is due to us! . . . We today are the conscience of the world. We . . . have confidence and are still waiting for your help.*
>
> *We were called "the inspiration of the fighting nations and the inspiration of the world." . . . We, as a nation, have a right to live. We demand that right! . . .* [4]

Both the Home Army and the civilian evacuation began on October 3, 1944, amidst the rubble of a devastated Warsaw. After sixty-three days of relentless fighting, many civilians fell to their knees as the columns of insurgents passed by. Other exhausted soldiers emerged from sewers and basements; some carried the wounded on their shoulders, others walked in a daze, unsure of where they were. Those insurgents who had no uniforms to identify them as AK soldiers were accepted as Polish combatants by the Germans if they were wearing red-and-white armbands or White Eagle badges. Women soldiers were given the option of either going to female POW camps or accepting civilian status. Members of the German Wehrmacht transported all POWs, but no one could know whether the SS and the Gestapo would later honor the agreement signed by representatives of the

German Army. The insurgents shouldered their weapons—anything from captured Schmeisser submachine guns, to Sten guns, rifles, and other arms—and they deposited them at specified sites where curious onlookers watched in silent amazement. The women insurgents carried first-aid kits, mailbags, and radio equipment. Their columns moved off in what seemed to be an endless procession on October 3, 4, and 5. A total of 11,668 insurgents surrendered, including some 2,000 women.[5]

Exhausted soldiers of the Home Army appear from sewers and basements after two months of grim fighting.

A young German officer described the capitulation in a letter to his parents and characterized the Polish insurgents this way:

In truth they fought better than we did. . . . Nothing sensible can come from this kind of subjugation of an entire nation. Sad but true! We don't have a monopoly on fortitude, spirit, patriotism, and sacrifice (We can't take the Poles' credit away from them). That a city can defend itself for months on end, with much heavier losses on the attacker's side . . . and much can be learned from this by a neutral observer.[6]

In a letter to his mother, that same German soldier wrote the following lines:

In spite of everything, the most heroic fighting, given the conditions, was done by the bandits themselves. ('Bandit' remained the standard German term for the insurgents.) . . . The insurgents deserved to be treated like soldiers. The Poles had nothing left to hope for, after the loss of their statehood and all their means of defense. . . . Then they marched by in step, four abreast, avoiding the tear-stained and pain-ridden faces of the women, with their weapons ready to be surrendered. All done without a sign of despair, heads held high with national pride. Exemplary![7]

After the military evacuation, the civilian survivors were an equally moving and somber sight. Emerging from a wilderness of desolation, thousands of dirty, exhausted, starving, and bewildered Warsaw citizens wearily made their way along streets flanked by wooden crosses that marked the shallow graves of loved ones and friends who had not survived. Under the watchful eyes of German guards were the men, women, and children, including the sick, the wounded, emaciated, blinded, bandaged, bloodstained, and limping, whom Providence had selected to live on. One survivor provided the following description of the exodus on the street:

> *On the way to the Western Station a crowd blackening into a large seething mass moves slowly, weighted down with packages clutched in complete silence. Expressionless, it does not let the watching Germans see the tragedy unfolding inside every one of us.*
>
> *The guards spaced out along the length of the street do not sneer, but watch with interest and even admiration. Warsaw has set a new record, beating the length of Stalingrad's resistance by a few days, even though the odds had been more heavily stacked against us. We are rather proud of that.*
>
> *We walk past burnt-out houses. On the pavements, the charred bodies of people and animals tell a tragic tale. As we walk through the city of vampires our consciousness is gradually permeated by the pompous tones of Chopin's funeral march. Someone passing us whistles it through gritted teeth.*[8]

After the uprising, the Red Army remained at the gates of Warsaw a full four months—from September until the middle of January—before entering the city. Large numbers of Varsovians who had not been placed in captivity or had somehow escaped the dragnet were left to their own self-reliance. They were homeless, and many had sick or young dependents. They traveled where possible, to the mountains, to the far south, or to the homes of relatives and friends as far from the war-ravaged front as possible. Others went to suburban towns west of Warsaw where reception centers awaited them in schools and parish halls.[9]

While Germany razed Warsaw to the ground, the Soviet Army

watched contentedly from the other side of the Vistula just outside of the city. Throughout that time the Germans, on Hitler's orders, completed the demolition of Warsaw, not leaving a stone standing. All those districts west of the Vistula remained largely under German control. The city became an empty shell.

Then on January 12, 1945, Soviet General Georgy Zhukov launched a winter offensive across Poland. German forces were overwhelmed. By the end of January 1945 the German armies were virtually confined within their own territory except for an insecure hold in Hungary and northern Italy, while in Romania and Bulgaria the Soviets had established a firm military grip. Everything west of the Vistula that had been in German hands fell to the Soviet Army, and after Warsaw fell to the Soviets, they dominated practically all of Poland. And as Churchill later remarked in his memoirs, "Poland, though liberated from the Germans, had merely exchanged one conqueror for another."[10] But the British prime minister also said that despite the fact that Poland had been overrun by two of the Great Powers . . . *they were unable to quench the spirit of the Polish nation. The heroic defense of Warsaw shows that the soul of Poland is indestructible, and that she will rise again like a rock, which may for a time be submerged by a tidal wave, but which remains a rock.*[11]

SOURCES AND BIBLIOGRAPHY

Archives

Nuremberg Trial Proceedings. Volume 4. Thursday, 20 December 1945. Document 2751-PS. New Haven, CT: Yale Law School Avalon Project.

Memoirs, special studies, and general works

Army Times, ed. *Heroes of the Resistance: Adventures of Underground Fighters in Europe during World War II*. New York: Dodd, Mead & Company, 1967.

Blet, Pierre. *Pius XII and the Second World War: According to the Archives of the Vatican*. New York: Paulist Press, 1997.

Bor-Komorowski, T. *The Secret Army*. Nashville, TN: The Battery Press, 1984.

Braun, Kazimierz. *A History of Polish Theater 1939–1989: Spheres of Captivity and Freedom*. Westport, CT: Greenwood Press, 1996.

Brzezinski, Zbigniew. *Out of Control: Global Turmoil on the Eve of the 21st Century*. New York: Scribner, 1993.

Budrewicz, Olgierd. *Introduction to Poland*. Miami: American Institute of Polish Culture, 1985.

Chodakiewicz, Marek Jan. *Between Nazis and Soviets: Occupation Politics in Poland 1939–1947*. Lanhan, MD: Lexington Books, 2004.

Churchill, Winston S. *The Gathering Storm*. Boston: Houghton Mifflin Company, 1948.

———. *Triumph and Tragedy*. Boston: Houghton Mifflin Company, 1987.

Coole, W. W. and M. F. Potter, eds. *Thus Spake Germany*. London: George Routledge and Sons, 1941.

Cynk, Jerzy B. *The Polish Air Force at War*. Atglen, PA: Schiffer Publishing, 1998.

Davies, Norman, *God's Playground: A History of Poland*. Volume 2. New York: Columbia University Press, 1982

———. *Heart of Europe: A Short History of Poland*. Oxford: Clarendon Press, 1984.

———. *Rising '44: The Battle for Warsaw*. New York: Penguin Books, 2003.

Dziewanowski, M. K. *Poland in the 20th Century*. New York: Columbia University Press, 1977.

Ellul, Jacques. *Propaganda: The Formation of Men's Attitudes*. New York: Vintage Books, 1965.

Ford, Charles and Robert Hammond. *Polish Film: A Twentieth Century History*. Jefferson, NC: McFarland & Company, Inc. Publishers, 2005.

Furst, Alan. *The Polish Officer*. New York: Random House, 1995.

Garlinski, Josef. *Poland, SOE and the Allies*. London: George Allen and Unwin Ltd., 1969.

———. *The Survival of Love: Memoirs of a Resistance Officer*. Oxford: Basil Blackwell Ltd., 1991.

Gehler, Michael and Kaiser Wolfram. *Christian Democracy in Europe Since 1945*. New York: Routledge, 2004.

Giertych, Jedrzej. *In Defense of My Country*. London: The Roman Dmowski Society, 1981.

Graham, Robert A. *The Pope and Poland in World War Two*. London: Veritas Foundation Publishing Centre, n. d.

Gross, Tomasz. *Polish Society Under German Occupation: The Generalgouvernment 1939–1944*. Princeton, NJ: Princeton University Press, 1979.

Gutman, Yisrael. *The Jews of Warsaw 1939–1943*. Bloomington, IN: Indiana University Press, 1982.

Haestrup, Jorgen. *Europe Ablaze: An Analysis of the History of the European Resistance Movements 1939–1945*. Odense, Denmark: Odense University Press, 1978.

Halecki, O. *A History of Poland*. New York: David McKay Company, Inc., 1976.

Hanson, Joanna K. M. *The Civilian Population and the Warsaw Uprising of 1944*. London: Cambridge University Press, 1982.

Hart, B. H. Liddell. *History of the Second World War*. New York: G. P. Putnam's Sons, 1970.

Hitchcock, William I. *The Bitter Road to Freedom*. New York: Free Press, 2008.

Hlond, August. *The Persecution of the Catholic Church in German-Occupied Poland*. London: Burns Oats, 1941.

Howarth, Patrick. *Undercover: The Men and Women of the SOE*. London: Phoenix Press, 1980.

Iranek-Osmecki, Kazimierz. *He Who Saves One Life*. New York: Crown Publishers, Inc., 1971.

Jacobson, Douglas W. "Poland Fights: The Dark and Silent Ones." *Am-Pol Eagle: Voice of Polonia*, 2012.

Johnson, Paul. *Modern Times: The World from the Twenties to the Eighties*. New York: Harper & Row Publishers, Inc., 1983.

Juchniewicz, Mieczyslaw. *Poles in the European Resistance Movement 1939–1945*. Warsaw: Interpress Publishers, 1972.

Karolak, Tadeusz. *John Paul II, The Pope from Poland*. Warsaw: Interpress Publishers, 1979.

Karski, Jan. *Story of a Secret State*. Boston: Houghton Mifflin Company, 1944.

Kennan, George F. *Russia and the West Under Lenin and Stalin*. Boston: Little Brown Company, 1961.

Klukowski, Zygmunt. *Diary from the Years of Occupation 1939–1944*, Urbana, IL: University of Illinois Press, 1993.

Knuth, Rebecca. *Libricide: The Regime-Sponsored Destruction of Books and Libraries in the Twentieth Century*. Westport, CT: Greenwood Publishing Group, 2003.

Komorowski, Krzysztof. *Polish Resistance in World War II No. 29*. London: London Branch of the Polish Home Army Ex-Servicemen Association, 2004.

Korbonski, Stefan. *Fighting Warsaw: The Story of the Polish Underground State, 1939-1945*. New York: Hippocrene Books, Inc., 1956.

Kulski, Julian Eugeniusz. *Dying, We Live: The Personal Chronicle of a Young Freedom Fighter in Warsaw 1939–1945*. New York: Holt, Rinehart and Winston, 1979.

Kwiatkowski, Bohdan. *Sabotaz i dywersja*. London: Bellona, 1949.

Lane, Arthur Bliss. *I Saw Poland Betrayed*. Belmont, MA: Bobbs-Merrill Company, 1948.

Lorit, Sergius. *The Last Days of Maximilian Kolbe*. New York: New City Press, 1982.

Lowe, Roy. *Education and the Second World War: Studies in Schooling and Social Change*. London: Falmer Press, 1992.

Lukas, Richard C. *The Forgotten Holocaust: The Poles Under German Occupation, 1939–1944*. Lexington, KY: University Press of Kentucky, 1986.

Madajczyk, Czeslaw. *Politics of the Third Reich in Occupied Poland*. Part Two. Panstwowe: Wydawnictwo Naukowe, 1970.

Malinski, Mieczyslaw. *Pope John Paul II: The Life of Karol Wojtyla*. New York: Image Books, 1982.

Manchester, William. *The Last Lion Winston Spencer Churchill Alone 1932–1940*. Boston: Little Brown and Company, 1988.

Marks, Leo. *Between Silk and Cyanide: A Codemaker's War 1941–1945*. New York: The Free Press, 1998.

McInerney, Ralph. *The Defamation of Pius XII*. South Bend, IN: St. Augustine's Press, 2001.

Michel, Henri. *The Shadow War: European Resistance 1939–1945*. New York: Harper & Row Publishers, 1972.

Michener, James. *Poland*. New York: Random House, 1983.

Milosz, Czeslaw. *Native Realm: A Search for Self-Definition*. New York: Farrar, Straus and Giroux, 1968.

Neugebauer, Norwid. *The Defense of Poland: September 1939*. London: Kolin Ltd., 1942.

Nicolson, Nigel, ed. *Letters and Diaries of Harold Nicolson*. Vol. II *The War Years, 1939–1945*. New York: Atheneum, 1967.

Nurowski, Roman. *War Losses in Poland 1939–1945*. Poznan: Wydawnictwo Zachodnie, 1960.

Oram, James. *The People's Pope: The Story of Karol Wojtyla of Poland*. San Francisco: Chronicle Books, 1979.

Orska, Irene. *Silent is the Vistula*. New York: Longmans, Green and Co., Inc., 1946.

Ostasz, Grzegorz. *Polish Underground State's Patronage of the Arts and Literature 1939–1945 No. 22*. London: London Branch of the Polish Home Army Ex-Servicemen Association, 2004.

Panek, Christine Zamoyska. *Have You Forgotten? A Memoir of Poland 1939–1945*. New York: Doubleday, 1989.

Parada, Joseph. *Invasion of Poland*. http://www.actungpanzer.com/invasion-of-poland-fall-weiss.htm.

Parker, Christine S. "History of Education Reform in Post-Communism Poland, 1989–1999: Historical and Contemporary Effects on Educational Transition." Dissertation at Ohio State University, 2003.

Piotrowski, Tadeusz. *Poland's Holocaust: Ethnic Strife, Collaboration with Occupying Forces and Genocide in the Second Republic, 1918–1947*. Jefferson, NC: McFarland & Company, 1997.

Plokhy, S. M. *Yalta: The Price of Peace*. New York: Viking, 2010.

Pogonowsky, Iwo Cyprian. *Poland: An Illustrated History*. New York: Hippocrene Books, Inc., 2000.

Polish Ministry of Information. *The German New Order in Poland*. London: Hutchinson and Co., 1941.

Raack, Richard. *Stalin's Drive to the West 1938–1945*. Stanford, CA: Stanford University Press, 1995.

Radzilowski, John. *A Traveller's History of Poland*. Northampton, MA: Interlink Publishing Group, 2007.

Rees, Laurence, documentary director. *Behind Closed Doors: Stalin, the Nazis and the West,* BBC History of World War II. Russian State Archives for Film and Photographic Documents, 2009.

Robertson, K. G., ed. *War, Resistance and Intelligence: Essays in Honour of M. R. D. Foot*. South Yorkshire, Great Britain: Cooper, 1999.

Rychlak, Ronald J. *Hitler, the War and the Pope*. Columbus, MS: Genesis Press, Inc., 2008.

Sendler, Irene. *Unsung Polish Heroine.* unsung-polish-heroine-irene-sendler.html.

Sharp, Samuel L. *Poland: White Eagle on a Red Field.* Cambridge, MA: Harvard University Press, 1953.

Shirer, William L. *The Rise and Fall of the Third Reich.* New York: Simon and Schuster, 1960.

Slawinski, Andrzej. *Polish Resistance in World War II No. 20.* London: London Branch of the Polish Home Army Ex-Servicemen Association. 2004.

Smith, C. Peter. *Ju 87 Stuka.* Volume One. *Dive Bomber Units 1939–1941.* Hinckley, UK: Classic Publications, 2006.

Stafford, David. *Secret Agent: The True Story of the Covert War Against Hitler.* Woodstock, NY: The Overlook Press, 2000.

Stone, Harry. *Writing in the Shadow: Resistance Publications in Occupied Europe.* London: Frank Cass & Co., Ltd., 1996.

Watt, Richard M. *Bitter Glory: Poland and Its Fate 1918–1939.* New York: Simon and Schuster, 1979.

Wdowinski, David. *And We Are Not Saved.* New York: Philosophical Library, 1963.

Weigel, George. *Witness to Hope.* New York: Harper Collins Publishers, Inc., 1999.

Wheal, Elizabeth-Anne, Stephen Pope, and James Taylor. *Encyclopedia of the Second World War.* Secaucus, NJ: Castle Books, 1989.

Wilmot, Chester. *The Struggle for Europe.* Herfordshire, England: Wordsworth Editions Ltd., 1977.

Wittekowna, Maria. *Polish Forums/History of Poland.* www. Polishforums.com/history-poland-34maria-wittekowna-other-polish-women-ak.

Wrobel, Piotr. *The Devil's Playground: Poland in World War II.* Montreal: The Canadian Foundation for Polish Studies of the Polish Institute of Arts & Sciences, 1999.

Zaloga, Stephen and Victor Madej. *The Polish Campaign 1939.* New York: Hippocrene Books, Inc., 1985.

Zawodny, J. K. *Nothing but Honour: The Story of the Warsaw Uprising, 1944.* Stanford, CA: Hoover Institution Press, 1978.

Journal articles and editorials

Dalin, David G. "Pius XII and the Jews, A Defense." *The Weekly Standard,* February 26, 2001.

Jacobson, Douglas. "Poland Fights: The Dark and Silent Ones," *Am-Pol Eagle: Voice of Polonia*, June 28, 2012.

END NOTES

Introduction

1. George Weigel, *Witness to Hope* (New York: Harper Collins Publishers, Inc., 1999), 46.

2. Olgierd Budrewicz, *Introduction to Poland* (Miami: American Institute of Polish Culture, 1985), 23.

Chapter One: The Polish Phoenix

1. M. K. Dziewanowski, *Poland in the 20th Century* (New York: Columbia University Press, 1977), 29.

2. Elizabeth-Anne Wheal, Stephen Pope, and James Taylor, *Encyclopedia of the Second World War* (Secaucus, NJ: Castle Books, 1989), 123. See also *Danzig and the Polish Corridor*, http://www. robinsonlibrary.com/history/history/worldwar1/danzig1919.htm.

3. Dziewanowski, *Poland in the 20th Century*, 85–86.

4. This carefully hidden relationship between the two dictatorial powers was to continue in one form or another until 22 June 1941 when Germany invaded Soviet Russia. It is one of the ironies of history that German specialists first taught Soviet Communism how to make excellent tanks, a weapon used to overwhelm Germany in 1943–45. Paul Johnson, *Modern Times: The World from the Twenties to the Eighties* (New York: Harper & Row Publishers, Inc., 1983), 76, 139.

5. Dziewanowski, *Poland in the 20th Century*, 86.

6. Ibid., 98–99.

7. Ibid.

8. Ibid.

9. Ibid., 99–100.

10. In March 1936 Hitler ordered the German troops to retreat from the Rhineland in the event of armed resistance by the French. "But the lethargic, almost suicidal reluctance to oppose first German rearmament and then later German acts of aggression was a guiding principle of French and British policy throughout the 1930s." Ibid.

11. William L. Shirer, *The Rise and Fall of the Third Reich* (New York: Simon and Schuster, 1960), 82–83.

12. Ibid., 212–13.

13. Ibid., 322ff.

14. Ibid., 421.

15. Ibid., 448.

16. B. H. Liddell Hart, *History of the Second World War* (New York: G. P. Putnam's Sons, 1970), 11–12.

17. Richard M. Watt, *Bitter Glory: Poland and Its Fate 1918–1939* (New York: Simon and Schuster, 1979), 402.

18. Shirer, *The Rise and Fall of the Third Reich*, 532.

19. Hart, *History of the Second World War*, 12.

20. S. Aster, *1939: The Making of the Second World War*, 313. As cited in Watt, *Bitter Glory: Poland and Its Fate 1918–1939*, 408.

21. Watt, *Bitter Glory: Poland and its Fate 1918–1939*, 417–18.

22. Hart, *History of the Second World War*, 32.

Chapter Two: The September Campaign

1. Nuremberg Trial Proceedings, volume 4, (Thursday, 20 December 1945), Document 2751-PS, (New Haven, CT: Yale Law School Avalon Project). Sworn affidavit of Alfred H. Naujocks who stated that he was ordered to organize the Gleiwitz incident by Reinhard Heydrich, chief of the German Security Police. See also John Radzilowski, *War, Occupation and the*

Holocaust 1939–46, A Traveller's History of Poland (Northampton, MA: Interlink Publishing Group, 2007), 190.

2. John Radzilowski, *Invason of Poland 1 September 1939–6 October 1939*, http://ww2db.com/battle_spec.php?battle_id=28. Source: Stephen Zaloga and Victor Madej, *The Polish Campaign 1939* (New York: Hippocrene Books, Inc., 1985). See also Watt, *Bitter Glory: Poland and its Fate 1918–1939*, 420–24.

3. Zaloga and Madej, *The Polish Campaign 1939*.

4. Samuel L. Sharp, *Poland: White Eagle on a Red Field* (Cambridge, MA: Harvard University Press, 1953), 153.

5. "When Hitler marched into Poland, he had reserve stocks of oil for less than six months of active operations. His total oil 'income' in the next twelve months, some seven and a half million tons, proved only just sufficient to meet the demands at home and in the field, even though half this period was that of the inactive 'twilight war.'" Chester Wilmot, *The Struggle for Europe* (Hertfordshire: Wordsworth Editions Ltd., 1977), 22.

6. Watt, *Bitter Glory: Poland and Its Fate 1918–1939*, 419–20.

7. Zaloga and Madej, *The Polish Campaign 1939*. See also Lt. General M. Norwid Neugebauer, *The Defense of Poland: September 1939* (London: Kolin Ltd., 1942).

8. Ibid.

9. Zaloga and Madej, *The Polish Campaign 1939*, 145–49.

10. Jerzy B. Cynk, *The Polish Air Force at War* (Atglen, PA: Schiffer Publishing, 1998). See also C. Peter Smith, *Ju 87 Stuka*, volume one, *Luftwaffe Ju 87 Dive Bomber Units 1939–1941* (Hinckley, UK: Classic Publications, 2006).

11. John Radzilowski, *A Traveller's History of Poland*, 190–91.

12. Zaloga and Madej, *The Polish Campaign 1939*, 110–12.

13. Ibid.

14. Watt, *Bitter Glory: Poland and Its Fate 1918–1939*, 421.

15. Ibid., 422–23.

16. Ibid., 424–25.

17. Norman Davies, *Rising '44: The Battle for Warsaw* (New York: Penguin Books, 2003), 84–85.

18. Watt, *Bitter Glory: Poland and Its Fate 1918–1939*, 427.

19. Ibid., 429.

20. Ibid., 430–31.

21. Ibid., 432–33.

22. Sharp, *Poland: White Eagle on a Red Field*, 154.

23. Radzilowski, *A Traveller's History of Poland*, 192–93.

24. Ibid.

25. Jan Nowak, *Courier from Warsaw* (London: Collins/Harvill, 1982), 58.

26. Radzilowski, *A Traveller's History of Poland*, 193.

27. Watt, *Bitter Glory: Poland and Its Fate 1918–1939*, 439.

28. Norman Davies, *Heart of Europe: A Short History of Poland* (Oxford: Clarendon Press, 1984), 67. See also Sharp, *Poland: White Eagle on a Red Field*, 156.

Afterthoughts on the September Campaign

1. Revisionist historian A. J. P. Taylor, in his *Origins of the Second World War* (1961), stated that "only Danzig prevented cooperation between Germany and Poland." But as Hitler bluntly told his military chiefs in the spring of 1939, "*Danzig is not the subject of the dispute at all. It is a question of expanding our living space in the East; of securing our food supplies. . . . There is no other possibility in Europe.*" Shirer, *The Rise and Fall of the Third Reich*, 484. To Hitler, the heightened sense of grandeur to which, in his view, the new German state would be elevated could only be solved by *Lebenstraum* in Europe, which was impossible without invading other countries in the East.

2. William Manchester, *The Last Lion Winston Spencer Churchill Alone 1932–1940* (Boston: Little Brown and Company, 1988), 26.

3. Ibid.

4. Nigel Nicolson, ed., *Letters and Diaries of Harold Nicolson*, vol. II, *The War Years, 1939-1945* (New York: Atheneum 1967).

5. Manchester, *The Last Lion Winston Spencer Churchill Alone 1932–1940*, 588.

6. Ibid., 589.

Chapter Three: The Occupation under Nazi Rule

1. Dziewanowski, *Poland in the 20th Century*, 114.

2. Ian Kershaw, "War and 'Ethnic Cleansing': The Case of the 'Warthegau,'" in *War, Resistance and Intelligence: Essays in Honour of M. R. D. Foot*, ed. K. G. Robertson (South Yorkshire, Great Britain: Cooper, 1999), 84, 91.

3. Ibid., 92.

4. O. Halecki, *A History of Poland* (New York: David McKay Company, Inc. 1976) 312–13.

5. Nowak, *Courier from Warsaw*, 69.

6. James Michener, *Poland* (New York: Random House, 1983), 455.

7. Ibid.

8. Sharp, *Poland: White Eagle on a Red Field*, 156.

9. Norman Davies, *God's Playground: A History of Poland,* vol. 2 (New York: Columbia University Press, 1982), 445.

10. Ibid., 446.

11. Ibid.

12. Christine Zamoyska-Panek, *Have You Forgotten? A Memoir of Poland 1939–1945* (New York: Doubleday, 1989), 113.

13. Davies, *God's Playground: A History of Poland*, vol. 2, 441.

14. Davies, *Rising '44: The Battle for Warsaw*, 85–86.

15. Zygmunt Klukowski, *Diary from the Years of Occupation 1939–1944* (Urbana, IL: University of Illinois Press, 1993), 115.

16. *Thus Spake Germany*, ed. Coole and Potter (London: George Routledge and Sons, 1941), 369–70.

17. Mieczyslaw Malinski, *Pope John Paul II: The Life of Karol Wojtyla* (New York: Image Books, 1982), 40.

18. Stefan Korbonski, *Fighting Warsaw* (New York: Hippocrene Books, Inc., 1956), 15.

19. Tadeusz Karolak, *John Paul II, The Pope from Poland* (Warsaw: Interpress Publishers, 1979), 45–50. As cited in Weigel, *Witness to Hope*, 54.

20. James Oram, *The People's Pope: The Story of Karol Wojtyla of Poland* (San Francisco: Chronicle Books, 1979), 50. As cited in Weigel, *Witness to Hope*, 54.

21. Kershaw, "War and 'Ethnic Cleansing': The Case of the 'Warthegau,'" 91.

22. Davies, *God's Playground: A History of Poland*, vol. 2, 447.

23. "Poland Fights Back," *Heroes of the Resistance: Adventures of Underground Fighters in Europe during World War II*, ed. Army Times (New York: Dodd, Mead & Company, 1967), 57–58.

Chapter Four: Life under Soviet Rule

1. *Behind Closed Doors: Stalin, the Nazis and the West*, BBC History of World War II, Russian State Archives for Film and Photographic Documents, Laurence Rees, documentary director, 2009.

2. Davies, *God's Playground: A History of Poland*, vol. 2, 444.

3. Ibid., 447.

4. Tadeusz Piotrowski, "Polish Collaboration," *Poland's Holocaust: Ethnic Strife, Collaboration with Occupying Forces and Genocide in the Second Republic, 1918–1947* (Jefferson, NC: McFarland & Company, 1997), 11. See also Richard Raack, *Stalin's Drive to the West, 1938–1945* (Stanford: Stanford University Press, 1995), 58.

5. Michael Gehler and Kaiser Wolfram, *Christian Democracy in Europe since 1945* (New York: Routledge, 2004), 118.

6. Davies, *God's Playground: A History of Poland*, vol. 2, 448.

7. Josef Krauski, "Education as Resistance: The Polish Experience of Schooling During the War," in Roy Lowe, *Education and the Second World War: Studies in Schooling and Social Change* (London: Falmer Press, 1992), 128–3

8. Marek Jan Chodakiewicz, *Between Nazis and Soviets: Occupation Politics in Poland 1939–1947* (Lanhan, MD: Lexington Books, 2004).

9. Davies, *God's Playground: A History of Poland*, vol. 2, 448.

10. ———, *Heart of Europe: A Short History of Poland*, 67.

11. Davies, *God's Playground: A Short History of Poland*, vol. 2, 452.

12. Nowak, *Courier from Warsaw*, 255.

13. Richard C. Lukas, *Forgotten Holocaust: The Poles Under German Occupation 1939–1944* (Lexington, KY: University Press of Kentucky, 1986), 72.

14. Nowak, *Courier from Warsaw*, 132.

15. Davies, *God's Playground: A History of Poland*, vol. 2, 452.

16. *Behind Closed Doors: Stalin, the Nazis and the West*, BBC History of World War II, Russian State Archives for Film and Photographic Documents, Laurence Rees, documentary director, 2009.

17. *Diary of German General Franz Halder*, chief of the German General Staff, July 31, 1940, as cited in Wilmot, *The Struggle for Europe*, 56–57.

Chapter Five: The Civilian Resistance

1. John Radzilowski, *A Traveller's History of Poland* (Northampton, MA: Interlink Publishing Group), 199.

2. Lukas, *Forgotten Holocaust: The Poles Under German Occupation 1939–1944*, 117.

3. Jorgen Haestrup, *Europe Ablaze: An Analysis of the History of the European Resistance Movements 1939–1945* (Odense, Denmark: Odense University Press, 1978), 147.

4. Henri Michel, *The Shadow War: European Resistance 1939–1945* (New York: Harper & Row Publishers, 1972), 246.

5. Ibid., 245.

6. Lukas, *Forgotten Holocaust: The Poles Under German Occupation 1939–1944*, 97.

7. Michel, *The Shadow War: European Resistance 1939–1945*, 78.

8. Jan Karski, *Story of a Secret State* (Boston: Houghton Mifflin Company, 1944), 301.

9. Lukas, *Forgotten Holocaust: The Poles Under German Occupation 1939–1944*, 99.

10. Haestrup, *Europe Ablaze: An Analysis of the European Resistance Movements, 1939–1945*, 131.

11. Lukas, *Forgotten Holocaust: The Poles Under German Occupation 1939–1944*, 97–98.

12. Ibid.

13. Haestrup, *Europe Ablaze: An Analysis of the European Resistance Movements 1939–1945*, 146.

14. Nowak, *Courier from Warsaw*, 61.

15. Alan Furst, *The Polish Officer* (New York: Random House, 1995), 46.

16. Nowak, *Courier from Warsaw*, 79, 164.

17. Haestrup, *Europe Ablaze: An Analysis of the European Resistance Movements 1939–1945*, 132–33.

18. Lukas, *Forgotten Holocaust: The Poles Under German Occupation 1939–1944*, 100–01.

19. Czeslaw Milosz, *Native Realm: A Search for Self-Definition* (New York: Farrar, Straus and Giroux, 1968), 230.

20. Nowak, *Courier from Warsaw*, 61.

21. Stefan Korbonski, *Fighting Warsaw: The Story of the Polish Underground State, 1939–1945* (New York: Hippocrene Books, Inc. 2004), 200–01.

22. Ibid., 202–03.

23. Ibid., 205–06.

24. Black propaganda is false, misleading information that claims to be from a source on one side of a conflict, but that actually comes from the other side. Its major characteristic is that the intended recipients of the information are not aware that they are being influenced and do not feel that they are being pushed in a certain direction. Jacques Ellul, *Propaganda: The Formation of Men's Attitudes* (New York: Vintage Books, 1965), 16.

25. Nowak, *Courier from Warsaw*, 68–75.

26. Ibid., 78.

27. Ibid. In May 1941, without any prior authorization from Hitler, Rudolf Hess flew on a lone "mission of humanity" to Britain under the delusion that Hitler did not want to defeat England and wanted to stop the fighting—so long as Britain would give Germany a free hand in Europe. Hess asserted that if the war continued, Germany would win, and the results for the British would be disastrous. Hitler gave orders for Hess to be shot when he returned to Germany. However, he was held as a prisoner of war in Britain until the end of the war and later was sentenced to life imprisonment at the Nuremberg Trial. Shirer, *The Rise and Fall of the Third Reich*, 834–38.

28. Nowak, *Courier from Warsaw*, 79–80.

29. Ibid., 167.

30. Lukas, *Forgotten Holocaust: The Poles Under German Occupation 1939–1944,* 101.

31. Nowak, *Courier from Warsaw*, 81.

32. Ibid., 85.

33. Lukas, *Forgotten Holocaust: The Poles Under German Occupation 1939–1944,* 102.

34. Nowak, *Courier from Warsaw*, 109.

35. Jan Tomasz Gross, *Polish Society under German Occupation: The Generalgouvernment 1939–1944* (Princeton, NJ: Princeton University Press, 1979), 213.

Chapter Six: The Underground State

1. Karski, *Story of a Secret State* (Boston: Houghton Mifflin Company, 1944), 89.

2. Dziewanowski, *Poland in the 20th Century*, 116.

3. Stefan Korbonski, *Fighting Warsaw: The Story of the Polish Underground State, 1939–1945* (New York: Hippocrene Books, Inc., 2004), 200–01. 27.

4. Karski, 129–30.

5. Ibid., 235.

6. Korbonski, *Fighting Warsaw: The Story of the Polish Underground State, 1939–1945*, 37.

7. Ibid., 29.

8. Ibid., 38.

9. Ibid., 40.

10. Nowak, *Courier from Warsaw*, 67.

11. Karski, *Story of a Secret State*, 131.

12. Gross, *Polish Society Under German Occupation: The Generalgouvernment1939–1944,* 265.

13. Ibid., 264.

14. Ibid., 266–67.

15. Ibid.

16. Lukas, *Forgotten Holocaust: The Poles Under German Occupation 1939–1944*, 59–60.

17. Ibid., 95–96.

18. Korbonski, *Fighting Warsaw: The Story of the Polish Underground State 1939–1945*, 166.

19. Ibid., 167–68.

20. Ibid., 117.

21. Ibid., 116–18.

22. Ibid., 124–25.

23. Karski, *Story of a Secret State*, 235.

24. Korbonski, *Fighting Warsaw: The Story of the Polish Underground State, 1939–1945*, 126–27.

25. Ibid., 130–31.

26. T. Bor-Komorowski, *The Secret Army* (Nashville, Tennessee: The Battery Press, 1984), 117.

27. Korbonski, *Fighting Warsaw: The Story of the Polish Underground State, 1939–1945*, 131

28. Ibid., 140–41.

29. Ibid., 144.

Chapter Seven: The Underground Army

1. Davies, *God's Playground: A History of Poland,* vol. 2, 464.

2. Davies, *Rising '44: The Battle for Warsaw*, 172.

3. Ibid., 171.

4. Karski, *Story of a Secret State*, 234.

5. General Rowecki was arrested by the Gestapo on June 30, 1943 and executed in Oranienburg concentration camp in August 1944 Nowak, Courier from Warsaw, 455–56.

6. Bor-Komorowski, *The Secret Army*, 143–44.

7. Haestrup, *Europe Ablaze: An Analysis of the History of the European Resistance Movements 1939–1945*, 23.

8. Milosz, *Native Realm: A Search for Self-Definition*, 242.

9. Haestrup, *Europe Ablaze: An Analysis of the History of the European Resistance Movements 1939–1945*, 472.

10. Karski, *Story of a Secret State*, 254.

11. Nowak, *Courier from Warsaw*, 170.

12. Dziewanowski, *Poland in the 20th Century*, 117.

13. Ibid., 118.

14. Nowak, *Courier from Warsaw*, 170.

15. Ibid., 82.

16. Ibid.

17. Furst, *The Polish Officer*, 91.

18. Lukas, *Forgotten Holocaust: The Poles Under German Occupation, 1939–1944*, 64–65.

19. Karski, *Story of a Secret State*, 258.

20. Ibid.

21. Bohdan Kwiatkowski, *Sabotaz i dywersja* (London: Bellona, 1949), vol. 1, 21.

22. Bor-Komorowski, *The Secret Army*, 153–54.

23. Korbonski, *Fighting Warsaw: The Story of the Polish Underground State, 1939–1945,* 214–15.

Chapter Eight: Poland and the SOE

1. Josef Garlinski, *Poland, SOE and the Allies* (London: George Allen and Unwin Ltd., 1969), 28.

2. Haestrup, *Europe Ablaze: An Analysis of the History of the European Resistance Movements 1939–1945*, 271.

3. Garlinski, *Poland, SOE and the Allies,* 28.

4. Leo Marks, *Between Silk and Cyanide: A Codemaker's War 1941–1945* (New York: The Free Press, 1998), 530.

5. Garlinski, *Poland, SOE and the Allies*, 43.

6. Haestrup, *Europe Ablaze: An Analysis of the History of the European Resistance Movements 1939–1945*, 273.

7. Garlinski, *Poland, SOE and the Allies*, 43.

8. David Stafford, *Secret Agent: The True Story of the Covert War Against Hitler* (Woodstock, New York: The Overlook Press, 2001), 27.

9. Garlinski, *Poland, SOE and the Allies*, 29.

10. Haesrup, *Europe Ablaze: An Analysis of the History of the European Resistance Movement 1939–1945*, 273.

11. Garlinski, *Poland, SOE and the Allies*, 48.

12. Ibid., 49.

13. Haestrup, *Europe Ablaze: An Analysis of the History of the European Resistance Movements 1939–1945*, 273.

14. Garlinski, *Poland, SOE and the Allies*, 92.

15. Ibid., 95.

16. Ibid., 96.

17. Ibid., 101–102.

18. Ibid., 110–111.

19. Ibid., 111–112.

20. Ibid., 112–113.

21. Ibid., 114.

22. Douglas W. Jacobson, "Poland Fights: The Dark and Silent Ones," *Am-Pol Eagle*, Thursday, 28 June 2012.

23. Patrick Howarth, *Undercover: The Men and Women of the SOE*, (London: Phoenix Press, 1980), 65ff.

24. Garlinski, *Poland, SOE and the Allies*, 140–41.

25. Ibid., 143.

26. Ibid., 147.

Chapter Nine: Women in the Polish Resistance

1. J. K. Zawodny, *Nothing but Honour* (Stanford, CA: Hoover Institution Press, 1978), 44.

2. Marek Ney Krwawicz, "Women Soldiers of the Polish Home Army," *Polish Resistance in World War II* (London: London Branch of the Polish Home

Army Ex-Servicemen's Association, 2004), www.polishresistance-ak. org/12/%20article.htm.

3. Ibid.

4. Most of the material concerning Bisia Krasicka was obtained from written correspondence to the author from her son, Toni Reavis.

5. Zawodny, *Nothing but Honour,* 4

6. *Polish Forums/History of Poland*

7. Ibid.

8. Poland, Resistance during World War II, *Women and Combatants/Military Personnel,* as cited in Shelley Saywell, *Women in War* (Markham, Ontario: Penguin Books, 1985), 102–03. See also Zawodny, *Nothing but Honour: The Story of the Warsaw Uprising, 1944,* 47.

8. Karski, *Story of a Secret State,* 281

9. Ibid., 281.

10. Ibid., 282

11. Ibid., 285.

12. "Polish Greatness (Blog)" *Famous Polish Spies–Elzbieta Zawacka,* polishgreatness.blogspot.com/2011/02/spy-week-famous-polish-spies-Elzbieta.html. See also "Axis History Forum," *Polish General Elzbieta Zawacka Dies,* http://forum.axishistory.com/viewtopic. php?f=52&t=148217.

13. Karski, *Story of a Secret State,* 282–83.

Chapter Ten: The Jews and the Ghetto Uprising

1. Encyclopedia of the Holocaust as cited in *Warsaw Ghetto,* http://www. deathcamps.org/occupation/wars%20ghetto.html.

2. Ibid.

3. Nowak, *Courier from Warsaw,* 106.

4. Kazimierz Iranek-Osmecki, *He Who Saves One Life* (New York: Crown Publishers, Inc., 1971) 22.

5. Ibid., 21–23.

6. Ibid.

7. Nowak, *Courier from Warsaw,* 105.

8. Iranek-Osmecki, *He Who Saves One Life*, 82.

9. Yisrael Gutman, *The Jews of Warsaw 1939–1943* (Bloomington, IN: Indiana University Press, 1982), 307.

10. Iranek-Osmecki, *He Who Saves One Life*, 91. See also David Wdowinski, *And We Are Not Saved* (New York: Philosophical Library, 1963), 222.

11. Gutman, *The Jews of Warsaw 1939–1943*, 313.

12. Ibid.

13. Ibid., 311.

14. Iranek-Osmecki, *He Who Saves One Life,* 92.

15. Gutman, *The Jews of Warsaw 1939–1943*, 320–21.

16. Ibid., 315–16.

17. Ibid., 367.

18. Ibid.

19. Iranek-Osmecki, *He Who Saves One Life*, 95.

20. Ibid., 95–96.

21. Ibid.

22. Ibid., 97.

23. Gutman, *The Jews of Warsaw 1939–1943*, 372.

24. Iranek-Osmecki, *He Who Saves One Life*, 98.

25. Gutman, *The Jews of Warsaw 1939–1943*, 372.

26. Moshe Arens, *Who Defended the Ghetto?* The Jerusalem Post, http:www.jewishvirtuallibrary.org/sourcr/biography.org/jsource/Holocaust/Strooptoc.html. The Stroop Report: Table of Contents Jewish Virtual Library.

27. Gutman, *The Jews of Warsaw 1939–1943*, 375.

28. Ibid., 381.

29. Iranek-Osmecki, *He Who Saves One Life*, 101–02.

30. Ibid.

31. Ibid., 103.

32. Ibid., 105–06.

33. Ibid., 107.

34. Ibid., 108.

35. Andrzej Slawinski, "Those Who Helped Polish Jews during WWII," *Polish Resistance in World War II* (London: London Branch of the Polish Home Army Ex-Servicemen Association).

Chapter Eleven: Persecution of the Catholic Church

1. Weigel, *Witness to Hope*, 52.

2. Robert A. Graham, *The Pope and Poland in World War Two* (London: Veritas Foundation Publishing Centre, n.d.), 17. See also Ronald J. Rychlak, *Hitler, the War and the Pope*, (Columbus, MS: Genesis Press, Inc., 2000), 168.

3. Pierre Blet, *Pius XII and the Second World War: According to the Archives of the Vatican* (New York: Paulist Press, 1997), 70.

4. Rychlak, *Hitler, the War and the Pope*, 168.

5. Graham, *The Pope and Poland in World War Two*, 19–20.

6. Rychlak, *Hitler, the War and the Pope*, 168.

7. Polish Ministry of Information, "The Catholic Church," *The German New Order in Poland*. (London: Hutchinson and Co., 1941), 3.

8. Ibid., 11.

9. Ibid., 14.

10. Ibid. 4.

11. August Hlond, *The Persecution of the Catholic Church in German-Occupied Poland* (London: Burns Oates, 1941), 124. This was a Vatican broadcast communiqué intended for America and broadcast on the night of January 21, 1940.

12. Graham, *The Pope and Poland in World War Two*, 21.

13. Ibid., 15.

14. Hlond, *The Persecution of the Catholic Church in German-Occupied Poland*, 21–22.

15. Polish Ministry of Information, *The German New Order in Poland*, 3–4.

16. Graham, *The Pope and Poland in World War Two*, 15–16.

17. Rychlak, *Hitler, the War and the Pope*, 136–37.

18. Ralph McInerny, *The Defamation of Pius XII* (South Bend, IN:St. Augustine's Press, 2001), 52–53.

19. Blet, *Pius XII and the Second World War*, 80.

20. McInerney, *The Defamation of Pius XII*, 53.

21. Ibid, 75.

22. Ibid.

23. Ibid., 82.

24. Graham, *The Pope and Poland in World War Two*, 21.

25. Weigel, *Witness to Hope*, 52.

26. Sergius C. Lorit, *The Last Days of Maximilian Kolbe* (New York: New City Press, 1982), 19.

27. Weigel, *Witness to Hope*, 53.

28. Ibid.

29. Graham, *The Pope and Poland in World War Two*, 26–28.

30. David G. Dalin, "Pius XII and the Jews: A Defense" *The Weekly Standard* volume VI, no. 23 (February 26, 2001). Professor Dalin is an ordained rabbi who completed seminary studies at the Jewish Seminary of America. He has written widely on the role of Jews in political history and lectured widely on Pope Pius XII and the Jews in World War II and is the author of *The Myth of Hitler's Pope*, published by Regnery.

31. Rychlak, *Hitler, the War and the Pope*, 175–76.

32. Ibid., 264.

33. Graham, *The Pope and Poland in World War Two*, 21.

34. Dalin, *Pius XII and the Jews: A Defense*.

35. Graham, *The Pope and Poland in World War Two*, 59–60.

36. Weigel, *Witness to Hope*, 52. See also Zbigniew Brzezinski, *Out of Control* (New York: Scribners, 1993), 7–18. As cited and compiled by Withold J. Lukaszewski, "Polish Losses in World War II," *Sarmatian Review*, vol. XVIII (April 1998).

Chapter Twelve: Resistance through Culture

1. Rebecca Knuth, *Libricide: The Regime-Sponsored Destruction of Books and Libraries in the Twentieth Century* (Westport, CT.: Greenwood Publishing

Group, 2003), 86–89. See also Antoni Symonowicz, "Nazi Campaign Polish Culture," in *War Losses in Poland 1939–1945*, ed. Roman Nurowski (Poznan: Wydawnictwo Zachodnie, 1960), 73.

2. Piotr Wrobel, *The Devil's Playground: Poland in World War II* (Montreal: The Canadian Foundation for Polish Studies of the Polish Institute of Arts & Sciences, 1999), 16–17.

3. Symonowicz, "Nazi Campaign Polish Culture," *War Losses in Poland 1939–1945*, 74.

4. Iwo Cyprian Pogonowski, *Poland: An Illustrated History* (New York: Hippocrene Books, Inc., 2000), 202–09.

5. Josef Garlinski, *The Survival of Love: Memoirs of a Resistance Officer* (Oxford: Basil Blackwell Ltd., 1991), 1–2.

6. Czeslaw Madajczyk, *Politics of the Third Reich in Occupied Poland, Part Two* (Panstwowe Wydawnictwo Naukowe, 1970), 155–56.

7. Karski, *Story of a Secret State*, 305.

8. Ibid.

9. Salmonowicz, *Polish Underground State*, 213.

10. Christine S. Parker, *History of Education Reform in Post-Communism Poland, 1989–1999: Historical and Contemporary Effects on Educational Transition*, dissertation at the Ohio State University (2003).

11. Salmonowicz, *Polish Underground State*. 213, 222.

12. Karski, *Story of a Secret State*, 305.

13. Weigel, *Witness to Hope*, 54–55.

14. Madajczk, *Politics of the Third Reich in Occupied Poland*, part two, 160–61.

15. Michel, *The Shadow War: European Resistance 1939–1945*. 144.

16. Ibid.

17. Karski, *Story of a Secret State*, 305.

18. Salmonowicz, *Polish Underground State*, 222–26.

19. Grzegorz Ostasz, "Polish Underground State's Patronage of the Arts and Literature 1939–1945," Article 22 *Polish Resistance in World War II* (London: London Branch of the Polish Home Army Ex-Servicemen Association, 2004).

20. Kazimierz Braun, *A History of Polish Theater 1939–1989: Spheres of Captivity and Freedom* (Westport, CT: Greenwood Press, 1996), 13.

21. Ostasz, "Polish Underground State's Patronage of the Arts and Literature 1939–1945."

22. Braun, *A History of Polish Theater 1939–1989: Spheres of Captivity and Freedom*, 16.

23. Weigel, *Witness to Hope*, 63, 66.

24. Ibid., 65.

25. Braun, *A History of Polish Theater 1939–1989: Spheres of Captivity and Freedom*, 17.

26. Mieczyslaw Malinski, *Pope John Paul II: The Life of Karol Wojtyla* (New York: Image Books, 1979), 24.

27. Weigel, *Witness to Hope*, 65.

28. Ibid.

29. Ibid., 62.

30. Ibid., 66–67.

31. Symonowicz, *War Losses in Poland 1939–1945*, 86–87.

32. Charles Ford and Robert Hammond, *Polish Film: A Twentieth Century History* (Jefferson, NC: McFarland & Company, Inc. Publishers 2005), 95.

33. Ibid., 101.

34. Pogonowski, *Poland: An Illustrated History*, 218.

35. Salmonowicz, *Polish Underground State*, 256–65.

36. Ostasz, "Polish Underground State's Patronage of the Arts and Literature 1939–1945."

37. Salmonowicz, *Polish Underground State*, 265.

38. Davies, *Rising '44: The Battle for Warsaw*, 188.

Chapter Thirteen: The Underground Press

1. Krzysztof Komorowski, "The Press in Occupied Poland," Article 29 *Polish Resistance in World War II* (London: London Branch of the Polish Home Army Ex-Servicemen Association, 2004).

2. Harry Stone, *Writing in the Shadow: Resistance Publications in Occupied Europe* (London: Frank Cass & Co., Ltd., 1996), 10–11.

3. Karski, *Story of a Secret State*, 265.

4. Ibid., 266.

5. Komorowski, "The Press in Occupied Poland."

6. Gross, *Polish Society under German Occupation: The Generalgouvernment 1939–1944*, 251.

7. Ibid., 252.

8. Michel, *The Shadow War: European Resistance 1939–1945*, 97.

9. Stone, *Writing in the Shadow: Resistance Publications in Occupied Europe*, 79–80.

10. Gross, *Polish Society Under German Occupation: The Generalgouvernment 1939–1944*, 254.

11. Komorowski, "The Press in Occupied Poland."

12. Karski, *Story of a Secret State*, 269.

13. Ibid., 270

14. Stone, *Writing in the Shadow: Resistance Publications in Occupied Europe*, 42.

15. Karski, *The Secret State*, 271.

16. Stone, *Writing in the Shadow: Resistance Publications in Occupied Europe*, 17, 19.

17. Ibid., 11, 12.

18. Ibid., 12, 13.

19. Karski, *The Secret State*, 273.

20. Ibid., 271–73.

Chapter Fourteen: The Allied Betrayal

1. Davies, *Rising '44: The Battle for Warsaw*, 195.

2. Dziewanowski, *Poland in the 20th Century*, 130.

3. See chapter four for a more detailed explanation of the Katyn Forest affair.

4. Lukas, *Forgotten Holocaust: The Poles Under German Occupation 1939–1944*, 73.

5. Davies, *Rising '44: The Battle for Warsaw*, 208.

6. Ibid., 208–09.

7. Ibid.

8. Zawodny, *Nothing but Honour*, 70.

9. Dziewanowski, *Poland in the 20th Century*, 119.

10. Ibid., 122.

11. William I. Hitchcock, *The Bitter Road to Freedom* (New York: Free Press, 2008), 152.

12. Dziewanowski, *Poland in the 20th Century*, 122.

13. This statement was taken from then-acting Foreign Minister Raczynski's diary and quoted by Jan Ciechanowski in *Defeat in Victory* (Garden City, NY: Doubleday, 1947), 93–94 and cited in Dziewanowski, *Poland in the 20th Century*, 123.

14. Arthur Bliss Lane, U.S. ambassador to Poland 1944–1947, *I Saw Poland Betrayed* (Belmont, MA: Bobbs-Merrill Company, 1948), 36.

15. Hitchcock, *The Bitter Road to Freedom*, 151.

16. Zawodny, *Nothing but Honour*, 70.

17. Ibid.

18. Bor-Komorowski, *The Secret Army*, 201, 203. 87.

19. Zawodny, *Nothing but Honour*, 87.

20. Ibid., 99.

21. Ibid., 89.

22. Ibid., 100.

23. Ibid., 105.

24. Dziewanowski, *Poland in the 20th Century*, 130–31.

25. Ibid.

26. Lane, *I Saw Poland Betrayed*, 23.

Chapter Fifteen: The Warsaw Uprising

1. Zawodny, *Nothing but Honour*, 114–15.

2. Kondracki, "The Warsaw Uprising," *Polish Resistance in World War II*, 1.

3. Zawodny, *Nothing but Honour*, 27.

4. Ibid., 26.

5. Korbonski, *Fighting Warsaw*, 352–53.

6. T. Bor-Komorowski, *The Secret Army* (Nashville, TN: The Battery Press, 1984), 216.

7. Ibid.

8. Irena Orska, *Silent is the Vistula* (New York: Longmans, Green and Co., Inc., 1946), 21.

9. Bor-Komorowski, *The Secret Army*, 216.

10. Zawodny, *Nothing but Honour*, 210–11.

11. Julian Eugeniusz Kulski, *Dying, We Live: The Personal Chronicle of a Young Freedom Fighter in Warsaw 1939–1945* (New York: Holt, Rinehart, and Winston, 1979), 201.

12. Davies, *Rising '44: The Battle for Warsaw*, 245.

13. Bor-Komorowski, *The Secret Army*, 217.

14. Ibid., 217–19.

15. Orska, *Silent is the Vistula*, 67.

16. Davies, *Rising '44: The Battle for Warsaw*, 247. See also Orska, *Silent is the Vistula*, 28–29.

17. Bor-Komorowski, *The Secret Army*, 233.

18. Ibid., 234.

19. Zawodny, *Nothing but Honour*, 58.

20. Ibid., 55.

21. Joanna K. M. Hanson, *The Civilian Population and the Warsaw Uprising of 1944* (London: Cambridge University Press, 1982), 87–92. As cited in Hitchcock, *The Bitter Road to Freedom*, 157.

22. Institut Marksizqma-Leninzma, *History of the Great Patriotic War of the Soviet Union*, vol. 4, 244. As cited in Zawodny, *Nothing but Honour*, 73.

23. Ibid.

24. Ibid., 74.

25. Ibid., 76.

26. Ibid., 78.

27. Bor-Komorowski, *The Secret Army*, 251.

28. Davies, *Rising '44: The Battle for Warsaw*, 279.

29. Ibid., 280.

30. Bor-Komorwoski, *The Secret Army*, 251.

31. Ibid., 252.

32. Orska, *Silent is the Vistula*, 75.

33. Lukas, *Forgotten Holocaust: The Poles Under German Occupation 1939– 1944*, 210.

34. Ibid.

35. Bor-Komorowski, *The Secret Army*, 302.

36. Zawodny, *Nothing but Honour*, 126.

37. Ibid., 130. See also Bor-Komorowski, *The Secret Army*, 342–43.

38. Lukas, *Forgotten Holocaust: The Poles Under German Occupation 1939– 1944*, 216.

39. Zawodny, *Nothing but Honour*, 173.

40. Ibid., 174.

41. Ibid., 177.

42. Ibid., 206–07.

43. Ibid., 210–11.

44. Ibid., 209.

Afterthoughts on the Uprising

1. Jedrzej Giertych, *In Defense of My Country* (London: The Roman Dmowski Society, 1981), 429–30. Poles who had escaped from Poland and Germany after September 1939 and who joined resistance movements in other countries of occupied Europe were recruited from Polish populated areas of the Soviet Union, Western Ukraine, Western Byelorussia, and the Vilna area, which had belonged to Poland until September 1939. Mieczyslaw Juchniewicz, *Poles in the European Resistance Movement 1939–1945* (Warsaw: Interpress Publishers, 1972), 67.

2. Tadeusz Kondracki, "The Warsaw Uprising," Article 4 *Polish Resistance in World War II* (London: London Branch of the Polish Ex-Servicemen Association, 2004).

3. Nowak, *Courier from Warsaw*, 447.

4. Ibid., 448.

5. Ibid., 449.

6. Davies, *God's Playground: A History of Poland*, vol. 2, 475.

7. Nowak, *Courier from Warsaw*, 449.

8. Ibid.

9. Ibid., 450.

10. Milosz, *Native Realm: A Search for Self-Definition*, 248.

11. Zawodny, *Nothing but Honour*, 53.

12. Davies, *God's Playground: A History of Poland*, vol. 2, 475.

13. Ibid.

14. Ibid., 476.

15. Ibid., 477.

16. Zawodny, *Nothing but Honour*, 131.

17. Davies, *God's Playground: A History of Poland*, vol. 2, 361.

18. Ibid., 358.

Chapter Sixteen: Tyranny Replaced: Yalta's Death Blow to Polish Hopes

1. *Behind Closed Doors: Stalin, the Nazis and the West*, BBC History of World War II, Polish Military Museum, Warsaw, Laurence Rees, documentary director, 2009.

2. George F. Kennan, *Russia and the West Under Lenin and Stalin* (Boston: Little Brown Co. 1961), 365.

3. Hitchcock, *The Bitter Road to Freedom*, 158–59.

4. Ibid.

5. Davies, *Rising '44: The Battle for Warsaw*, 444–45.

6. Ibid.

7. Hitchcock, *The Bitter Road to Freedom*, 159.

8. S. M. Plokhy, *Yalta: The Price of Peace* (New York: Viking, 2010), 29–31.

9. Ibid., 153.

10. Ibid., 166.

11. Ibid., 167.

12. Ibid., 243–44.

13. Ibid., 245.

14. Lane, *I Saw Poland Betrayed*, 62.

15. Plokhy, *Yalta: The Price of Peace*, 245–46.

16. Winston S. Churchill, *The Second World War*, vol. 6 *Triumph and Tragedy*, (Boston: Houghton Mifflin Company, 1981), 334.

17. Norman Davies, *God's Playground: A History of Poland,* vol. 2 (New York: Columbia University Press, 2005) 361.

18. Ibid., 358.

19. *Behind Closed Doors: Stalin, the Nazis and the West,* BBC History of World War II, Polish Institute and Sikorski Museum, London, Laurence Rees, documentary director, 2009.

Chapter Seventeen: Epitaph to a Defiant Nation

1. Zawodny, *Nothing but Honour*, 194.

2. Davies, *God's Playground: A History of Poland*, vol. 2, 356.

3. Zawodny, *Nothing but Honour*, 195.

4. Ibid.

5. Davies, *Rising '44: The Battle for Warsaw*, 437.

6. Tadeusz Sarnicki, *Warszawa heroiczna. Pamietnik z Powstania Warszawskiego.* As cited in Davies, *Rising '44: The Battle for Warsaw*, 481.

7. Ibid.

8. Ibid., 476.

9. Ibid., 478.

10. Winston S. Churchill, *Memoirs of the Second World War: An abridgement of the six volumes of the Second World War*, vol 6, *Triumph and Tragedy* (Boston: Houghton Mifflin Company, 1987), 911.

11. Winston S. Churchill, *The Second World War*, vol. 1, *The Gathering Storm*, (Boston: Houghton Mifflin Company, 1948), 448.